"Written by Bill Kynes, a longtime pastor and Will Kynes, *Wrestling with Job* is filled with ins... ...application of this rich biblical book that means so much to those who experience suffering—namely all of us. This book is a feast for all readers who want to understand Job and what it means for our lives, but I would highlight its importance for clergy whose congregations need to hear what Job has to say to them. Thank you, Bill and Will, for combining your skill and passion for Scripture to illuminate Job's message for us today."

Tremper Longman III, distinguished scholar and professor emeritus of biblical studies at Westmont College, author of *How to Read Daniel*

"The biblical book of Job takes a hard, honest look at the painful trials all of us suffer. In this exceptional guide to its main interpretations and applications, one of my favorite pastors (Bill Kynes) combines forces with a world-class scholar (Will Kynes) to produce a faith-building book for Bible teachers and the people they serve. Rather than attempting to solve the mysteries of evil and divine sovereignty, *Wrestling with Job* helps readers persevere through times of spiritual struggle with enduring trust in Almighty God, and in his Son, Jesus Christ."

Philip Ryken, president of Wheaton College

"A unique father-son double act, this challenging and yet nurturing rereading of Job by the Kyneses—one a pastor and the other a scholar—leads to a profound mixture of a personal, pastoral touch and strong scholarly foundations that impart key information for understanding this complex biblical book. Informed by a rich airing of intertexts and imbued with a strong sense of Christian ministry to those who suffer, the book of Job comes to life afresh in these pages with humor, sensitivity, and a deep engagement with Scripture across both testaments."

Katharine Dell, professor of Old Testament literature and theology at the University of Cambridge and fellow of St Catharine's College, Cambridge

"I don't know many preachers willing to tackle Job. But this book can embolden anyone to teach from one of the Bible's most challenging and rewarding books. The combination of homiletical and exegetical commentary not only addresses concerns about how to teach a series through Job but also answers many of the book's thorniest theological questions. I hope the Kynes duo will give us an encore."

Collin Hansen, vice president of content and editor in chief of The Gospel Coalition and host of the *Gospelbound* podcast

"This book will nourish your soul by giving you a glimpse of the glory of God. Its pages are filled with rich biblical insight communicated with deep pastoral feeling. I had to stop repeatedly to capture pearls of wisdom that I will pass on to others."

Colin S. Smith, senior pastor of The Orchard, founder and Bible teacher, Open the Bible

"The father-son duo of Bill and Will Kynes has produced the rare gem in the Christian book world: a study on Job that is full of scholarly insight yet also down to earth and rich in pastoral wisdom and application for pastor and layperson alike. Beautifully written with engaging discussion questions, it's perfect for small groups. While readers may not have all their *why* questions answered on the issues of suffering and evil, they will be inspired to persevere with Job-like faith and put their hope in the One who sacrificed all to redeem this fallen world."

Joel S. Woodruff, president of the C. S. Lewis Institute

"True Christian faith has nothing to do with wish fulfillment but everything to do with facing reality, which is why every believer, sooner or later, has to wrestle with Job—and with what Job had to wrestle with: the reality of inequitable suffering. Bill and Will Kynes, pastor-father and scholar-son, have coauthored a precious gift: a wise and edifying twofer that provides not mere 'answers' but guidance for reading Job with understanding, deepening our trust in God, and persevering in our faith, come what may."

Kevin J. Vanhoozer, research professor of systematic theology at Trinity Evangelical Divinity School

"Has anything like this ever appeared: a father-son duo teaming up on the book of Job? Even if one heard of such a thing with the hearing of the ear, now the eye can see it—and in the flesh! Across ten chapters covering all of Job, the elder Kynes, a pastor, offers wise ministerial exposition, with the younger Kynes, a biblical scholar, providing profound interpretive commentary. As the authors note, study of Job can be unsettling but, if done patiently and well, can at the end be challenging and encouraging. I found all that to be true—and then some—in this rich and moving book. I recommend it most highly."

Brent A. Strawn, professor of Old Testament and professor of law at Duke University

"*Wrestling with Job* is a superb guide to participating in Job's unsettling narrative, adopting Job's posture toward God, and ultimately persevering as Job persevered. Kynes and Kynes bridge the conventional gap between the academy and the pulpit, balancing nuanced commentary and informative exposition with distinctly Christian application. This book is a particularly helpful resource for those who read Job with a defiant faith, honestly challenging God in an effort to make sense of apparent unjust retribution in light of the benevolent character of God. If, like Job, you find yourself asking, 'Why, Lord?' this book will lead you to answers from Job by guiding you to the God of Job."

Dominick S. Hernández, associate professor of Old Testament and Semitics at Talbot School of Theology, Biola University, and author of *Proverbs: Pathway to Wisdom*

"*Wrestling with Job* brings together the experience of a seasoned pastor with the expertise of a premier scholar to render the book of Job relatable and approachable for today's readers. The volume's pastoral voice, sensitivity to contemporary questions, and expositional orientation make it a valuable resource for those preparing to preach from this challenging text."

Michelle Knight, assistant professor of Old Testament and Semitic languages at Trinity Evangelical Divinity School

"*Wrestling with Job* brings together the experience of a seasoned pastor with the expertise of a premier scholar to render the book of Job relatable and approachable for today's readers. The volume's pastoral voice, sensitivity to contemporary questions, and expositional orientation make it a valuable resource for those preparing to preach from this challenging text."

Michelle Knight, assistant professor of Old Testament and Semitic languages at Trinity Evangelical Divinity School

BILL KYNES AND WILL KYNES

WRESTLING
with
JOB

DEFIANT FAITH IN THE
FACE OF SUFFERING

ivp
Academic
An imprint of InterVarsity Press
Downers Grove, Illinois

InterVarsity Press
P.O. Box 1400 | Downers Grove, IL 60515-1426
ivpress.com | email@ivpress.com

InterVarsity Press® is the publishing division of InterVarsity Christian Fellowship/USA®. For more information,
visit intervarsity.org.

The publisher cannot verify the accuracy or functionality of website URLs used in this book beyond the date
of publication.

Cover design and image composite: David Fassett
Interior design: Daniel van Loon

ISBN 978-1-5140-0076-2 (print) | ISBN 978-1-5140-0077-9 (digital)

Printed in the United States of America ♾

Library of Congress Cataloging-in-Publication Data
A catalog record for this book is available from the Library of Congress.

29 28 27 26 25 24 23 22 | 8 7 6 5 4 3 2 1

To Susan Kynes—

We are grateful for her support and encouragement

as a true comforter.

CONTENTS

DIGGING DEEPER
COMMENTS

PREFACE

AFTER THIRTY-ONE YEARS of preaching in one church, I (Bill) finally summoned the courage to preach a series of sermons on the book of Job. Only after a sabbatical study leave, which gave me the opportunity to invest in preparation, did I take the plunge. I was fortunate, however, to have a partner in this project, my son Will. Will had done his Cambridge PhD research on Job,[1] and our weekly conversations provided insight and ideas that became an integral part of my preaching. This book attempts to share that process of integrating academic biblical scholarship with pastoral reflection that we enjoyed in those conversations. The main chapters are primarily in my pastoral voice, while the Digging Deeper comments that follow them present Will's more academic perspective, offering insight into the many debated issues surrounding the interpretation of the book.

Despite my sense of inadequacy to do justice to this challenging book, beginning after the Christmas holidays, I took our church on a Lenten journey through Job, culminating at Easter. The chapters that follow chart that journey, as I cover the whole of Job in ten chapters. Be encouraged, it could have been worse—John Calvin preached 159 sermons on Job, and one Puritan preached from Job for almost three decades!

---

[1]Published as *My Psalm Has Turned into Weeping: Job's Dialogue with the Psalms* (Berlin: de Gruyter, 2012).

We invite you to join in this journey through the book of Job, but we encourage you not to do it superficially or quickly. In fact, we would suggest reading and reflecting on only a chapter of this study per week as one way of allowing the length of Job's struggle to be experienced. To appreciate Job requires entering into his painful ordeal over time, enabling the power of his story to sink in. Job wrestles with God, and we must wrestle with him also. We assure you, the rewards will be great.

ACKNOWLEDGMENTS

I (BILL) WOULD LIKE TO THANK my friend Randy Newman and our editors at IVP for their helpful comments. And most of all, I would like to thank my brothers and sisters of Cornerstone Evangelical Free Church, who have been my spiritual family for the last thirty-six years. I have seen something of the beauty of Christ in your lives, and it has been my privilege to preach God's word to you week after week. Thank you for the encouragement I received from you to remain faithful to that task. This book would not have been possible without you. May the Lord continue to fill you with his grace and truth.

I (Will) have my father to thank for my love for studying the Bible, shaped over decades of hearing him preach scripturally rich sermons like those which form the basis of this book. What a delight it has been to write about my favorite biblical book with my favorite pastor! I would also like to thank my research assistant, Rachel Witmer, for her diligent work helping us prepare this book for publication. Finally, I'm immensely grateful to my wife, Vanessa, and three daughters, Karis, Charlotte, and Hannah, for saturating my life with a joy that helps sustain me through long hours of reading, reflecting, and writing on suffering.

one

THE BOOK OF JOB

A WINDOW INTO A WORLD OF SUFFERING AND FAITH

Will your long-winded speeches never end?
What ails you that you keep on arguing?

JOB 16:3

THE CHALLENGE OF JOB

The book of Job is, in many ways, a hard book.

The book is hard because it deals with an uncomfortable subject—suffering. And Job suffers terribly. His thousands of sheep, camels, and oxen are taken away from him; his many servants are all carried away by foreign invaders; his ten children all die when a house collapses on them; and finally Job himself is afflicted with painful sores that broke out over his entire body. This is gut-wrenching stuff—not for the faint of heart!

The book of Job is perplexing because it doesn't give us the answers we want. We want to know why good people suffer, and the book leaves that question entirely unaddressed.

The book is baffling because much of its central section is in the words of Job's friends, whom God says did not speak what was right. So how are you supposed to know what to learn from what they say?

And what about Job himself? In the seemingly endless dialogues, Job's way of talking to God seems more petulant than patient. He argues with God and complains about his situation. The book seems to be one long lament. Aren't Christians supposed to be joyful all the time?

Job is also challenging because 95 percent of the book is poetry. Poetic literature requires great sensitivity to the art of metaphor and simile, as well as to the subtle nuances of the various forms of Hebrew parallelism. Our ability to appreciate these features is made all the more challenging when crossing the vast cultural distance that separates us from the book's author.[1]

But Job's poetic character raises another problem. The book is not a philosophical treatise; it is a spiritual struggle of the most intense kind. Its poetic form reflects the emotional turmoil that Job experiences. And to appreciate its message the reader must somehow sympathize with that emotion. You cannot read this book dispassionately and expect to receive what it has to offer. You must allow yourself to feel something of what Job feels, as uncomfortable as that may be.

And, finally, Job is demanding simply because it has forty-two chapters! And most of those chapters are both repetitive and downright depressing. Job and his friends go on and on, back and forth, arguing with one another with neither side giving an inch. It reminds me of the US Congress. It's been said that "the traditional phrase, 'the patience of Job,' might better be [stated] as 'the patience of the reader of Job.'"[2] There may be truth to that.

WHY STUDY JOB?

In view of these difficulties, why should you devote yourself to the study of this ancient book? If nothing else, you will be encouraged with the thought that though you may not have "your best life now," at least it is better than Job's!

---

[1]On the author of Job, see Comment 1.3, "Date of Job."
[2]R. E. Murphy, "The Last Truth About God," *Review and Expositor* 99 (Fall 2002): 585. Much of the previous section can be found in my article "5 Ways to Rewardingly Read the Book of Job," The Gospel Coalition, February 3, 2020, www.thegospelcoalition.org/article/5-ways-read-job/.

In fact, you don't need any special reason for studying Job. The book of Job is a part of Holy Scripture; it is God's "breathed out" word to us—and as such, it is useful; it is profitable; it is beneficial to teach us and to train us so that we would be fully equipped and prepared for all that God wants from us (2 Tim 3:16-17).

Which leads us to ask, How is the book of Job profitable? What can we expect to gain from it? Among the many ideas that we'll be considering in the chapters ahead, the one I want to emphasize as we begin is this: the book of Job will encourage us, in whatever our circumstances, to persevere in faith to the very end.

Job teaches about perseverance. In the only explicit reference to Job in the New Testament, James presents Job as a model to emulate: "As you know, we count as blessed those who have persevered. You have heard of Job's perseverance and have seen what the Lord finally brought about. The Lord is full of compassion and mercy" (Jas 5:11). In his profound suffering and grief, Job is brutally honest in his relationship with God. He challenges God to make himself known to him and to give him some reason for his terrible affliction. He protests, he objects, he accuses, he laments, he cries out in his pain, and he even curses the day of his birth. But through it all, Job never turns his back on God—he refuses to curse God and die in despair.

Job perseveres—"You have heard of Job's perseverance," James says. Referring to Job's "patience," as the King James Version puts it, is too tame, too passive. Job struggles, he fights, he wrestles with God, but he doesn't give up. Regardless of how he feels, he holds up under an almost unbearable load, as he tries to reconcile before God his experience of intense suffering with the knowledge of his own innocence.

We can learn much from this book to help us persevere in our faith to the end. For the key question of the book is, Will you trust God—will you believe that he is good and worthy of your praise,

your adoration, your worship, and your love—regardless of your circumstances? Will your faith in God's goodness endure when it
is tested?

Make no mistake: in some way, your faith will be tested. Jesus
spoke of that in his parable about the four soils into which the
sower sows the seed of the Word of God. Jesus warns us that some
will receive the word with joy. The seed will sprout, and they will
believe for a while, but in the time of testing they will fall away
(Lk 8:13). Will that be true of you? What will that testing look like
in your life?

You may be tested with prosperity. "Wouldn't that be nice!" you
say. Yes, but wealth and pleasure can become like weeds that choke
the life of the seed. Prosperity can be deadly to faith when it results
in a sense of self-sufficiency and pride or when your faith in God
becomes dependent on his blessings. The book of Job challenges that
kind of self-serving faith.

Or your faith could be tested with simple distraction. You can
become preoccupied with paying the rent or getting promoted at
work or with fears about that lump under your skin or handing over
the car keys to your teenager. We can be overwhelmed by the cares
of this world and all the anxieties and fears that fill our minds. Even
the fear that you might become like Job could undermine your faith.

Or your faith could be tested by actual pain and suffering. And
this can be the toughest test of all, for nothing can call into question
our faith in the essential goodness of God like our suffering.
Hardship and affliction can become a trial, an examination, an eval-
uation. Can God be trusted? Is he really worthy of my worship? In
whatever form that testing comes, Jesus says, only those who persevere produce a crop (Lk 8:15).

The importance of perseverance. We can't overstate the importance of
perseverance in our faith. Paul says, "If we endure, we will also reign

with [Christ]" (2 Tim 2:12). In Hebrews we read, "You need to persevere so that when you have done the will of God, you will receive what he has promised" (Heb 10:36). And again, "Therefore, since we are surrounded by such a great cloud of witnesses, let us throw off everything that hinders and the sin that so easily entangles. And let us run with perseverance the race marked out for us" (Heb 12:1). James says, "Blessed is the one who perseveres under trial because, having stood the test, that person will receive the crown of life that the Lord has promised to those who love him" (Jas 1:12). Twice in Matthew's Gospel, Jesus says that only "the one who stands firm to the end will be saved" (Mt 10:22; 24:13).

Simply put, without an enduring faith we are lost. The book of Job is a lesson in perseverance in the face of incredible suffering—inexplicable suffering, innocent suffering. For suffering—especially suffering that seems to come upon us for no reason, suffering that seems to make no sense, suffering that is too random or too evil—that is a supreme challenge to our faith.

On the one hand, suffering can make us angry and defiant before God. History is littered with the anti-Christian testimonies of atheists who point to the reality of pain and suffering as the ground of their unbelief, who curse the God whom they say they no longer believe in.

On the other hand, suffering can dampen and deaden our faith. It can make us lethargic and lifeless in our relationship with God. We no longer look to him as our loving Father. Instead, he becomes a distant caretaker of the cosmic order with no personal concern for a little minion like me. We find ourselves no longer on speaking terms.

But for others, for those with the courage to hold on—their suffering can become a gateway to a deepened faith. As Viktor Frankl, who endured the unbearable suffering of a Nazi concentration camp, observed, "just as the small fire is extinguished by the storm while a large fire is enhanced by it—likewise a weak faith is weakened by predicaments and catastrophes, whereas a strong faith is strengthened by them."[3]

We will suffer, you can be sure of it. And in our suffering—whether physically or emotionally—we must learn from Job if we are to endure faithfully to the end.

WHAT KIND OF BOOK IS JOB?

So as we approach this book, we must first ask, What kind of a book is it? I've already mentioned its artistic quality. In the ordering of our Bibles, it is listed with other poetic books—the Psalms, Proverbs, Ecclesiastes, and Song of Songs. It is often considered one of the Wisdom books, but that's too limiting—it has more in common with lament psalms than with Proverbs.[4]

Some have described Job as a "lawsuit drama" or as "skeptical, protest literature."[5] But again, Job resists neat classification. Commentator Francis Andersen writes, "The book of Job is an astonishing mixture of almost every kind of literature to be found in the Old Testament."[6] The book also shows some fascinating parallels to other ancient Near Eastern books.[7] Though they share some themes, the differences outweigh the similarities. One writer concludes, "Perhaps part of the fascination of the book of Job is that there is no other book like it, even in the ancient world."[8] It's a book that in many respects must be understood on its own terms.[9]

---

[3]Viktor E. Frankl, *Man's Search for Ultimate Meaning* (New York: Perseus, 2000), 19.
[4]On the classification of Job as a Wisdom book, see Comment 1.1, "The Demise of 'Wisdom Literature.'"
[5]See Comments 5.4, "Job as Lawsuit" and 5.5, "Parody."
[6]Francis I. Andersen, *Job: An Introduction and Commentary* (Downers Grove, IL: InterVarsity Press, 1976), 33.
[7]See Comment 4.1, "Dialogues in the Ancient Near East."
[8]Wilson, *Job*, 7.
[9]See Comment 1.2, "The Genre(s) of Job."

Who wrote the book? Its author is never mentioned, which leads us to believe that authorship isn't critical to the interpretation of the book.

Its setting is in the land of Uz, but no one knows where Uz was. One writer observed, "One might just as well search for the Land of Oz."[10]

When was it written? The book appears to be set in patriarchal times, in part because of its silence regarding the land of Israel, the priesthood, and the temple. But it was still connected to Israelite faith—with its insistence on the justice of God, and the denial of bowing to idols like the sun and the moon (cf. Job 31:26-28). At least in the prologue and the divine speeches, the narrator of the story uses the covenant name Yahweh—the name by which God revealed himself to Israel.[11] And very early this book became a part of Jewish Scripture. But its message is not linked to any particular event or setting in Israel's history. This broadens its message, setting it free from the bounds of time or place.

The story appears to be set in the time of the patriarchs, but when was it actually written? Again, we don't know. All attempts to date the book have been inconclusive. All we can say with certainty is that it was written after Job's death since the writer tells us that Job lived 140 years. But the way that Job appears to allude to other biblical books, like Isaiah, Jeremiah, and especially the Psalms,[12] suggests a much later date—perhaps even after the exile.[13]

---

[10]Dermot Cox, *Man's Anger and God's Silence: The Book of Job* (Slough: St. Paul Publications, 1990), 21. Note also the comment of David Clines: "The importance of the name Uz lies not in where such a place is, but in where it is not. Israelites themselves may not have known its precise location, but they will have known, as we do, that it is not in Israel" (*Job*, 3 vols. [Nashville: Thomas Nelson, 1989–2011], 1:10).

[11]Though this name is almost never on the lips of the characters in the dialogue (found only in Job 12:9).

[12]See Comment 1.4, "Allusion and Intertextuality."

[13]See Comment 1.3, "Date of Job."

Should we read the book of Job as a precise verbatim record of what transpired in Uz between Job and his friends? That seems unlikely—people generally don't argue in poetic verse.

Job seems to have been a historical figure. He is mentioned as a righteous man by the prophet Ezekiel (Ezek 14:14, 20), but that doesn't mean that this book is what we would call strictly historical. The divinely inspired author could well have retold a well-known story about a famous man to explore the deepest questions of the human relationship with the God who made us and who rules this world. However it came about, the author of this God-breathed book has explored these questions in a most profound way.

The richness of Job's message can't be simply explained. It can't be captured in the 280 characters of a tweet or even in one thirty-minute sermon. Instead, the message must be experienced. The reader must identify with the real experience of suffering, and what that means for one's relationship with God. That's why there are forty-two chapters. That's why it's best not to rush through it. You must enter into the narrative—you must feel what Job feels. The book of "Job is to be lived in and not just studied."[14]

Christopher Ash, in his reflections on the book of Job, speaks of the difference between asking the "armchair questions" of the scholar and asking the "wheelchair questions" of the sufferer.[15] Job is asking "wheelchair questions." He is in desperate straits, and somehow we need to enter into his suffering to understand his struggle. The fact that the characters speak in poetry rather than prose means that their words are meant to touch our hearts as well as our heads. "Poetry doesn't lend itself to summing up in tidy propositions, bullet points, neat systems, and well-swept answers," Ash contends. "We need to let a poem get to work on us—we must immerse ourselves in it."[16]

---

[14]Christopher Ash, *Job: The Wisdom of the Cross* (Wheaton, IL: Crossway, 2014), 23.
[15]Ash, *Job*, 18.
[16]Ash, *Job*, 22-23.

Job is also a very long book, and that, too, is significant. The book consists of forty-two chapters because there is no quick-fix easy answer to the questions it raises. There is no instant release from grief. We must go through the process. The book's length invites the reader into the process of reflection; it takes us on a journey, and a journey takes time.[17] It invites us to join in an exploration of the process of loss and grief. In that process our faith may be reworked and our lives may be transformed, as Job's were.

Beware: a study of Job may unsettle you. But in the end, you will be challenged and encouraged by it in all sorts of ways.

And the first encouragement we need from Job is the encouragement to persevere in faith to the end. We will be taken down a road of intense suffering—with all of the emotional and spiritual turmoil that creates—to come to a new appreciation of the God who is there all along. A journey through Job becomes almost like an extended Lenten observance on a path to Jerusalem. In this journey, we can see Jesus as a kind of Job—the ultimate innocent sufferer, who, on the cross, pronounces his own cry of desperation and dereliction: "My God, my God, why have you forsaken me?" (Mt 27:46).

But as in Job, the gospel gives us a happy ending. We must see what the Lord finally brings about—the suffering of Good Friday gives way to the vindication of Easter morning. He is risen; he is risen indeed!

Yes, "the Lord is full of compassion and mercy" (Jas 5:11). We will see how Job wrestles with God until he gets that blessing.

DIGGING DEEPER

1.1. The demise of "Wisdom Literature." For more than a hundred years, first in biblical scholarship, then in the church, it has been common to refer to Job, along with Proverbs and Ecclesiastes, as

---

[17]On the way the literary form of the book is a part of its meaning, see Comment 1.5, "Mimesis."

belonging to a distinct category of biblical and ancient Near Eastern texts known as "Wisdom Literature." According to this widespread view, these texts are the product of the universal search for wisdom. Rather than interpreting the world from the perspective of the Israelites' special relationship with their God as presented in the Law, History, and the Prophets, these texts are said to offer insights, available to all, from the reasoned analysis of life. According to his view, in addition to being universalistic and rationalistic, these texts are occasionally empirical, basically secular, frequently skeptical, and fundamentally humanistic and individualistic.

Recently, biblical scholars have begun to question this consensus for a number of reasons.[18] From a historical perspective, recent work has identified when biblical scholarship first grouped those specific texts together as a distinct "Wisdom" category, the mid-nineteenth century in Germany, a time and place in which the constellation of ideological values associated with the category—universalism, rationalism, humanism, and so on—were particularly popular. The suspicious similarity between the values of scholars at that time and those they attributed to the "wise men" who they thought wrote those books suggests this may be yet another example of nineteenth-century biblical scholars looking into the well and seeing their own reflections.[19]

From a literary perspective, the view of genre used to classify these texts into a single genre that sets them apart from others in the canon does not reflect how genres actually work. In fact, texts may be grouped together in many ways, depending on the similarities readers find significant among them. German scholars after the Enlightenment may have been interested in finding texts that were universalistic, rationalistic, and humanistic, but other

---

[18]See Will Kynes, *An Obituary for "Wisdom Literature": The Birth, Death, and Intertextual Reintegration of a Biblical Corpus* (Oxford: Oxford University Press, 2019).
[19]See Comment 6.2, "Defining Wisdom."

readers, including those who lived closer to the time when the texts were actually written, when those ideas were not as popular, have noticed other significant affinities they have with other texts. Each of those genre groupings highlights a different feature of the texts; fully understanding them, then, requires not classifying them in a single genre (particularly not one first imposed for self-serving reasons in the nineteenth century), but learning from as many of them as possible. The Wisdom Literature category has cordoned off the texts associated with it from the rest of the Bible and its theology for over a century; the category's death offers an opportunity to reexamine what they mean.

1.2. The genre(s) of Job. A genre is "a group of texts gathered together due to some perceived significant affinity between them."[20] Most texts can be grouped into multiple genres depending on which features have attracted our attention. These perceived similarities between texts shape our expectations as we read, and, at their best, help us to understand texts better. Grouping sonnets together enables us to recognize their structure; grouping love poems together highlights how they express their passion rhetorically. Some poems will be in both of those genre groupings and our reading expectations should be shaped by both. However, when we treat genres as exclusive categories, such that a text can only *be* one genre, and forget that these genre groupings result from our culturally located perceptions, genres can actually distort our interpretations.

Job is a prime example of both the distorting power of reading a text according to a single genre and the illuminating potential of reading it as participating in many genres. Though the general consensus for more than a century has been that Job is best classified as Wisdom Literature, it wears that label uncomfortably. A number of scholars have noticed this, and an increasing

---

[20]Kynes, *Obituary for "Wisdom Literature,"* 107.

acknowledgment that Job's meaning cannot be contained with Wisdom Literature has contributed to the demise of the category as a whole.

Before the Wisdom genre category was invented in the mid-nineteenth century, Job was never exclusively grouped with Proverbs and Ecclesiastes, or its message characterized by the philosophical ideas now associated with wisdom. Traditional Jewish reading put Job in a collection with Psalms and Proverbs called the *Sifrei Emet*, which highlights how much it shares with both those books.[21] Early Christian tradition generally grouped Job with other books of poetry: Psalms, Proverbs, Ecclesiastes, and Song of Songs. This underscores the book's poetic nature. However, both Jewish and Christian ancient canon lists also occasionally grouped Job with the histories, either near Judges at the beginning or Esther at the end, which encouraged readers to note connections between Job and various figures from Israel's history. The closest historical connections to Job are found in the genealogy of Esau in Genesis 36.[22] This link to Genesis also connects the book to the Torah (or Pentateuch) and Moses. Early readers, such as Ben Sira and Josephus, also grouped Job with the Prophets.

In recent scholarship, as the Wisdom category has begun to lose its influence, all of these groupings have been resurrected to some degree or another, as scholars have started to notice how comparing Job to these other collections of texts uncovers significant features that the category had buried. Even more genre groupings have been added, such as drama,[23] epic, lament, lawsuit,[24] apocalyptic, and parody.[25] None of these genres can fully encompass the book's meaning (which is

---

[21]Job's speeches in particular often sound very similar to psalmic laments; see Comments 7.4, "Appeals to Innocence in the Psalms" and 7.5, "The Biblical Tradition of Defiant Faith."

[22]See Comment 1.3, "Date of Job."

[23]See Comment 2.4, "Job as a Drama."

[24]See Comment 5.4, "Job as Lawsuit."

[25]See Comment 5.5, "Parody."

generally the case with genres), but each highlights important features of it.[26] So, just as the Wisdom category highlights the emphasis on the concept of wisdom in the book, these other genres underscore other significant features, such as Job's laments or the legal metaphor that drives his conflict with God. Only by reading the book in multiple genres can its full meaning be comprehended.

1.3. Date of Job. Many consider Job to be one of if not the oldest book in the Bible. This common view primarily results from the setting the book depicts, which appears similar to that of the patriarchs in Genesis. In fact, in the genealogy of Esau in Genesis 36, we encounter an Eliphaz (Gen 36:10), a Teman (Gen 36:11), a Zepho (translated in the Greek as "Zophar"; Gen 36:11), an Uz (Gen 36:23), a Bedad and a Bilhan (Gen 36:25, 27), which together remind one of Bildad, and a Jobab (Gen 36:33), which an addition to the end of the Greek translation explicitly connects with Job (Job 42:17). Like Abraham, Isaac, and Jacob, Job appears to offer his own sacrifices apart from the cultic trappings of tabernacle, temple, or priests. Indeed, the law, history, and covenants of Israel are never explicitly mentioned. The Hebrew of the book also has a number of archaic features. There is even a term used for money (*qesitah*) in Job 42:11 that only appears elsewhere in Genesis 33:19 and Joshua 24:32. Fittingly, a Jewish tradition developed that Moses was the author of the book.

However, this evidence is hardly definitive, and, even if it proved that the book was set in the patriarchal period, it would not indicate that it was written at that time. Thus, the rabbis consider a number of dates for Job: the time of Jacob, Moses, the judges, David, the Sabaeans (or possibly the queen of Sheba), the Chaldeans, and Ahasuerus.[27]

---

[26]For more on the various genres of Job and their contributions to its interpretation, see Kynes, *Obituary for "Wisdom Literature,"* 149-78.

[27]Bava Batra 14b, 15a-b.

Lacking explicit reference to historical events, to determine the book's date, scholars have been forced to rely primarily on intra-biblical parallels, linguistic evidence, and the development of Israel's religion. However, conclusions based on evidence in each of these categories are tenuous. The evidence on which they rely can often be interpreted to support multiple and even contradictory conclusions. For example, the many allusions to other texts in the Old Testament contribute to arguments that Job is one of the latest texts in the Old Testament.[28] However, in many cases, those allusions could go in the other direction, with other texts alluding to Job, even if in Job's frequent parodies it makes much better sense to conclude that Job is the later text, twisting earlier texts toward his rhetorical purposes.[29] Discussions of the inconclusive nature of the evidence for Job's date have, therefore, become standard fare in commentaries.[30]

The limited indisputable evidence for the date of Job includes the existence of several fragments of the book discovered at Qumran, which date back as early as the late third century BCE. These indicate Job must have been composed sometime before that. In recent scholarship, the book's date is generally placed after the exile, between the fifth and third centuries BCE, based on cumulative evidence, particularly the book's language, mention of a Satan figure (which is considered a late theological development), and challenge of a developed view of retribution, though the occasional argument for a seventh-century date may be found. Some even argue different parts of the book, such as the prose narrative, poetic dialogues, or Elihu speeches, were written at different times. David Clines, a leading Job scholar, summarizes the situation well: "Of [Job's] author or date of composition I frankly know nothing, and my

---

[28]See Comment 1.4, "Allusion and Intertextuality."
[29]See Comment 5.5, "Parody."
[30]E.g., Habel, *Job*, 40-42.

speculations are not likely to be worth more than the many guesses that already exist."[31]

1.4. Allusion and intertextuality. Unlike a quotation, which explicitly identifies itself, often with a citation, an allusion is "an intentional implicit reference to an earlier expression."[32] This implicit nature draws readers deeper into the interpretive process by relying on their ability to recognize how significant words, imagery, or structure in one text refer to an earlier text, creating a dialogue between them. Quotations and allusions are two of the many ways that all texts are interconnected with one another, either by their authors or their readers, both of whom are constantly using other texts to express or interpret meaning. The term for this broad phenomenon is "intertextuality."[33] Though all texts are intertextual to some degree, Job is particularly tightly woven into a web of textual interconnections. Recognizing this is vital for reading the book well.

The author of Job constantly alludes to other texts in the Old Testament. To understand the book fully, readers must tune their ears to hear these notes from elsewhere in the melody of Israel's story as they harmonize with Job's tale. There are potential allusions to a broad swath of texts beyond Wisdom Literature, including Genesis, Exodus, Deuteronomy, 1 Samuel, Isaiah 40–55, Jeremiah, Amos, Psalms, and Lamentations.[34]

Allusions are so pervasive within the text that Job appears to be what one scholar has termed a "citational text," in which readers can justifiably suppose that the author intentionally cited a number of earlier texts with the expectation that the public would

---

[31]Clines, *Job*, 1:xxix.

[32]Will Kynes, *My Psalm Has Turned into Weeping: Job's Dialogue with the Psalms* (Berlin: de Gruyter, 2012), 36.

[33]See Will Kynes, "Intertextuality: Method and Theory in Job and Psalm 119," in *Biblical Interpretation and Method: Essays in Honour of Professor John Barton*, ed. Katharine J. Dell and Paul M. Joyce (Oxford: Oxford University Press, 2013), 201-13.

[34]See, e.g., Katharine Dell and Will Kynes, eds., *Reading Job Intertextually* (New York: Bloomsbury T&T Clark, 2013).

recognize those allusions as relevant to the text's presentation and meaning.[35] Biblical examples would include Isaiah 40–55 and Revelation.[36] Modern texts of this type include the poetry of T. S. Eliot and the novels of James Joyce.

Because allusions, unlike quotations, are implicit, they are easy to miss, and just as easy to see mistakenly when they were not actually intended by the author (the unintentional resonances that readers recognize between texts are better referred to as "echoes"). However, some allusions are fairly clear, and, because they involve meaningful parodies, they can legitimately be considered intentional. The most famous is Job's "bitter parody" of the psalmist's praise of God's concern for humanity in Psalm 8:5 to lament God's oppressive presence (Job 7:17-18).[37] Enough significant connections between Job and other biblical texts are evident in Job that careful readers should expect to find more as they read and then should pay attention to how Job and the friends are interpreting those earlier texts.

1.5. Mimesis. Fundamentally, mimesis means imitation, and the term may be used to describe various imitative aspects of literary works. One particular understanding of mimesis that contributes significantly to our understanding of Job is the way that literary works can be written to imitate life. The book of Job accomplishes this in various ways. The most striking are the length of the dialogue between Job and his friends, the confusion it engenders in the conflicting answers it provides, and the abrupt mood swings that pervade Job's responses, all of which reflect

---

[35]Marko Juvan, *History and Poetics of Intertextuality*, trans. Timothy Pogačar (Indianapolis: Purdue University Press, 2008), 146.

[36]See Patricia Tull Willey, *Remember the Former Things: The Recollection of Previous Texts in Second Isaiah* (Atlanta: Scholars Press, 1997); Benjamin D. Sommer, *A Prophet Reads Scripture: Allusion in Isaiah 40–66* (Stanford, CA: Stanford University Press, 1998); Steve Moyise, *The Old Testament in the Book of Revelation* (Sheffield, UK: Sheffield Academic, 1995).

[37]For other examples, see Comments 2.2, "The Prologue and Genesis 2–3"; 3.2, "Job's Counter-cosmic Curse"; 5.1, "The Question of Integrity"; 5.5, "Parody"; 7.2, "Allusions to Adam"; and 7.3, "Allusions to Deuteronomy."

the real experience of enduring suffering, which frequently feels long, confusing, and emotionally jarring.

The Job poet demonstrates impressive psychological insight, both in his depiction of Job's progressive responses to his suffering and the friends' attempts to comfort their companion, which devolves from education to accusation. Even the lack of a definitive explanation for Job's suffering in the book as a whole, along with God's refusal to clarify how it can be reconciled with his power and justice, represents well human experience in a fallen world, in which answers to these questions elude us and we are forced simply to trust God.[38]

---

[38]See Comment 9.2, "Why Doesn't God Explain?"

two

THE CYNIC'S TAUNT

JOB 1–2

Does Job fear God for nothing?

JOB 1:9

ONE WORD COULD CAPTURE our current cultural climate: cynical. Sunny optimism is out; cloudy pessimism is in. Cynicism—that disposition of disbelief in the sincerity or goodness of all human motives—is the new norm.

In part, this climate change can be attributed to the postmodern turn in the second half of the last century. We have experienced a significant cooling of our modern confidence in human reason and scientific discovery to solve all our problems. The Enlightenment foundation, which seemed so firm around 1900, has crumbled after two world wars, two atomic bombs, Vietnam, Watergate, ongoing struggles for racial justice, and a global pandemic. The disillusionment that took place, both intellectually and culturally, has given rise to a new age of doubt and distrust. We live in an increasingly cynical age. *The Cynic's Dictionary* defines a cynic this way: "An idealist whose rose-colored glasses have been removed, snapped in two and stomped into the ground, immediately improving his vision."[1]

Cynicism begins with a wry assurance that everyone has an angle. Behind every silver lining is a cloud. The cynic is always observing,

---

[1]Rick Bayan, *The Cynic's Dictionary* (Edison, NJ: Castle Books, 1994), 53.

critiquing, and complaining, but never engaging, loving, and hoping. Journalists today are bred to be suspicious of everyone, and their motto is always, "Follow the money," or, "Expect the worst and you will probably find it."

You see this cynical mood in the satire and parody of today's comedy, made popular a generation ago by the likes of Bart Simpson and David Letterman. They gave us humor with a smirk instead of a smile.

In the universities, literary critics constantly engage in "deconstructing" texts, seeking the author's hidden agenda and those underlying power dynamics that lie behind the words. Claims to truth are viewed as mere instruments of manipulation and assertions of one's power over others.[2]

Religion is especially vulnerable to this cynical onslaught. It's the common view that all religious people are hypocrites at heart. Ambrose Bierce once defined a saint as "a dead sinner revised and edited." In his 2008 documentary film *Religulous,* Bill Maher doesn't hide his own disdain for religion. "The irony of religion," he says, "is that because of its power to divert man to destructive courses, the world could actually come to an end. The plain fact is, religion must die for mankind to live."[3]

This cynicism is clear and undisguised in the attack of the "new atheists." Christopher Hitchens's book title says it all: *god* [sic] *Is Not Great: How Religion Poisons Everything.* I think also of Richard Dawkins's cynical contempt in his book *The God Delusion.* "The God of the Old Testament," he says, "is arguably the most unpleasant character in all fiction: jealous and proud of it; a petty, unjust, unforgiving control-freak; a vindictive, bloodthirsty ethnic cleanser; a misogynistic, homophobic, racist, infanticidal, genocidal, filicidal, pestilential, megalomaniacal, sadomasochistic, capriciously malevolent

[2]For an excellent academic diagnosis of the life-threatening metastasis of criticism in universities, see Rita Felski, *The Limits of Critique* (Chicago: University Press, 2015).
[3]Bill Maher, "The irony of religion," Ask Atheists, www.askatheists.com/85280.

bully."[4] So there! He adds, "The universe we observe has precisely the properties we should expect if there is, at bottom, no design, no purpose, no evil and no good, nothing but blind, pitiless indifference."[5] That's cynicism.

Cynicism, in its essence, is a denial of the good, the true, and the beautiful; that's why it is ultimately a denial of God. A character in a Robert Louis Stevenson story makes a most perceptive observation—"I hate cynicism a great deal worse than I do the devil, unless, perhaps, the two were the same thing?"[6] Are they?

I call the central question posed by the book of Job "The Cynic's Taunt." It is the question asked by the satanic accuser—"Does Job fear God for nothing?" In other words, is there really such a thing as a true believer? Aren't all those religious people just in it for the divine blessings?

This raises an even more pressing question: Is there really a true God? Is there a God who is worthy of our worship, our love, our trust—regardless of our circumstances? That's what the book of Job is about—and that is the question we must all answer. There is none more important in all of life.

In the first two chapters, we encounter the dramatic stage that is set for the struggle to come. We'll consider it in three parts: First, in the opening verses, is the description of Job as a godly man. Then comes the entrance of the mysterious satanic figure and his cynical accusation. And finally, we'll look at God's role in all this—which may be the most challenging part of all. I call it the divine gambit—the bargain that is made, the test that is set, to see if the cynic will indeed have the last word. We'll wait to consider all that happens to Job and his reactions to it until the next chapter.

[4]Richard Dawkins, *The God Delusion* (London: Bantam, 2006), 51.
[5]Dawkins, *River Out of Eden* (New York: Basic Books, 1995), 133.
[6]Robert Louis Stevenson, "An Inland Voyage," in *The Works of Robert Louis Stevenson*, vol. 2 (Boston: Jefferson Press, 1895), 30.

A RIGHTEOUS MAN

So, finally, we turn to the book of Job: "In the land of Uz there lived a man whose name was Job. This man was blameless and upright; he feared God and shunned evil" (Job 1:1).

This verse sets the scene for all that follows. Without this premise, the rest of the story loses all its dramatic power. There is no uncertainty in the author's mind—this man Job is a godly man. This fact is expressed in a fourfold litany of praise unparalleled in the Bible, and its cumulative effect is powerful.

The description of Job's piety comes in two pairs. First, he is said to be "blameless and upright"—characterizing him as a man of untarnished character and genuine faith.[7] The word for "blameless" does not mean that Job was without sin—Job himself refers to "the sins of my youth" in Job 13:26, and "my sin" in Job 14:16. "Blameless" here simply points to Job's moral character. It speaks of his genuineness and authenticity. There is nothing hypocritical about him. Job was a man of "personal integrity, not sinless perfection."[8]

The next term, "upright," is similar, but it shifts the focus away from Job's own character to the way he treated other people. He acted fairly in his dealings with others; he showed mercy to those in need.

The second pair of descriptions turns toward his relationship with God. "His religion was shaped by humble piety"[9]—"he feared God and shunned evil." The poem about wisdom later in Job will proclaim this the very definition of wisdom (Job 28:28).[10] This "fear of God" is often depicted in the Bible as the supreme mark of the godly

---

[7]This pair of traits appears in descriptions of God (Deut 32:4) and of David, linked to his complete obedience to God's commands (1 Kings 9:4), as the ground of the psalmist's confidence before God (Ps 25:21; cf. Ps 37:37), and repeatedly in Proverbs, where these traits are associated with protection (Prov 2:7; 2:21), guidance (Prov 11:3, 5), and the target of the wicked (Prov 28:10; 29:10).

[8]John E. Hartley, *The Book of Job* (Grand Rapids, MI: Eerdmans, 1988), 31.

[9]Christopher Ash, *Job: The Wisdom of the Cross* (Wheaton, IL: Crossway, 2014), 32.

[10]See Comment 6.4, "Wisdom and the Fear of the Lord (Job 28:28)."

person. It is the beginning of wisdom (Prov 1:7; 9:10), and it creates the proper posture of the human being in reverence and awe before their Creator. Fundamentally, it means respecting God as God and treating him accordingly.

And as a result, Job "shunned evil." Job's religion issues into a godly morality. He maintained a constant repentant heart, habitually turning away from evil in his thoughts, words, and deeds.[11] There is no question—Job is a genuine believer, a model of godliness.

Again, this is not to say that Job was a perfect man, a sinless man— only one man who ever lived fits that description. But Job's condition is like that of Noah. In Genesis 6:9 Noah was said to be "a righteous man, blameless among the people of this time, and he walked faithfully with God." But in the book of Hebrews, Noah is especially commended for his faith—for, the writer tells us, it was by faith that he heeded God's warning and built an ark, and so he became "heir of the righteousness that is in keeping with faith" (Heb 11:7). Noah was righteous by faith, and so was Job—and so is any sinner before God,[12] and all the evidence of Job's life confirmed the reality of that faith.

This superlative assessment of Job's condition is clear. It is never contradicted by the narrator, and it is affirmed by God himself twice in the book's first two chapters and then again in the last (Job 1:8; 2:6; 42:7, 8). Only his friends will deny it. So hold on to it. You will miss the point of the book if you forget it. Job is a godly man.

A GREAT MAN

In Job 1:1 our author asserts that Job was a good man; in the following verses he describes his greatness: "He had seven sons and three daughters, and he owned seven thousand sheep, three

---

[11]Ash, *Job*, 32.
[12]Ash, *Job*, 32.

thousand camels, five hundred yoke of oxen and five hundred donkeys, and had a large number of servants. He was the greatest man among all the people of the East" (Job 1:2-3).

Here is a picture of "the good life" in the currency of that age—great wealth in family and possessions, along with a high social stature in the community. Today we might speak of someone having a loving family, while being a CEO with thousands of employees, with a penthouse in Manhattan or a horse farm in Virginia. They would be a generous philanthropist, an elder in their church, one whose advice was sought by governors and senators, and who had their own podcast with a multitude of Twitter followers. What else could anyone want? By any standard, Job was a great man.

In a sense, this is just what you would expect. A man of such character before God should be blessed with such abundance. You get the distinct impression that Job's goodness is the cause of his greatness, for doesn't the psalmist in Psalm 1 tell us that

> [The righteous person] is like a tree planted by
>   streams of water,
>   which yields its fruit in season
> and whose leaf does not wither
>   —whatever they do prospers. (Ps 1:3)

Shouldn't piety lead to prosperity? But we are left with the question—If Job is great because he is good, will he continue to be good when he is no longer great?

The final illustration of Job's character in Job 1:4-5 reinforces what I have just said. After each of the joyous family feasts (probably birthday parties), Job would make it his habit to sacrifice a burnt offering for each of his children, just in case: "Perhaps [God forbid!] my children have sinned and cursed God in their hearts." Surely, this is a mark of piety, but might it also suggest that something isn't quite right in the way Job approaches his relationship with God—that anxiety outweighs faith, and fear is divorced from trust? Does Job suppose that by offering sufficient sacrifices he can protect himself and those he loves from suffering?

Such was the heart of Job. He was ever mindful of what it means to be righteous before God, even in the hearts of his children. This is the man whose life is about to be turned upside down.

A CYNICAL TAUNT

In Job 1:6, the story suddenly veers in another direction, as the setting shifts from earth to heaven, and we listen in on a dramatic interchange that Job is never privy to: "One day the angels came to present themselves before the LORD." Here we have some sort of heavenly council, as the company of angels, "the sons of God," appear before the Lord, ready to do his bidding.[13] But this verse ends in a rather foreboding manner: "and Satan also came with them."[14]

Who is this Satan figure? The Hebrew word *satan* means "adversary" or "accuser" (the Greek translation is *diabolos* or "devil"), and here the word comes with the definite article "the," giving emphasis to the role of this figure. He is "the accuser." Along with the angelic council comes one who stands against God's people in some way.[15]

In Job 1:7, it is the Lord who initiates the interchange. He says to this adversary, "Where have you come from?" What have you been up to? What is your business here? "Satan answered the LORD, 'From roaming throughout the earth, going back and forth on it.'"

We get the impression that the earth, not heaven, is his designated sphere of activity. In the New Testament, Jesus speaks of the devil as

---

[13]Cf. Zech 6:5: "The angel answered me, 'These are the four spirits of heaven, going out from standing in the presence of the Lord of the whole world.'"

[14]The Hebrew is not clear whether "the satan" is a part of this council or not. Because of the question addressed to him, I think it best to consider him an outsider. See Francis Anderson, *Job* (London: Inter-Varsity Press, 1976), 82.

[15]See Comment 2.1, "'The Satan' and the Heavenly Council."

"the prince of this world" (Jn 12:31; 14:30; 16:11), and Peter's words fit well with what we see in Job: "Your enemy the devil prowls around like a roaring lion looking for someone to devour" (1 Pet 5:8).

So the Satan was up to no good—looking for someone to accuse, someone on God's side to sabotage and subvert, some way to undermine faith in the supposed goodness and glory of God. That shouldn't be too hard, for in Satan's view, there can be no such thing as a genuine believer.

But God begs to disagree. "Then the LORD said to Satan, 'Have you considered my servant Job? There is no one on earth like him; he is blameless and upright, a man who fears God and shuns evil'" (Job 1:8). "I know Job's heart—he is faithful and loyal, a man of integrity and real godliness. He is truly 'my servant,'" God says. "There is no one like him. In all your efforts to discover if there is such a thing as a genuine believer, have you considered my servant Job?"[16]

Satan is unimpressed. "Does Job fear God for nothing?" he replies. "Have you not put a hedge around him and his household and everything he has? You have blessed the work of his hands, so that his flocks and herds are spread throughout the land. But now stretch out your hand and strike everything he has, and he will surely curse you to your face" (Job 1:9-11).

It's the cynic's taunt—"All this pious sanctity you see in your man Job—it's all a show, a pretense. He doesn't care about you, God, and your supposed glory and majesty. It's all about him, and how he reaps the benefits of all his religiosity—the sheep, the cattle, the camels, and all the rest. Take that away, and he will want nothing to do with you!" Satan, true to his role as accuser, points out to God what he sees as an apparent chink in Job's armor. He questions whether Job's faith will survive the suffering he has been so

---

[16]See Comments 2.2, "The Prologue and Genesis 2–3" and 5.1, "The Question of Integrity."

determined to avoid through his sacrifices and the security provided by his substantial nest egg of livestock.

So what are we to make of that taunt? Isn't it true that many around the world are hearing a message that promises just what Satan is describing—that putting your faith in God is but a means to health and wealth? Put your faith in God, and he will be at your beck and call. All you have to do is ask. If you are poor, God can make you rich; if you are sick, he can make you well.

And why wouldn't he? We're his beloved children, aren't we? What father, if his son asks for a fish, will give him a snake? Ask and you will receive. If you only have enough faith, it will all be yours. And, of course, the preachers of this prosperity gospel have to show by their extravagant lifestyle, with their fancy cars and big houses and private jets, that it works, and it can work for you, too.

Now, most of us are a little too sophisticated to swallow the health and wealth message. And, truth be told, we're wealthy enough already. But we have our own version of the prosperity gospel, in the form of the therapeutic gospel.[17] The reward that we count on is not material, but emotional; what Jesus promises is not objective wealth but subjective well-being. Invite Jesus into your heart, and he will fill you up with peace and hope and eternal joy. He will give you an "abundant life"—and we have lots of ways that we can define that abundance. Put your faith in Christ, and he will give you the life you want—"your best life now," with a no-hassle guarantee.

We don't fear God for nothing—no, we fear God for the blessings he gives. How right is Satan about Job? How right is Satan about you?

THE DIVINE GAMBIT

In this opening chapter, we have seen a godly man and a cynical taunt, and finally we want to look at what may be the most challenging part

---

[17]See Ash, *Job*, 19-21.

of the whole story. This is what I call the divine gambit—God's willingness to put Satan's claim to the test.

Satan had said, "Stretch out your hand and strike everything [Job] has, and he will surely curse you to your face" (Job 1:11). The Lord then says to Satan, "Very well, then, everything he has is in your power, but on the man himself do not lay a finger" (Job 1:12).

What? Did we hear this right—"everything he has is in your power"? "Go ahead," God is saying. "Bring this godly man, my servant Job, to utter ruin. Have all his sheep and cattle and camels and all his servants carried away by foreign invaders, then kill all ten of his children when the house collapses and crushes them as they are all together celebrating a birthday."

And that's just stage one. After that comes the bodily assault on poor Job. Satan gets to assail him with painful sores that cover his whole body.[18] Job is left to rot, as he sits among the ashes of the garbage heap. "He's all yours, Satan, go to it. And we'll see if you're right about my servant Job."

How is this possible? How could a good and just God possibly agree to such a deal?

Let's be clear. On the one hand, Satan is the bad guy in all this. He is the actual agent of destruction. It is his hand that directly afflicts Job. Some try to say that that gets God off the hook. They say that Job is wrong to complain to God at all. It is Satan that he ought to revile and rail against.

But that's too simple. Laying the blame for Job's distress on Satan makes no sense of the rest of the book. As we'll see, Job's complaint throughout is with God, not Satan. Job knows God to be ultimately responsible for what happens to him, and that assumption is nowhere contested—and certainly not by God when he finally speaks for himself (Job 38–41). In chapter two, God takes direct responsibility

---

[18]See Comment 3.1, "Job's Disease."

for what happens when he says that Satan incited him against Job to ruin him (Job 2:3), and at the end of the book, the narrator will likewise attribute the blame to God (Job 42:11).[19]

To be sure, God never acts with malicious intent, ever. But he is still in charge, even when secondary agents like Satan act badly. Satan must ask permission to harm poor Job. He has no authority on his own. God and Satan are not two equal powers vying for control of the universe. The devil exists, but as Martin Luther used to say, he is "God's devil." And God has him on a leash. He can only do what the Lord allows him to do. But throughout the Bible we see that whatever evil the Lord allows the devil to perpetrate, he can also use for his good purposes. At a number of places in the Bible, we have what you would call dual intentions at work—in the same act, the devil can intend evil, while God can intend good.

A classic biblical example of this is seen in the actions of Joseph's brothers in the book of Genesis. They acted cruelly in selling Joseph into slavery, but in the end, Joseph forgives them and says, "You intended to harm me, but God intended it for good to accomplish what is now being done, the saving of many lives" (Gen 50:20). One act performed by two different actors with two different intentions: one evil and one good. And, of course, the ultimate example of this is found in the crucifixion of God's own Son, Jesus Christ. It was a most evil act—perpetrated by evil men; yet God acted through it to bring blessing to the whole world (cf. Acts 2:23-24; 3:18; 4:27-28).[20]

Satan brings about the sufferings that Job endures, and by them Satan intends to tempt Job to evil by cursing God to his face. But Satan drops out as a character in the rest of the book. The story revolves around God's intentions in all this. Why would he ever agree to such a bargain with the devil—a bargain that means inflicting

---

[19]See Comment 10.3, "God and Evil (42:11)."
[20]On this point, see Comment 2.3, "Calvin on Satan."

pain on an innocent man, not to mention all sorts of collateral death and destruction?

Some suggest that one way out of this theological dilemma is to see the book simply as a grand stylized drama. It is essentially a fictional morality play, one that paints the most extreme picture imaginable to heighten the tension in such a way as to make the spiritual struggle of Job with God as intense as possible. In other words: "Don't worry," they say, "no one was actually harmed in the making of this book."[21]

That's possible, but I don't think it is the case. Yes, the descriptions may be stylized, but I think Job was a real, well-known person, and surely something really bad must have happened to him to make him as famous as he was. In any event, you still have to wrestle with why God allows such bad things to happen—*even in the story.*

If you are troubled by God allowing the death of Job's children in this story you are exactly where the author wants you to be. That's the point. You should be unsettled and provoked by all this. You are exactly where Job was—wondering how a good and just God could allow such things to happen. This challenges our preconceived ideas about God, just like those of Job and his friends.

We want God to act in predictable and self-evidently good ways, don't we? God is supposed to act in the ways that we think a good God should act. But what do we do when he doesn't? God himself admits in Job 2:3 that he was incited to ruin Job "without any reason." Job was an innocent man; he was a godly man. There was no apparent justification—no reason based on any justice known to us—for God to have allowed Job to be ruined as he was. And this is exactly what the book is about. Can we hold on to God in faith, will we fear him, will we still worship him even when our treatment seems a mysterious travesty of justice?

---

[21]See Comment 2.4, "Job as a Drama."

"Does Job fear God for nothing?" Satan's question is a taunt, a provocation, even an insult. For behind Satan's question is not only the accusation that there is no such thing as a genuine believer—one who really worships God for who he is and not just for what they can get out of him. Though ostensibly a challenge to Job's faith, this accusation is ultimately leveled at the credibility of God.[22]

First, it is an accusation that God has been wrong to bless Job as he has, because Job's faith is not genuine anyway.

But even more, in this question we find the further implication that God himself is not really worthy of worship for his own sake rather than just for the good gifts he bestows. This statement is an assault on the intrinsic glory of God himself. God's willingness to engage in this gambit with Satan is ultimately about that—God's own glory. It's not just that Job's faith is on the line here. God's own glory is at stake. In some mysterious way, Job's worship of God in the face of his suffering will put God's own worthiness on public display. We see a reflection of this in Peter's words in the New Testament: "Now for a little while you may have had to suffer grief in all kinds of trials. These have come so that the proven genuineness of your faith—of greater worth than gold, which perishes even though refined by fire—may result in praise, glory and honor when Jesus Christ is revealed" (1 Pet 1:6-7).

The "praise, glory and honor" that rightly belongs to God is somehow demonstrated and displayed when the faith of God's people is tested and found genuine. Such faith manifests the truth that God is worthy of worship. This is what the cynic can never understand, for the cynic denies the reality of a goodness that is unassailable, a beauty that cannot be spoiled, and a truth that stands forever. The cynic denies a God who is worthy of all praise, glory, and honor.

---

[22]Gerhard von Rad, *Wisdom in Israel*, trans. James D. Martin (Harrisburg, PA: Trinity Press International, 1972), 221.

But that is just what the angelic chorus sings incessantly in heaven—"You are worthy, our Lord and God, to receive glory and honor and power" (Rev 4:11). But Satan, he never joins in. The question of this book is, Will Job? The question that it raises is, Will you?

DIGGING DEEPER

2.1. "The Satan" and the heavenly council. The name "Satan" derives from the Hebrew noun *satan*, meaning "adversary" or "accuser."[23] In the Old Testament, this term is applied to both human (1 Sam 29:4; 2 Sam 19:22; 1 Kings 5:4; 11:14, 23, 25; Ps 109:6) and celestial figures (Num 22:22, 32; 1 Chron 21:1; Job 1–2; Zech 3:1-7). Two ancient Near Eastern concepts contribute significantly to the developing understanding of Satan. First is the combat myth, in which a heroic, often divine, figure defeats a powerful adversary, such as Marduk's slaying of Tiamat in Enuma Elish or Baal's similar conquest of Yam in the Baal Cycle. References to this myth appear in the Bible, though without explicitly connecting the opponent and Satan (Ps 74:13-15; Is 27:1; 51:9). Second, the widespread ancient Near Eastern concept of the divine council introduces the role of celestial figures in the legal maintenance of earthly justice. Psalm 82 offers the clearest biblical example of this, as "God presides in the great assembly; he renders judgment among the 'gods'" (Ps 82:1) and admonishes these "gods" for their failure to instill justice before declaring that they will "die like mere mortals" (v. 7).

The four passages that use the term *satan* for a celestial figure all understand him primarily in terms of this motif, though they do not all necessarily refer to the same figure. In Zechariah 3:1-7, the celestial satan figure opposes the angel of the Lord in a dispute

---

[23]Much of this section is adapted from Will Kynes, "Satan," in *The Oxford Encyclopedia of the Bible and Theology*, ed. Samuel Balentine et al. (Oxford: Oxford University Press, 2015), 264-67.

over whether Joshua is worthy to serve as high priest. The Lord decides in Joshua's favor and rebukes the Satan (Zech 3:2). In Job 1–2, the Satan appears to play a similar prosecutorial role.

The implicit hostility between God and the Satan in Zechariah 3 and Job 1–2 becomes explicit in the New Testament, where Satan (now a proper name) is called an enemy (Mt 13:39), the evil one (Mt 13:38), an adversary (1 Pet 5:8), a murderer, and the father of lies (Jn 8:44). Yet, several texts present Satan as subject to God's will, as in Job. God uses him for discipline (1 Cor 5:5; 1 Tim 1:20), and Jesus' intercession delivers Peter from Satan's "sifting" (Lk 22:32). Revelation 12 promises Satan's eventual defeat while mixing together much of the earlier imagery used for Satan: "The great dragon was thrown down—that ancient serpent called the devil, or Satan, who leads the whole world astray. He was hurled to the earth, and his angels with him. . . . The accuser of our brothers and sisters . . . has been hurled down" (Rev 12:9-10; cf. Rev 20:2, 10; Mt 25:41). However, the collection of various hints at the nature of a supernatural adversary of God into a full "biography of Satan," from the fall of "Lucifer" due to his pride (Is 14:4-20; Ezek 28:11-19) and then his temptation of humanity in the Garden of Eden (Genesis 3) did not emerge until the early church.[24]

2.2. The prologue and Genesis 2–3. The prologue of Job is a mirror image of Genesis 2–3.[25] There, the serpent enters a peaceful paradise and leads a human figure to question whether God's internal motivation is to be trusted (Gen 3:5), and Adam blames his wife's influence for his disloyalty to God. Job, however, is thrust into dystopian chaos, but maintains his loyalty and encourages his wife to do the same, validating God's confidence in the integrity of his human servant.[26] This trust despite current

[24]Henry Ansgar Kelly, *Satan: A Biography* (Cambridge: Cambridge University Press, 2006).
[25]Sam Meier, "Job I–II: A Reflection of Genesis I–III," *Vetus Testamentum* 39 (1989): 183-93; Michael C. Legaspi, *Wisdom in Classical and Biblical Tradition* (New York: Oxford University Press, 2018), 87-91.
[26]See Comment 5.1, "The Question of Integrity."

appearances is what makes Job's response one of faith, which answers the Satan's challenge.[27] As a second Adam, Job passes the test the first human couple failed.[28] Reinforcing this connection, Job's words in Job 1:21 and 2:10 draw on significant language from Genesis 2–3, such as "naked," "good," and "evil."

2.3. Calvin on Satan. The role of Satan in the prologue is one of the more difficult theological challenges in Job. Given his robust reflection on the nature of divine sovereignty, John Calvin provides a helpful resource for reflecting on Satan theologically. Calvin describes Satan as "the instrument of God's wrath," who "bends himself hither and thither at His beck and command to execute His just judgments."[29] Calvin points to the affliction of Job, focusing in particular on the Chaldean raiders who stole his camels and killed his servants (Job 1:17), to distinguish the role that each actor plays in the same event, such that we may "attribute this same work to God, to Satan, and to man as author, without either excusing Satan as associated with God, or making God the author of evil."[30] To do so, he claims that we must distinguish the purpose and manner of each participant in the event: "The Lord's purpose is to exercise the patience of His servant by calamity; Satan endeavors to drive him to desperation; the Chaldeans strive to acquire gain from another's property contrary to law and right."[31] Each also has a different manner of acting: "The Lord permits Satan to afflict His servant; He hands the Chaldeans over to be impelled by Satan, having chosen them as His ministers for this task. Satan with his poison darts arouses the wicked minds of the Chaldeans to execute that evil deed. They dash madly into

---

[27]See Michael V. Fox, "The Meanings of the Book of Job," *Journal of Biblical Literature* 137 (2018): 17-18.

[28]See Comment 7.2, "Allusions to Adam."

[29]John Calvin, *Institutes of the Christian Religion*, ed. John T. McNeil (Louisville, KY: Westminster John Knox Press, 1960), 2.4.2, 311.

[30]Calvin, *Institutes*, 2.4.2, 310.

[31]Calvin, *Institutes*, 2.4.2, 310.

injustice, and they render all their members guilty and befoul them by the crime."[32]

In one act, three different agents, with three different purposes and three different manners of acting, converge. Yet, Calvin claims that the different purposes and manners give this one act three different moral qualities. For God, the act is good, while for Satan and the Chaldeans it is evil. Rather than flattening out the moral quality of an act and declaring it absolutely evil for all involved, Calvin's nuanced approach so differentiates between the agents in an act that it becomes difficult to call it the same act in reference to each—God is building endurance and deepened faith, Satan is trying to tear down faith, and the Chaldeans are on a camel raid. The way Calvin distinguishes the agency within this single event demonstrates the hierarchical view of causation that he uses to explain God's relationship to evil, including Satan. God can direct both Satan and humanity and Satan can direct humanity (when allowed by God), but humans cannot direct either. The undertakings are not equal; God's reigns supreme and provides the ultimate purpose for the action. However, Satan and sinful humans are still responsible for their behavior. According to Calvin, Satan's purposes do not frustrate God's; they are merely an instrument for our good and God's glory.

2.4. Job as a drama. Job has long been associated with drama. Already in the fifth century, Theodore of Mopsuestia (d. 428 CE) was said to believe that Job was composed in imitation of Greek tragedy. Though this dramatic interpretation was condemned in the early church, it found a number of prominent supporters in the sixteenth century and was widespread from the seventeenth into the nineteenth centuries.[33] This often led Job to be associated with the Song of Songs, which also was interpreted as a drama during this period. This interpretation virtually disappeared as the

---

[32]Calvin, *Institutes*, 2.4.2, 310.
[33]C. L. Seow, *Job 1–21: Interpretation and Commentary* (Grand Rapids, MI: Eerdmans, 2013), 48.

Wisdom Literature category gained greater prominence in the twentieth century.

Recently, however, the dramatic reading of Job has been resurrected. Some see the book as a tragedy, though they will admit the book's happy ending violates that genre. Others appeal to the ending along with the incongruity and irony throughout to associate the book with comedy, though they acknowledge the book's message still has a tragic ring. Interpreting the book as drama in a more general sense serves heuristically, at least, to draw the audience into the impassioned "intellectual action" of the book,[34] even if its lack of actual action and character development make it difficult to imagine Job being performed on stage.

Dramatic interpretations also account well for the central role dialogue plays in the book and the numerous plays it has inspired. For example, in *The Masque of Reason*, Robert Frost imagines a forty-third chapter for the book of Job in which God appears in a flaming bush to justify himself to Job and his wife. In Archibald MacLeish's Pulitzer Prize–winning play *J.B.*, a wealthy New York banker loses everything, rejects the comfort of three characters representing history, science, and religion, respectively, and finds solace, not in God's eventual offer to restore his prosperity in exchange for his obedience but in the love of his wife. The book has also been adapted cinematically numerous times, including in the recent films *The Tree of Life*, *A Serious Man*, and *Bruce Almighty*. All these adaptations reflect not merely the dramatic nature of the book, but also the dramatic effect it has on readers, as it engages them intellectually and emotionally, incorporating them into the interplay between its characters.

---

[34]Luis Alonso Schökel, "Toward a Dramatic Reading of the Book of Job," *Semeia* 7 (1977): 45–61.

three

THE INNOCENT SUFFERER

JOB 1–3

Catastrophic loss wreaks destruction like a massive flood. It is unrelenting, unforgiving, and uncontrollable, brutally erosive to body, mind, and spirit. Sometimes loss does its damage instantly, as if it were a flood resulting from a broken dam that releases a great torrent of water, sweeping away everything in its path. Sometimes loss does its damage gradually, as if it were a flood resulting from unceasing rain that causes rivers and lakes to swell until they spill over their banks, engulfing, saturating, and destroying whatever the water touches. In either case, catastrophic loss leaves the landscape of one's life forever changed. My experience was like a dam that broke. In one moment I was overrun by a torrent of pain I did not expect.[1]

So begins theology professor Jerry Sittser in his book *A Grace Disguised*. In this book Sittser tells the gripping story of his life after the car he was driving collided head-on with a drunk driver, and Sittser's wife, his mother, and his daughter were all killed. "In one moment my family as I had known and cherished it was obliterated," he wrote. "Three generations—gone in an instant!"[2]

As I write this, I feel distinctly unqualified to expound the book of Job. Who am I to talk about the challenge to faith that comes from

---

[1]Jerry L. Sittser, *A Grace Disguised: How the Soul Grows Through Loss* (Grand Rapids, MI: Zondervan, 2004), 24.
[2]Sittser, *Grace Disguised*, 27.

intense suffering? I have lived a blessed life. Sure, I have suffered loss. I am now older than my father when he died of stomach cancer, and my older brother was diagnosed with the same disease just one year later, and he died at age forty. The same year my father died, Susan and I lost a premature stillborn baby, a little girl. We all suffer in various ways—this is a fallen world. But I feel that my pain has been minimal compared to many others.

I read about people who have really suffered—people like Jerry Sittser, or like Trinity Evangelical Divinity School professor John Feinberg. In 1987, after fourteen years of marriage and with three young boys at home, Feinberg's wife, Pat, was diagnosed with a rare disease that causes a deterioration of the brain—with both physical and mental devastation. There is no treatment for the disease, much less a cure. More than that, it is genetic—and it is caused by a dominant gene—which meant that there was a 50 percent chance that each of their boys would also become its victims. And they would not know if they had the gene until the symptoms begin to appear in their late twenties or early thirties. Pat became progressively worse. In 2001 she had to have a feeding tube put in, in 2006 she could no longer be cared for at home and needed to be put in a nursing home, and from 2010 she was unable to speak a word. Feinberg writes about his experience in 2016 with brutal honesty in his book *When There Are No Easy Answers*.[3]

Certainly, I have my emotional ups and downs, but my afflictions have been more of the vicarious kind. In my role as a pastor I have shared in the sufferings of others—the trials of many in our church who experience intense anguish, emotional heartache, pain that persists, grief that leaves a lasting hole in one's life that will never be filled. Some of them have experienced those times when there are

---

[3]John Feinberg, *When There Are No Easy Answers: Thinking Differently About God, Suffering, and Evil* (Grand Rapids, MI: Kregel, 2016).

no easy answers. I weep with those who weep, but their pain was not mine. What have I suffered compared to that?

JOB SUFFERS GREATLY

And then there is Job. The author of the book wants us to see Job's suffering as, in a sense, the most extreme case imaginable. It is extreme both in the height from which he fell and in the depths to which he descended, magnified by the suddenness of it all.

As we have seen, he sets us up for the tragedy to come by first extolling Job for his godliness—Job "was blameless and upright; he feared God and shunned evil" (Job 1:1). And in what appears to follow from that, he describes Job's greatness—displayed in his immense wealth and high social status (Job 1:2-3).

But then, almost in an instant, it was all taken away:

One day when Job's sons and daughters were feasting and drinking wine at the oldest brother's house, a messenger came to Job and said, "The oxen were plowing and the donkeys were grazing nearby, and the Sabeans attacked and made off with them. They put the servants to the sword, and I am the only one who has escaped to tell you!"

While he was still speaking, another messenger came and said, "The fire of God fell from the heavens and burned up the sheep and the servants, and I am the only one who has escaped to tell you!"

While he was still speaking, another messenger came and said, "The Chaldeans formed three raiding parties and swept down on your camels and made off with them. They put the servants to the sword, and I am the only one who has escaped to tell you!"

While he was still speaking, yet another messenger came and said, "Your sons and daughters were feasting and drinking wine at the oldest brother's house, when suddenly a mighty wind swept in from the desert and struck the four corners of the house. It collapsed on them and they are dead, and I am the only one who has escaped to tell you!" (Job 1:13-19)

There is a comprehensiveness to this description. It involves human agents—Sabean and Chaldean raiders—and natural forces—lightning, a mighty desert wind. The disasters strike from all four points of the compass—south, west, north, east.[4]

"While he was still speaking," we read in Job 1:16. And again in the next verse. And again in Job 1:18. One blow of the hammer after another—bang, bang, bang—with no time to take it in, and no time to adjust, to reflect, or even to pray. Each shock increased in intensity, culminating in the death of all his children. All of the objects that reflected God's blessing in his life were whisked away, as if by a thunderous tsunami, and after each calamity is the repeated refrain: "and I am the only one who has escaped to tell you!" (Job 1:15, 16, 17). "It is as if the life of [each] messenger is spared only so that Job can be told and his suffering made worse."[5] Suddenly, Job, this great man, was reduced to nothing.

But this was not all. On another day, we read in Job 2:7, "Satan went out from the presence of the LORD and afflicted Job with painful sores from the soles of his feet to the crown of his head."[6] Not only are his great possessions carried away, and not only are his children crushed, but his own body is ravaged by excruciating pain. He sat "among the ashes"—a burning dump outside the town, a place of isolation, degradation, and humiliation. What an ugly and pitiful sight.

Job's friends, when they saw him from a distance, could hardly recognize him. They must have been overwhelmed, not unlike

---

[4]Lindsay Wilson, *Job* (Grand Rapids, MI: Eerdmans, 2015), 35.
[5]Wilson, *Job*, 35.
[6]For further discussion, see Comment 3.1, "Job's Disease."

Allied troops entering the Nazi death camps and discovering the survivors' decimated bodies. Here is suffering in its extreme.

Job is devastated in every area of his life. Physically, his body is racked by painful sores. Emotionally, he grieves the loss of all his children. Socially, he has plummeted from wealthy landowner sitting at the city gates to pariah languishing in the ash heap. Job is an outcast, a pariah. In fact, he will say later that he was now mocked in song by the young men, and "they do not hesitate to spit in my face" (Job 30:9-10). Even his own wife appears to have turned against him.

And then there was the spiritual suffering—Where was his God in all this? Job is suffering inexplicably—"without any reason." Job was innocent, he had done nothing to deserve this—and, being privy to that exchange in heaven, we know this to be true. God himself admits it (Job 2:3)!

The magnitude of that suffering is beyond anything we can imagine. We are meant to resonate with the feelings of Job's friends, who were speechless in the presence of such a pathetic and appalling figure (Job 2:13).

So how can any of us relate to Job? We might be tempted to use him simply as a foil. Job's suffering diminishes the significance of our own pain. "You think you've got it bad? That's nothing—just look at Job! So just quit complaining and buck up!"

But that wouldn't be right simply because suffering can't be quantified; it can't be compared. We all do it, of course. When a tragedy occurs, we talk about the number of people killed or injured, the time spent in the hospital, the severity of the abuse, and the inconveniences of the illness. But we forget that suffering is personal; it is very subjective; and its intensity can't be computed by somehow measuring the circumstances that cause it. For those affected, there may be no difference in the amount of suffering caused by a terrorist attack that kills a hundred people, and a heart attack that kills just one.

Yes, there are differences in degrees, but the truth is, we all suffer, and we all will suffer. That's true for the simple reason that every human relationship we enjoy and cherish will one day be destroyed by death—the death of the one we love or our own. Jesus himself tells us that we will suffer. "In this world you will have trouble," he says (Jn 16:33). Job's suffering is in the extreme, but in the end, Job's struggles are just human struggles. For everyone suffers—and each in a unique way. Make no mistake—our suffering is real, and it is hard.

But there is more going on here. Job's struggles are not just human struggles; they are also the struggles of the believer—the man or woman of faith. They are the struggles of God's own children. Remember, Job doesn't suffer in spite of his godliness. No, he suffers because of it. It is God who volunteers Job for this most hazardous assignment, only because he knew Job to be the most capable soldier in his army.

What we see is not how God treats his enemies, but how God treats his friends (which is why, someone has suggested, he has so few of them!). We all suffer—so don't let the magnitude of Job's suffering distance you from the message of this book. For, in fact, the message is not primarily about how we deal with suffering but about how we relate to God.

JOB RESPONDS SUBMISSIVELY

So how does Job relate to God in the midst of this incredible trial? Let's be clear that from the outset, Job is not unmoved by it all. He is no Stoic who simply takes it all in without emotion, a passionless rock unmoved by the world. Job is deeply grieved by his loss, and he immediately enters into a state of mourning.

Every culture has its own way of recognizing death and its effects. We here in America are rather sparse in this regard, but we have our funeral customs—people wear black; they send flowers or notes of condolence; they visit the bereaved and perhaps bring a casserole. Those most affected will generally take some time off from work, refraining from some usual entertainments as an expression of their grief.

Other cultures have much more elaborate rituals, involving a period of relative isolation. Some Jews observe a mourning period, called *shiva*, for the seven days following the funeral, modeled on Joseph mourning the death of his father Jacob for seven days (Gen 50:10; cf. Job 2:13). In some cultures, this grieving period lasts for as much as forty days before the bereaved are reintegrated into society.

We see something of Job's grief in the ritual acts he performs. When he first hears the news of disaster, "Job got up and tore his robe and shaved his head" (Job 1:20). Tearing one's clothes is a common sign of grief or even outrage in the Bible.[7] Shaving the head has the same sense.[8]

Then in Job 2:8 we read that "Job took a piece of broken pottery and scraped himself with it as he sat among the ashes." Sitting among the ashes is also a ritual of grief,[9] for dust and ashes are signs of death, and it is to dust and ashes that we all return.[10]

And though most commentators think of Job scraping himself with broken pottery as simply a physical reaction to the sores that covered his body as a means of trying to ease the pain, a case can be made that this, too, is a ritual act—a form of self-laceration, reflecting the bodily losses he has sustained. In Jeremiah 48:37, for example, the prophet speaks of the lamenting of the Moabites:

---

[7]This can be found sixteen times in the Bible. See, e.g., Gen 37:29, 34; Judg 11:35; 2 Sam 3:31; 13:19; Esther 4:1.

[8]Cf., e.g., Is 15:2; Jer 16:6; Ezek 27:31; Amos 8:10; Mic 1:16.

[9]Cf. Ezek 27:30; Is 61:3; Jer 6:26; Jn 3:6; Esther 4:1.

[10]Cf. Job 30:19—"He throws me into the mud, and I am reduced to dust and ashes." For dust and ashes as a sign of total deprivation, cf. Ps. 113:7.

Every head is shaved
  and every beard cut off;
every hand is slashed
  and every waist is covered with sackcloth.[11]

Job is engaging in the rituals of mourning, and his friends will join with him. When they saw him, "they began to weep aloud, and they tore their robes and sprinkled dust on their heads. Then they sat on the ground with him for seven days and seven nights." His friends, then, take on the ritual responsibility to "sympathize with him and comfort him" (Job 2:12-13) and to move Job on from his mourning ritual into a ritual re-entrance into community and a normal state of life, signified by feasting and gift giving, which we eventually see in the epilogue (Job 42:11-12).[12]

So Job is no Stoic. He is not unmoved by his tragic circumstances. He grieves, but his initial reaction to all this is clearly one of humble submission. When he first received the mind-numbing news of one horrific event after another, we read in Job 1:20-21,

He fell to the ground in worship and said:

"Naked I came from my mother's womb,
  and naked I will depart.
The Lord gave and the Lord has taken away;
  may the name of the Lord be praised."

Again, after his body is afflicted with horrible sores, in Job 2:9 we read of his wife almost taunting him: "Are you still maintaining your integrity? Curse God and die!" "Why go on with this torture? Just

---

[11]Cf. Jer 16:6; 41:5; 47:5. But cf. Deut 14:1—"You are the children of the Lord your God. Do not cut yourselves or shave the front of your heads for the dead."

[12]On the ritual understanding of Job's mourning, see David A. Lambert, "The Book of Job in Ritual Perspective," *Journal of Biblical Literature* 134, no. 3 (Fall 2015): 557-75; Heath A. Thomas, "Job's Rejection and Liminal Traverse: A Close (Re)reading of Job 42:6," in *The Unfolding of Your Words Gives Light: Studies on Biblical Hebrew in Honor of George L. Klein*, ed. Ethan C. Jones (University Park, PA: Eisenbrauns, 2018), 155-74.

put an end to it!" It's as if she can't stand to see her husband suffer any longer. But Job will have none of it: "Shall we accept good from God, and not trouble?" he says (Job 2:10).

Such faith! What more could you possibly want from someone in such circumstances? This is piety in its purest form.

What unwavering devotion to God. What humble submission to God's will. Job is a model believer: "In all this, Job did not sin by charging God with wrongdoing" (Job 1:22). What an inspiration Job is!

Certainly Job inspired Matt Redman and Beth Redman, who wrote that well-known praise song "Blessed Be Your Name." It speaks of blessing God in good times and bad, both when "streams of abundance flow" and when "I'm found in the desert place." Through it all, "Still I will say, blessed be the name of the Lord! Blessed be your glorious name!"[13] That's a wonderful song. I love that song! And that's the song on Job's lips in the midst of the most extreme form of suffering we could ever imagine. Thank you, Job, for your encouragement and your uplifting inspiration. The book could end right there, and we would extol its lofty message. Job has passed the test of faith; God can be worshiped apart from his blessings. Take that, Satan! Game over!

JOB PROTESTS BOLDLY

But, of course, the problem is the book doesn't end right there. Far from it. At the end of Job 2, his three friends show up to sympathize with him and comfort him. They sit on the ground with him silently for seven days and nights. But then we read in Job 3:1—"After this, Job opened his mouth"—and what comes out of it is not at all what we expect. Instead of pious praise come words of bitter cursing. Job

---

[13]Matt Redmond, "Blessed Be Your Name," by Matt Redman and Beth Redman, *Where Angels Fear to Tread*, Worship Together, 2002.

engages in what one writer called "a retrospective contraceptive wish applied to his own existence."[14] In other words, Job wishes he had never been born:

> May the day of my birth perish,
>   and the night that said, "A boy is conceived!"
> That day—may it turn to darkness;
>   may God above not care about it;
>   may no light shine on it. (Job 3:3-4)

Of course, in seeking to rewrite the past, Job is asking for something that is impossible. This is a cry of the heart, expressing his extreme frustration with his condition and the disorder he is experiencing. Life is not supposed to be like this. Job's cry is "a bitter irony, a perverse upside-down version of Happy Birthday to Me."[15] Indeed, his despair expands into a wish for the un-making of creation itself.[16]

And if his birth couldn't have been prevented, why couldn't he at least have experienced an early death—

> Why did I not perish at birth,
>   and die as I came from the womb? (Job 3:11)
> . . .
> For now I would be lying down in peace;
>   I would be asleep and at rest. (Job 3:13)
> . . .
> Or why was I not hidden away in the ground like
>   a stillborn child,
>   like an infant who never saw the light of day?
> There the wicked cease from turmoil,
>   and there the weary are at rest. (Job 3:16-17)

---

[14]Christopher Ash, *Job: The Wisdom of the Cross* (Wheaton, IL: Crossway, 2014), 74.
[15]Daniel Simundson, *The Message of Job* (Minneapolis: Augsburg, 1980), 47.
[16]See Comment 3.2, "Job's Countercosmic Curse."

Why? Why? Why? The question haunts Job in his anguish.

> Why is light given to those in misery,
>> and life to the bitter of soul,
> to those who long for death that does not come,
>> who search for it more than for hidden treasure,
> who are filled with gladness
>> and rejoice when they reach the grave?
> Why is life given to a man
>> whose way is hidden,
>> whom God has hedged in? . . .
> What I feared has come upon me;
>> what I dreaded has happened to me. (Job 3:20-23, 25)

Wait a minute! What happened to that pious Job, that patient Job, that Job who was able to praise God even in the midst of his tears? This is a protesting Job.

And, as we shall see, it gets worse—much worse—and Job will appear, at times, disrespectful, impertinent, even brazen and brash in the way he deals with God.

What happened? We can only surmise that reality has sunk in. Job's initial response to his suffering was good and right. It is what you would expect from Job, the godly man that he is. It is what he had been trained to say, and he was trained to say it because it was true.

> The LORD gave and the LORD has taken away;
>> blessed be the name of the LORD. (Job 1:20)

But those words of pious truth were not the truth that he was now experiencing. The flood waters have receded, and he is now surveying the full extent of the damage. Job is overwhelmed by it all. He is agitated and agonizing; and he longs for rest. Such rest in the Bible speaks of that divine order—the world as it is supposed to be.

This rest points us to that time when God rested from his work on the seventh day.[17] The initial flash of light that Job experiences quickly fades, and a deep darkness sets in—a dark night of the soul.[18]

In Job 3 we see how he is really feeling. He is in anguish at what he is going through. He is torn up inside. And who wouldn't be? These are words of deep lament, or as one writer describes it, "a spine-chilling howl of despair."[19]

You may be shocked at such language, but you shouldn't be. Part of our concern may simply come from a certain cultural vantage point—particularly those of us with a northern European heritage. We tend to prize emotional restraint, a stiff upper lip, always remaining cool, calm, and collected. Emotional outbursts of any kind tend to make us nervous. Job's words certainly challenge "the bourgeois etiquette that has dominated the mores of western Christendom, especially in the Puritan tradition."[20] Self-control, Francis Anderson continues, is "no guide to the rightness of Job's speech. . . . The Lord's testing is not to find out if Job can sit unmoved like a piece of wood."[21]

Job laments, and he laments boldly. And as we read our Bible, Job is not alone in voicing words of lament.[22] We quite often see passionate expressions of grief and sorrow in the Psalms. Consider Psalm 38, for example. This is a psalm of David, but it could just as well have come from Job.

> My wounds fester and are loathsome . . .
> I am bowed down and brought very low;
>   all day long I go about mourning.

---

[17]See Comment 3.3, "Rest in the Bible."
[18]See Comment 7.1, "The Hiddenness of God."
[19]T. J. Gorringe, "Job and the Pharisees," *Interpretation* 40 (1986): 19.
[20]Francis Anderson, *Job* (London: Inter-Varsity Press, 1976), 100.
[21]Anderson, *Job*, 101.
[22]See Comment 7.5, "The Biblical Tradition of Defiant Faith."

My back is filled with searing pain;

    there is no health in my body.

I am feeble and utterly crushed;

    I groan in anguish of heart. (Ps 38:5-8)

Even more to the point, consider the lament of the prophet Jeremiah:

Cursed be the day I was born!

    May the day my mother bore me not be blessed!

Cursed be the man who brought my father the news,

    who made him very glad, saying,

    "A child is born to you—a son!" (Jer 20:14-15)

. . .

Why did I ever come out of the womb

    to see trouble and sorrow

    and to end my days in shame? (Jer 20:18)

In fact, the Old Testament has a whole book of lament, called Lamentations, grieving the destruction of the temple in Jerusalem by the Babylonians.

Even in the New Testament we see evidence of the agony of life in this fallen world. In 2 Corinthians 1, Paul says, "We do not want you to be uninformed, brothers and sisters, about the troubles we experienced in the province of Asia. We were under great pressure, far beyond our ability to endure, so that we despaired of life itself. Indeed, we felt we had received the sentence of death" (2 Cor 1:8-9). Later in that letter, he says, "I wrote you out of great distress and anguish of heart and with many tears" (2 Cor 2:4).

And didn't Jesus himself, in his sharing of our human experience, feel that same agony? He weeps at the tomb of his friend Lazarus. We read that "he was deeply moved in spirit and troubled" (Jn 11:33). In the Garden of Gethsemane, he lamented, "My soul is overwhelmed with sorrow to the point of death" (Mt 26:38), and he prayed "in anguish," and his sweat was like drops of blood (Lk 22:44).

And on the cross, we hear those most harrowing words of grief, when the full weight of the fallenness of this world falls on his shoulders: "My God, my God, why have you forsaken me?" (Mt 27:46). This is reality—Jesus, the ultimate innocent sufferer, wrestling with God at the moment of his greatest test of faith.

In Job 3, the patient Job becomes the protesting Job. We shouldn't be surprised at his changing mood. Consider the nineteenth-century theologian Robert Dabney.[23] In a matter of about a month, in two separate incidents, he lost two of his sons, Jimmy and Bobby. He wrote this in a letter: "When my Jimmy died, the grief was painfully sharp, but the actings of faith, the embracing of consolation, and all the cheering truths which ministered comfort to me were just as vivid."[24] Here Dabney shares the experience of the "patient Job"— "Blessed be the name of the Lord." But Dabney continues in the same letter, "But when the stroke was repeated, and thereby doubled, I seem to be paralyzed and stunned. I know that my loss is doubled, and I know also that the same cheering truths apply to the second as to the first, but I remain numb, downcast, almost without hope and interest."[25]

Jerry Sittser writes, similarly, "I felt punished by God and thought death would bring welcomed relief."[26] This is Job 3—the protesting Job. Here is Job in the depths of despair, lamenting the agony of the life that he was now living, cursing the day of his birth.

But note well—Job does not curse God, and he won't. Job never goes there, but he grieves, he laments, and he protests. He does so

---

[23]Dabney was also known as a defender of Southern slavery.
[24]Thomas Cary Johnson, *The Life and Letters of Robert Lewis Dabney* (Edinburgh: Banner of Truth, 1977), 172.
[25]Johnson, *Life and Letters*, 172.
[26]Sittser, *Grace Disguised*, 256-57.

boldly, almost brazenly, but he never curses God. He never denies
God's goodness, or his worthiness to be worshiped. He never treats
God as his enemy. In fact, it is Job's conviction that God is good and
that God is just that creates this crisis of faith in the first place.

MRS. JOB AND JOB'S BEWILDERMENT

We will have much more to say about Job's response to God as we go
on, but let me share one thought that may provide a clue to where
this is going. Look back at Job's interaction with his wife, Mrs. Job.
She appears to act as a tempter, when she says, "Are you still maintaining your integrity? Curse God and die!"[27] That's exactly what
Satan wants him to do. But Job resists: "You are talking like a foolish
woman" (2:9-10). Notice, he says *like* a foolish woman. He knows
she's *not* a foolish woman. This is *Job's* wife, after all. Job would never
have married a fool. But in speaking to him as she does, Job recognizes a discrepancy between what he knows to be true about her and
the way she is acting toward him.

And isn't that Job's problem with God? He knows God to be good
and just, so how could God be treating him as if he were a cruel and
unjust God? That's his struggle, and that struggle is a sign of his faith,
and of his hope—for he never gives up his conviction that God is
good and just. That's why he asks "Why?" in the first place. In the
end, Job's "why?" is never answered, but he is still commended by
God as one who has spoken rightly.

PIOUS PRAISE, LAMENT,
AND THE HUMAN EXPERIENCE

There is much more to come—and that itself says to us that grief is
a process. Job can't snap out of his lament in a moment. It will take
time, and it won't be easy. And we will see that his three "friends"

---

[27]See Comment 2.2, "The Prologue and Genesis 2-3."

won't make it any easier. In this process of grief, we must work through the pain, and we must be honest with ourselves, and honest with God. But be assured, God can take it.

There is a certain stream within the broader Christian church that has no place for sorrow or lament. Some call it clap-happy Christianity. The only emoji allowed is a smiley face. Unfortunately, this attitude only doubles people's pain, for now their sorrow is compounded by guilt. They reproach themselves for not being able somehow to rise above it all, and to shake off their gloomy feelings and to be joyful and full of praise. Isn't that what true believers do? Job tells us otherwise. In its depiction of our human experience of faith and trust in the face of the mysterious ways of God, the book of Job is very realistic about the struggle we all face in a world in which we will all suffer. That's important, for in the end, a relationship—a real relationship—requires that it be the real you relating to the real God.

So if that's true, what are we to make of that wonderful Redman song?

Every blessing You pour out I'll
Turn back to praise.
When the darkness closes in, Lord,
Still I will say, "Blessed be your name."[28]

Can you sing that? Can you sing that even when you don't feel like it—even when you are struggling with God, and those words ring hollow in your heart? I think you can—for I will admit there are many times when I sing the words of songs that are far above my experience. It may be hard, but I sing them anyway. For I consider them songs of aspiration—almost prayers. In my head I say, "Lord, help me to experience what I am singing right now. Work in me so

---

[28]"Blessed Be Your Name," by Redman and Redman.

that this becomes true in my heart, for in my heart of hearts, I know they speak truth."

Job still has a long way to go. His initial burst of praise has turned into a prolonged lament. But he won't give up. We shouldn't either. Though, as we shall see, persevering in faith doesn't always come without a fight.

DIGGING DEEPER

3.1. Job's disease. Though a condition known as "Job's Syndrome" (technically hyperimmunoglobulin E syndrome), which involves a rare genetic mutation that makes the immune system overreact to pathogens, often causing boils and lesions, was discovered in 1966, the disease that afflicted Job himself is unknown. The Hebrew term *shekhin*, which describes Job's physical affliction, could refer to "running sores," "severe boils," or "painful sores" (Job 2:7).[29] Whatever they are, they cover Job's body completely, from head to foot. The other symptoms Job describes in the dialogue include sleeplessness (Job 7:4) and nightmares (Job 7:14), repeatedly erupting pustules (Job 7:5), emaciation (Job 13:28; 19:20), bad breath (Job 19:17), joint aches (Job 30:17, 30), and fever (Job 30:30).

As painful as his physical affliction was, Job complains much more about his emotional and spiritual torment as a result of social ostracization (e.g., Job 19:13-19) and divine alienation (e.g., Job 23:8-17). Those working in disability studies observe that mental and social suffering commonly compound physical maladies.[30] This may help explain why the Satan's afflictions of Job culminate in an attack on his health, which is highlighted as the ultimate test in the prologue. This leads one scholar to declare, "It

---

[29]See Katharine J. Dell, "What Was Job's Malady?," *Journal for the Study of the Old Testament* 41 (2016): 61-77.

[30]See, e.g., Rebecca Raphael, "Things Too Wonderful: A Disabled Reading of Job," *Perspectives in Religious Studies* 31 (2004): 399-424; J. Schipper, "Healing and Silence in the Epilogue of Job," *Word and World* 30 (2010): 16-22.

is in a real sense a book about sickness, if only because it singles out this type of human misfortune as one that is especially personal and acute."[31] Though the limited attention given to the actual nature of Job's sickness suggests it would be more accurate to say that Job's personal and acute pain becomes the means through which the book explores the spiritual dimensions of suffering. Like many of the lament psalms, which are similarly vague about the nature of the illnesses the psalmists are battling, readers facing any type of affliction can relate to Job's trials.

3.2. Job's countercosmic curse. Job's curse of the day of his birth is a form of complaint echoed by others who face intense suffering, from the prophet Jeremiah (Jer 20:14-18) to the spirituals sung by enslaved African Americans, which lament, "Wish I'd died when I was a baby, O Lord rock a' jubilee, Wish I'd died."[32] However, Job intensifies its effect by expanding his birthday curse into a countercosmic incantation that aims to unmake creation itself. His pain is so acute, so all-encompassing, that he expresses it through a wish that all of creation be unmade along with him. Similarly, another spiritual proclaims, "Great God, then, if I had-a my way . . . I'd tear this building down."[33]

Job expresses his nihilistic despair by inverting the creation account in Genesis 1.[34] Jeremiah also does something similar, but reverses Genesis 1 to describe the day of judgment, in which the earth becomes "formless and empty," the heavens have no light, the mountains and hills quake, humans disappear, birds fly away, and the fruitful land becomes a desert, as God's wrath comes rather than his rest (Jer 4:23-26).

---

[31]Ronald E. Clements, *Wisdom in Theology* (Grand Rapids, MI: Eerdmans, 1992), 86.

[32]Cited in Albert J. Raboteau, *Slave Religion: The "Invisible Institution" in the Antebellum South* (New York: Oxford University Press, 1978), 259.

[33]Cited in James H. Cone, *The Spirituals and the Blues: An Interpretation* (New York: Seabury Press, 1972), 66.

[34]See Michael Fishbane, "Jeremiah IV 23–26 and Job III 3–13: A Recovered Use of the Creation Pattern," *Vetus Testamentum* 21 (1971): 151-67.

In Job's conjuring of uncreation, he wishes for darkness (Job 3:4a) rather than the first day's light (Gen 1:3); for God above not to care about his day beneath (Job 3:4b) rather than the second day's firmament separating the waters above and below (Gen 1:7); for his day not to be included among the days of the year (Job 3:6) rather than the fourth day's lights in heavens to mark sacred times, days, and years (Gen 1:14); for those who rouse Leviathan to curse his day (Job 3:8) rather than the fifth day's "great creatures of the sea" (Gen 1:21); for his life to have been extinguished at birth (Job 3:11) rather than the sixth day's creation of humankind (Gen 1:26); and for the rest of death (Job 3:13) rather than God's seventh-day rest from all his labors (Gen 2:2). Though Job here attempts to declare "Let there not be" and reverse creation with his speech, God will reverse his reversal with God's own creation language in the divine speeches.[35]

3.3. Rest in the Bible. Job mentions "rest" three times while cursing the day of his birth. First, he claims he would not enjoy it if he had perished at birth (Job 3:13). Second, the weary find rest "in the ground," an apparent reference to Sheol (Job 3:16). Finally, in the chapter's last verse, he concludes, "I have no rest, but only turmoil" (Job 3:26). In light of his reversal of the creation imagery of Genesis 1–2:4, including the rest with which it culminates (Job 3:13; cf. Gen 2:2), Job appears aware of the importance of Sabbath rest. However, in each case, he uses the Hebrew word *nuakh* for "rest," rather than *shavat*, from which the "Sabbath" derives its name (Gen 2:2-3). Though the verb *nuakh* is used to describe Sabbath "rest" (Ex 20:8-11; 23:12; Deut 5:12-15), it most frequently refers to rest from turmoil (as in Job 3:10, 17, 26) and adversity, so Job is likely referring to the ultimate "rest" of death (Is 57:2; Dan 12:13; Prov 21:6).[36] What Job most dreads is "turmoil," but that is what he receives and the word that concludes his speech rather than the "rest" he longs for (Job 3:26).

---

[35]See Gerald Janzen, *Job* (Atlanta: John Knox Press, 1985), 67.
[36]C. L. Seow, *Job 1–21: Interpretation and Commentary* (Grand Rapids, MI: Eerdmans, 2013), 358.

Those who have faced enduring affliction can relate with Job's desire to have his troubles replaced with rest. As Hamlet famously expresses it,

> To take arms against a sea of troubles
> And, by opposing, end them. To die, to sleep—
> No more, and by a sleep to say we end
> The heartache, and the thousand natural shocks
> That flesh is heir to—'tis a consummation
> Devoutly to be wished. To die, to sleep.
> To sleep, perchance to dream.[37]

Yet, like Hamlet, Job resists the longing to put himself into that sleep. He commits to find his rest only through receiving divine vindication.[38] In fact, his desire for "rest" (*nuakh*) is supplanted with a stronger longing for "consolation" (*nakham*; Job 7:13; 16:2; 21:34), consummated after the Lord's appearance (Job 42:6).

---

[37] William Shakespeare, *Hamlet*, 3.1.61-67.
[38] See Comment 5.3, "Job's Death Wish."

four

COLD COMFORT

You are miserable comforters, all of you!
Will your long-winded speeches never end?

JOB 16:2-3

IF JOB WERE TO BE MADE into a TV series, I have discovered
the perfect corporate sponsor: Despair, Inc.[1] This company declares
that "it proudly profits on the negative in all of us."

Despair, Inc., advertises a host of profoundly depressing products.
For example, you might want the Pessimist's Mug—a crystal-clear
mug with a line at the halfway point, with the words, "The glass is
half-empty. Deal with it."

You might also like their Demotivational Posters. You know those
motivational posters—suitable for framing, with beautiful pictures,
focusing on uplifting themes like, "Shoot for the moon. Even if you
miss it you will land among the stars." These posters are a little different. One says, "Despair: It's always darkest just before it goes pitch
black." Or there's this: "Defeat: For every winner, there are dozens of
losers. Odds are you're one of them." Or "Procrastination—'Hard
work often pays off over time, but laziness always pays off now.'"
Here's one that fits Job pretty well—"Challenges: I expected times
like this—but I never thought they'd be so bad and so long and so

---

[1]Despair, Inc., https://despair.com.

frequent." And then there is this one, which is particularly appropriate for this chapter's topic—"Mistakes: It could be that the
purpose of your life is only to serve as a warning to others."

In this chapter we consider the friends who come to comfort Job
in his suffering. They make many mistakes, and it could be, and I
think it highly likely, that their primary purpose in the book is to
serve as a warning to us. Let's see how we can profit from their failure.

THEY ARE REAL FRIENDS

Before we disparage these three men, Eliphaz, Bildad, and Zophar,
we must first appreciate their noble intentions. They are real
friends of Job. When they heard about all the troubles that had
come upon him, they set out to comfort him (Job 2:11). When they
saw him, they were overwhelmed by his plight, and they joined in
his grief (Job 2:13).

As we noted previously, Job had entered into the rituals associated
with mourning, and it was the role of comforters not only to provide
emotional support but also to serve the social function of helping to
bring the bereaved person back into the society of the living.[2] We
don't know how long Job had already been grieving, but when they
arrived, they demonstrated their concern by simply sitting with Job
in silence. So far, so good.

The problem comes when they break their silence and start to
speak. But notice that it is Job, not the friends, who initiates this
interchange. And what they heard from him was quite disturbing,
to say the least.

JOB'S DESPAIRING COMPLAINT

When Job opens his mouth in Job 3, he howls in despairing lament.
But what is most offensive to the friends, and what sets them off, is

---

[2]This is something the Lord does for Israel—cf. Jer 31:13.

Job's insinuation that all that had happened to him was God's fault, and that he didn't deserve any of it.

Job says,

Why is life given to a man
  whose way is hidden,
  whom God has hedged in? (Job 3:23)

The God who had once "put a hedge around him" to protect him (Job 1:10) had now hedged him in to afflict him. Job claimed to be suffering for no reason, and God was responsible. This provokes Job's pious friends. They just can't let that kind of talk stand unchallenged, and so begins this lengthy war of words with this broken man who resists their efforts to console him.[3]

The writer presents this dialogue in a highly stylized literary form.[4] First, it is written in poetry, rather than prose. Then it is a very orderly exchange—unlike our televised political debates, none of the speakers interrupts the others; each speaks in turn, finishing his speech before the next speaker begins. And in the three cycles of speeches, they each speak in the same order. You could almost imagine something like this taking place in the US Senate chambers. This is no ordinary argument—at least not like any argument I've ever been a part of. It reads more like a theater production than a documentary.[5]

And though each of the friends comes from a different location and comes at Job from a slightly different angle, there is a common agreement among them. It's clearly three against one. And we get the impression that the three friends represent the consensus viewpoint—what the polls would show to be the community

---

[3]Cf. the way Jacob resists the efforts of his sons to console him when it appears that Joseph has been killed (Gen 37:35; cf. also Is 22:4; Ps 77:2).

[4]Tremper Longman III, *Job* (Grand Rapids, MI: Baker Academic, 2012), 55. See also Comment 4.1, "Dialogues in the Ancient Near East."

[5]See Comment 2.4, "Job as a Drama."

standard. Job is in the minority. In fact, he stands alone. It is Job against the world, and the friends certainly pile it on poor Job.

Job's friends saw themselves as the heirs of the wisdom of their ancestors, gained from carefully observing human society. And this wisdom gave them confidence that they understood the way God acted in the world.

Their fundamental conviction is quite simple: God is just—he is always just, and he will always be seen to be just—in the here and now. In theological terms, they insist on the principle of retributive justice.[6] God will see to it that people get what they deserve. How could he do otherwise and still be just? If you fear God, you will be blessed, and if you sin, you will suffer.

This principle can easily be turned around. If you are blessed, it must be because you have feared God, and if you suffer, it must be because you have sinned. This must be true, because God is just. The wise recognize this and live accordingly.

All three friends insist on this principle of God's retributive justice, and so does Job. The difference between Job and his friends is simply the conclusion that they take from it. The friends look at Job's suffering and determine that there must have been some sin in his life to cause such pain. What else could it be?

Job, on the other hand, is sure that he has not sinned—at least not to any degree that would merit the treatment he has received—so God must be treating him unjustly. Or at the very least, something is fundamentally wrong with the way God is running the universe, and Job desperately wants to find out from God what he's up to. That's the gist of it. And they will go back and forth making their case for the next twenty-four chapters, and in the end, neither side will have budged an inch. Again, a lot like the US Senate.

---

[6]See Comment 4.2, "Retribution in the Old Testament."

ROUND ONE

Eliphaz begins his response to Job respectfully and almost deferentially in Job 4:2. "Uh, excuse me," he seems to be saying. "If someone ventures a word with you, will you be impatient?" But, after what he has just heard from Job, he asks, "Who can keep from speaking?"

Eliphaz then honors Job for the way he has spoken to others in the past:

> Think how you have instructed many,
> 　　how you have strengthened feeble hands.
> Your words have supported those who stumbled;
> 　　you have strengthened faltering knees. (Job 4:3-4)

Then in Job 4:5-6 comes the jab—physician, heal thyself:

> But now trouble comes to you, and you are discouraged;
> 　　it strikes you, and you are dismayed.
> Should not your piety be your confidence
> 　　and your blameless ways your hope?

Then Eliphaz goes straight to the point. God is just, so, Job, just deal with it:

> Consider now: Who, being innocent, has ever perished?
> 　　Where were the upright ever destroyed?
> As I have observed, those who plow evil
> 　　and those who sow trouble reap it. (Job 4:7, 8)

This is the way the world works—just look around and you will see it's true. You reap what you sow.

Don't question the ways of God.

> Can a mortal be more righteous than God?
> 　　Can even a strong man be more pure than his Maker?
> 　　　(Job 4:17)

God works out his just ways in the world. The wicked may prosper for a while, but it won't last. Suddenly hardship will overtake them (Job 5:3-6).

No, Job, suffering comes from the hand of a just God, who "thwarts the plans of the crafty" and "catches the wise in their craftiness" (Job 5:12-13).

Maybe the Lord is just disciplining Job through his suffering, Eliphaz suggests.

Blessed is the one whom God corrects;
so do not despise the discipline of the Almighty. (Job 5:17)

If Job is indeed righteous, his suffering should soon end.

Eliphaz concludes with this exhortation to Job:

We have examined this, and it is true.
So hear it and apply it to yourself. (Job 5:27)

Quit complaining, Job! Simply apply this wisdom to your situation, and you will be restored.

But Job will have none of it. He responds in Job 7:11,

Therefore I will not keep silent;
I will speak out in the anguish of my spirit,
I will complain in the bitterness of my soul.

So the dispute goes on. Eliphaz had been rather gentle with Job. Bildad is up next, and when he hears Job's response, he turns up the heat. He says,

How long will you say such things?
Your words are a blustering wind.
Does God pervert justice?
Does the Almighty pervert what is right?
When your children sinned against him,
he gave them over to the penalty of their sin. (Job 8:2-4)

"Beware, Job," he seems to be saying. "Your children got what was coming to them and what happened to them may happen to you!" Not the most gracious way of putting it!

He continues,

> But if you will seek God earnestly
>   and plead with the Almighty,
> if you are pure and upright,
>   even now he will rouse himself on your behalf
>   and restore you to your prosperous state.
> Your beginnings will seem humble,
>   so prosperous will your future be. (Job 8:5-7)

Just turn from your sin, Job, and God will again bless.

Job still won't back down, so when it is his turn, Zophar is harsher still:

> You say to God, "My beliefs are flawless
>   and I am pure in your sight."
> Oh, how I wish that God would speak,
>   that he would open his lips against you
> and disclose to you the secrets of wisdom,
>   for true wisdom has two sides.
>   Know this: God has even forgotten some of your sin.
>   (Job 11:4-6)

Zophar seems to attack Job: "God has let you off easy—you deserve worse than you have been given!" (That's a very comforting thought!) "Job, your only hope is to repent," Zophar says,

> Yet if you devote your heart to [God]
>   and stretch out your hands to him,
> if you put away the sin that is in your hand
>   and allow no evil to dwell in your tent,

then, free of fault, you will lift up your face;
    you will stand firm and without fear.
You will surely forget your trouble,
    recalling it only as waters gone by.
Life will be brighter than noonday,
    and darkness will become like morning. (Job 11:13-17)

So it goes on and on. And Job gives as good as he gets. He responds to each friend in an increasingly unfriendly manner. Job says,

I have heard many things like these;
    You are miserable comforters, all of you!
Will your long-winded speeches never end?
    What ails you that you keep on arguing? (Job 16:2-3)

ROUND TWO

In the second round of this heavyweight fight, Eliphaz, Bildad, and Zophar become increasingly provoked and irritated by Job's insistence on his innocence—his justifying himself before God.

Zophar, for example, is indignant.

My troubled thoughts prompt me to answer
    because I am greatly disturbed.
I hear a rebuke that dishonors me,
    and my understanding inspires me to reply. (Job 20:2-3)

He continues,

Surely you know how it has been from of old,
    ever since mankind was placed on the earth,
that the mirth of the wicked is brief,
    the joy of the godless lasts but a moment. . . .
    His prosperity will not endure.
In the midst of his plenty, distress will overtake him;
    the full force of misery will come upon him. . . .

When he has filled his belly,
   God will vent his burning anger against him
   and rain down his blows on him. (Job 20:4, 5, 21-23)

"Job," Zophar seems to say, "maybe your previous prosperity was not a sign of your godliness at all!"

ROUND THREE

In round three the gloves are off. Eliphaz, who began so gently, lets Job have it, full force:

Is it for your piety that [God] rebukes you
   and brings charges against you? (Job 22:4)

No, Job, that's not it at all.

Is not your wickedness great?
   Are not your sins endless? (Job 22:5)

And then, like an accusing prosecuting attorney, Eliphaz actually lists Job's supposed offenses—including withholding water from the weary and food from the hungry, with no heart for widows or orphans.

That is why snares are all around you,
   why sudden peril terrifies you,
why it is so dark you cannot see,
   and why a flood of water covers you. (Job 22:10-11)

In the end, all he can do is urge Job to repent:

Submit to God and be at peace with him;
   in this way prosperity will come to you. . . .
If you return to the Almighty, you will be restored:
   If you remove wickedness far from your tent.
      (Job 22:21, 23)

In chapter twenty-five, in his last speech, Bildad has almost run out of things to say, so he just repeats what Eliphaz has already said in his first two speeches—affirming unapproachable awe of God.

> How then can a mortal be righteous before God?
>> How can one born of woman be pure?
> If even the moon is not bright
>> and the stars are not pure in his eyes,
> how much less mortal, who is but a maggot—
>> a human being, who is only a worm! (Job 25:4-6)

Not very flattering—this "worm theology." No one is righteous before God, and Job should just accept that he is a sinner and repent. This is the shortest speech of the book, and in this third round, Zophar doesn't even speak at all.[7] The argument has clearly run out of steam. Both sides are entrenched in their position. It's useless to argue anymore. The friends just give up and fade away.

WHAT TO MAKE OF JOB'S FRIENDS

As I mentioned, we're going to look at Job's side in all this in the next chapter, but what are we to make of what the friends have to say? In their fundamental conviction, Job's friends do speak truth[8]—God *is* just, and the Bible throughout affirms his retributive justice. This theme is found repeatedly in the Old Testament. Moses speaks of it clearly in Deuteronomy 30:15—"See, I set before you today life and prosperity, death and destruction." If you keep the Lord's commands, then you will live and increase, and the Lord your God will bless you. "But if your heart turns away and you are not obedient, and if you are drawn away to bow down to other gods and worship them, I declare to you this day that you will certainly be destroyed" (Deut 30:17-18).

---

[7]See Comment 4.3, "The Breakdown of the Dialogue's Third Cycle."
[8]The only passage in the entire book of Job that is quoted in the New Testament contains words spoken by Eliphaz. See Comment 4.4, "Paul's Citation of Eliphaz."

And Solomon, in the Proverbs, conveys the same message:

My son, do not forget my teaching,
    but keep my commands in your heart,
for they will prolong your life many years
    and bring you peace and prosperity. . . .
Do not be wise in your own eyes;
    fear the LORD and shun evil.
This will bring health to your body
    and nourishment to your bones. (Prov 3:1-2, 7-8)

God's retributive justice is found very clearly in the New Testament too. Paul affirms it in no uncertain terms—"Do not be deceived: God cannot be mocked. A man reaps what he sows" (Gal 6:7).

Yes, it's true—God is just, and he acts justly. God does act according to retributive justice. But at the end of the book of Job, God will declare that these friends have not spoken of him what is right as his servant Job has (Job 42:7-8).[9] Why? What was wrong with what they had to say?

A simplistic view of God's retributive justice. Several answers come to mind. First, these friends of Job are rebuked by God because, though they speak the truth, it is not the whole truth. While it is true that God never acts unjustly, it is also true that God does not always exercise his retributive justice in an immediate and recognizable way. Additionally, God may have other reasons for his actions that are not explained by his justice. God cannot be put in some neat little moralistic box, such that his actions are entirely predictable based on our behavior. We like to think the world is that way. We assume there is some intelligible moral order that gives a clear-cut reason for everything that happens.

---

[9]See Comment 10.2, "God's Verdict (42:7-8)."

It's like that song in *The Sound of Music* sung by Maria when she falls in love with Captain Von Trapp and muses that she must have done something to deserve such a good thing in her life:

Perhaps I had a wicked childhood;
Perhaps I had a miserable youth;
But somewhere in my wicked, miserable past
There must have been a moment of truth.

This must be true, for, as she sings, "Nothing comes from nothing; nothing ever could." That's an expression of retributive justice.[10] Maria must assume some past act of virtue to explain her present good fortune, but usually it's the other way around. It's only when bad things happen that we complain about what we've been given!

Hinduism, with its doctrine of reincarnation, explains everything according to this rule: you get what you deserve, even if it is based on what you did in a previous life. But the Bible speaks otherwise. There is no simplistic moral equation that dictates how the principle of retributive justice must be applied. Suffering may come in the service of discipline. Even Eliphaz recognizes that (Job 5:17).

God can use suffering to teach us.[11] And God can also use suffering simply to magnify his own glory. When Jesus' disciples saw a man born blind from birth, they assumed this principle of retributive justice that "Nothing comes from nothing." So they asked Jesus, "Who sinned, this man or his parents?" "Neither," Jesus said, "but this happened so that the works of God might be displayed in him" (Jn 9:2, 3).

Getting what you deserve is not the whole truth. And when you think about it, a simplistic application of retributive justice would mean there could never be grace. That's why strict moralists don't like the notion of grace. It just doesn't fit, for grace can

---

[10]Ash, *Job*, 92.
[11]See Comment 8.4, "Suffering as Educational."

never be deserved. Grace seems to interrupt the moral order of
the cosmos.

The fear of the disruption of the moral order. Bildad simply can't
believe that God would treat a godly man the way Job has been
treated. That would throw the whole moral fabric of the universe
into disarray; the very foundations, the rocks on which he has built
his life, would be demolished. He says to Job,

> You who tear yourself to pieces in your anger,
>> is the earth to be abandoned for your sake?
>> Or must the rocks be moved from their place? (Job 18:4)

To admit that Job was suffering righteously would be too discom-
forting, too distressing, and Job himself points this out to them—

> Now you . . . have proved to be of no help;
>> you see something dreadful and are afraid. (Job 6:21)

Job's situation makes them afraid that their whole view of God
and the world is going to be crushed. That's frightening. Within
a simplistic view of God's retributive justice, we can control what
happens to us. Our prosperity is within our power. But Job's
case "shatters the myth that our own righteousness can protect
us from unjust suffering."[12] By blaming Job, the friends are trying
to protect themselves.

We do this all the time. When we see someone suffering, our first
response is often to distance ourselves from them. When we read
about a murder in the paper, we may be tempted to think, "Oh, that
was gang-related. That doesn't affect me." Or when we hear about
someone getting cancer, we may look for a cause in their life that
isn't found in ours. We want to separate ourselves from sufferers.

---

[12]J. Reitman, *Unlocking Wisdom: Forming Agents of God in the House of Mourning* (Springfield, MO:
21st Century Press, 2008), 63.

We want reasons for suffering. We want to establish why what happened to them won't happen to us, or at least we want to see how we can keep it from happening to us. What we fear is inexplicable suffering, random suffering—which is just what makes terrorism so full of terror. Terrorism's violence can affect anyone at any time.

A God who seems to act mysteriously, even randomly as seemed to be the case at times in the Covid-19 pandemic, becomes terrible to us. While holding to a simplistic view of God's retributive justice, both Job and his friends are struggling to avoid that awful possibility.

Yes, Job's friends speak the truth, but it's not the whole truth. God doesn't always just give people what they deserve. There is such a thing as innocent suffering.

The friends' misapplied truth. And more than that, Job's friends speak the truth, but in this case, it is misapplied truth.[13] It is misapplied, first, to Job's objective moral state. We know that his suffering was not the result of his sin. He *is* innocent. And paradoxically, since that is the case, the friends' exhortation to repent so that he can again enjoy God's blessing was nothing but a temptation for Job. If he did repent of sins he knows he did not commit, it would prove Satan to be right—Job would be abandoning his own integrity and would just be using God for his own self-interest.[14] To his credit, Job refuses to go there.

Second, the friends' truth is also misapplied to Job's subjective state of mind. What they gave Job was not what he needed. Job was in an abyss of despair—and for good reason. Everything that he valued—his property, his position in society, his entire family, his health, even his wife's loyalty—had been taken from him. And his God was nowhere to be found. He speaks out of the anguish of his heart, but the friends respond to him as if they were in a

---

[13]See Comment 4.5, "The Friends as Foolish 'Wise Men.'"
[14]See Comment 5.1, "The Question of Integrity."

theology classroom. The friends "rationalize rather than sympathize."[15] They speak from the detached security of the academic armchair, while Job is writhing in the pain of the sufferer's wheelchair.[16] Christopher Ash writes, "True words may be thin medicine for a man in the depths."[17] Their insistence that their truth applies to Job's situation only makes his anguish even more agonizing. No wonder Job calls them "miserable comforters" (Job 16:2).

And don't these friends also display the kinds of thoughts (and accusations) that come into our own heads in times of suffering? This dialogue reflects the internal conflict that we are all prone to.

WHAT CAN WE LEARN FROM THEIR MISTAKES?

As a foil to Job, it appears that the friends' sole purpose in the book is to serve as a warning to us. So what can we learn from their mistakes? Let me suggest four areas of application if you want to avoid being a miserable comforter as you minister to someone who is suffering.

First, be sensitive and be patient. Be attentive to the various emotional stages that a grieving person may go through. It may be shock, or denial, or anger, or depression—or all of them mixed together. Recognize that the suffering person may say things that they would never say in their more rational moments—and that's okay. Just be patient with them. This is not the time for a theology lecture.

I referred earlier to John Feinberg's case. He had written a PhD dissertation on the problem of evil, yet when evil came into his own life in the form of his wife's brutal illness, he wrote, "I had all these intellectual answers, but none of them made any difference in the way I felt."[18] And we need to be sensitive to that. We must learn to "mourn with those who mourn" (Rom 12:15). Sometimes—maybe most of the

---

[15]Norman Habel, *The Book of Job* (London: SCM, 1985), 299.

[16]Ash, *Job*, 18.

[17]Ash, *Job*, 123-24.

[18]John Feinberg, *When There Are No Easy Answers: Thinking Differently About God, Suffering, and Evil* (Grand Rapids, MI: Kregel, 2016), 37. See Comment 9.2, "Why Doesn't God Explain?"

time—the best thing we can do is simply show up. Our presence, our listening ears, and yes, our tears, may mean more than we know.

Feinberg makes some quick suggestions when you visit a person who is suffering deeply[19]—(1) don't minimize their pain; (2) don't glibly quote Bible verses; and (3) beware of saying, "I know how you feel." It's probably not true, and it probably doesn't matter. They don't want to know how you feel; they want to know that you care.

Second, be humble—don't presume to know more than you do. Job's friends thought they knew why Job was suffering, but they were wrong. The truth is, unless God has called you to be a prophet, none of us can know the mind of God in these matters. We cannot judge others based on the fact that they are suffering.

And related to this, beware of trying to defend God by speaking what is not true. This is what the friends were doing, and Job calls them on it, when he asks, "Will you speak wickedly on God's behalf?" (Job 13:7).[20] And this is the exact charge that God will finally bring against them (Job 42:7-8).

Being humble is actually quite freeing. Often we don't visit people who are suffering terribly simply because we don't know what to say. Well, you don't have to know what to say—and you can admit that. How much more helpful Job's friends could have been if they had just done that, and not presumed to know more than they did.

Third, be practical. In some cases that may mean acting to protect someone in danger. I think of situations where the suffering involves abuse of some kind. In such cases, those who are suffering need more than just a shoulder to cry on; they need someone to call the police.[21]

---

[19]Feinberg, *No Easy Answers*, 39-56.

[20]F. Campbell calls this "the ultimate sin that any theologian must fear" ("The Book of Job: Two Questions, One Answer," *Australian Biblical Review* 51 [2003]: 15-25, 24).

[21]D. A. Carson, *How Long, O Lord? Reflections on Suffering and Evil*, 2nd ed. (Grand Rapids, MI: Baker Academic, 2006), 224.

But more broadly, those who suffer often need practical help when tragedy strikes. People will often say, "If there is anything I can do, don't hesitate to call." That certainly expresses a helping heart, but in John Feinberg's experience that just puts a burden back on the sufferer. Much better, in his view, is actually thinking of something that needs doing and then asking if you can do it—bringing over a meal, picking up groceries, taking the kids to practice—these are little things that say you care. Offer hope for the future, but very practically help people live one day at a time.

And finally, be prayerful. You see, the central message of this dialogue with the friends, and in fact of the whole book, is that, in the end, only God himself could bring comfort to Job. The problem of suffering is ultimately intensely personal: we wonder if God really cares. Yes, God can use us as the instruments of his love, but we can't give people who suffer what they need most. That's why we must point them to the love of God, for it is God they need more than us.

Point people to the God who cares—the God who in his Son Jesus Christ has drawn near to us, and, in fact, shares in our suffering. Jesus is a high priest who is able to sympathize with our weaknesses, for he has been tempted in every way, just as we are (Heb 4:15). And in his suffering, he even asks our question—*Why?*

In our prayer for those who suffer, we long to connect them with the God and Father of our Lord Jesus Christ, the Father of compassion and the God of all comfort, who is able to comfort us in all our troubles (2 Cor 1:3, 4).

In 1940 at the height of the Battle of Britain in WWII, C. S. Lewis published his book *The Problem of Pain*. In the preface, he explained its purpose—to address certain intellectual problems associated with human suffering. And then he added this sentence: "For the far higher task of teaching fortitude and patience I was never fool enough to suppose myself qualified, nor have I anything to offer my readers except my conviction that when pain is to be borne, a little courage helps more than much knowledge, a little human sympathy more than much courage, and the least tincture of the love of God more than all."[22]

When people are in the depths of pain, some taste of the love of God is what they most need, but it is in that condition that many find it most difficult to pray. Shall we not pray for them? Would that Job's friends had done just that!

DIGGING DEEPER

4.1. Dialogues in the ancient Near East. The dialogue (or disputation) was a popular genre in the ancient Near East, particularly in Mesopotamia.[23] Generally, these works follow a tripartite structure: an introduction, in which the world, including the two opposing protagonists, is created, followed by an exchange of speeches between those protagonists over who is superior, and then, finally, the gods' or the king's declaration of the winner. The protagonists are generally nonhuman. Bird disputes with fish, date palm with tamarisk, copper with silver, and winter with summer. Though Job's content differs significantly, the book bears a notable structural similarity, as it also begins with an introduction that alludes to the creation account in Genesis 2–3,[24] proceeds to a contest between Job and his friends, and concludes with God's declaration of Job as the winner (Job 42:7-8).

Several other ancient Near Eastern texts, however, combine a dialogue format with an exploration of similar questions as Job. In these controversy dialogues, two friends debate a single, specific issue, though no divine answer is provided as in the other

---

[22]C. S. Lewis, *The Problem of Pain* (London: Collins, 1940), vii-viii.

[23]See Yoram Cohen and Nathan Wasserman, "Mesopotamian Wisdom Literature," in *The Oxford Handbook of Wisdom and the Bible,* ed. Will Kynes (New York: Oxford University Press, 2021), 121-40.

[24]See Comment 2.2, "The Prologue and Genesis 2–3."

dialogues. These include the Mesopotamian Dialogue of Pessimism, in which a master debates with his slave whether various tasks, such as hunting, marrying, or even living, are worthwhile, with the slave agreeing with his master even when he contradicts himself, and an Egyptian text known as "A Man and His Ba" or "The Man Who Grew Tired of Life," in which a man debates with his soul (ba) the merits of death over continuing a life of suffering. The closest parallel to Job, however, is the Babylonian Theodicy, in which a sufferer debates the doctrine of retribution with a friend. The sufferer expresses sentiments similar to Job's, such as "Those who do not seek a god go in the way of prosperity, (while) those who pray to a goddess become poor and destitute" (lines [ll.] 70-71; cf. Job 21:7-9), while his friend often sounds like Job's friends: "The divine mind is as remote as innermost heaven; it is difficult to understand, and people cannot know it" (ll. 256-57; cf. Job 11:2-9).[25] Job's contributions to the debate are more vitriolic than the sufferer in the Babylonian Theodicy, and his dialogue with his three friends degenerates into ad hominem attacks and the chaos of the third cycle, whereas the Babylonian Theodicy is measured and respectful throughout. Precedents exist, then, for both the dialogue form of Job and the questions with which the book wrestles, but the passion with which it struggles with those questions, and the appearance of God to provide an answer are unprecedented.

4.2. Retribution in the Old Testament. In the nineteenth and early twentieth century, the struggle with God's retributive justice in Job drew the book into conversation with texts across the Old Testament. For example, while discussing Job, Samuel Davidson claimed that retribution was "the genius of Mosaism"; W. T. Davison associated the doctrine with the Deuteronomic covenant, which became "the traditional teaching of law-givers, wise men, and prophets"; and Edouard Dhorme claimed that retribution is

---

[25]See C. L. Seow, *Job 1–21: Interpretation and Commentary* (Grand Rapids, MI: Eerdmans, 2013), 55.

"everywhere characteristic of Israelite theology."[26] Thus, Job's treatment of the issue does not restrict it to Wisdom Literature but "inevitably invites the reader to hear Job in the context of the entire Bible."[27] In that broader context, Job is clearly not the first to challenge this doctrine: "It is hard to suppose that the reader of the Bible is expected to conclude that Abel, Uriah the Hittite, and Naboth were murdered because they deserved to be."[28] However, as Wisdom Literature became established as a category, the genre boundary discouraged scholars from drawing these other texts into their interpretations of Job, making Proverbs into Job's main dialogue partner and limiting the book's links with retribution across Israel's law, covenant, and history. David Clines, for example, acknowledges Deuteronomy as the preeminent exponent of retribution, but takes Job's questioning of the doctrine as a confrontation of "the ideology of Proverbs."[29]

In the dialogue, Job criticizes God for not living up to the doctrine of retribution. However, without a belief in God's retributive justice, Job would have no case against God.[30] This conflict between his belief and his experiences pushes Job into a more nuanced conception of retribution, which will allow for the affliction of a righteous man like himself, at least for a time. The righteous must not always receive their reward nor the wicked suffer their punishment as immediately as his friends believe. In some cases, justice must be deferred to some future time when the hidden God finally comes to judge (Job 23:8-11). And thus, convinced of

---

[26]Samuel Davidson, *An Introduction to the Old Testament: Critical, Historical, Theological*, 2 vols. (London: Williams and Norgate, 1862), 217; W. T. Davison, *The Wisdom-Literature of the Old Testament* (London: Charles H. Kelly, 1894), 79; Edouard Dhorme, *A Commentary on the Book of Job*, trans. Harold Knight (London: Thomas Nelson and Sons, 1967 [1926]), cxxxvii, cxxxix.

[27]J. Clinton McCann, Jr., "Wisdom's Dilemma: The Book of Job, the Final Form of the Book of Psalms, and the Entire Bible," in *Wisdom, You Are My Sister: Studies in Honor of Roland E. Murphy, O. Carm., on the Occasion of His Eightieth Birthday*, ed. Michael L. Barré (Washington, DC: Catholic Biblical Association of America, 1997), 18.

[28]Harold Henry Rowley, *Job*, rev. ed. (Grand Rapids, MI: Eerdmans, 1976), 18.

[29]David Clines, *Job*, 3 vols. (Nashville: Thomas Nelson, 1989–2011), 1:lxi-lxii.

[30]James L. Crenshaw, *A Whirlpool of Torment: Israelite Traditions of God as an Oppressive Presence* (Philadelphia: Fortress Press, 1984), 62.

his righteousness (e.g., Job 31), Job pleads for that judgment (e.g., Job 31:35).

In fact, rather than representing the "traditional" view of retribution, the strict "mathematical equation" between deed and consequence the friends employ actually reflects a "developed form" of the doctrine.[31] Job's more nuanced view of retribution is what appears across the Old Testament. Even Proverbs, which many argue Job is responding to, "*undermines* . . . a simplified moral calculus."[32] The scholarly "oversimplification" of retribution in Proverbs overlooks the many proverbs that recognize the explanatory limits of retribution. Proverbs that privilege the poor (e.g., Prov 14:31; 19:17; 22:2) contradict a direct equivalence between wealth and righteousness. Rather than the strict retributive viewpoint of Job's friends, Proverbs teaches that "both the righteous and the wicked will *eventually* get what they deserve."[33] Thus, like the psalms of lament, "the book of Job was inevitable, not because Proverbs was too simplistic, but because life's inequities, as reflected in Proverbs, drive faith to argue with the Deity."[34] Even the so-called Wisdom psalms find their hope for justice in a future divine reckoning, whether or not this involves the afterlife.[35] However, as Psalm 73 demonstrates, more than justice is at issue. Though the psalmist is encouraged that the wicked will get what they deserve (Ps 73:18-20, 27), the ultimate source of his hope to face the present comes not from the future but from the immediate presence of God (Ps 73:23-26). When the Lord appears to Job in the whirlwind, he comes to a similar conclusion (Job 42:2-6). Job's arguments,

---

[31] E.g., Roland E. Murphy, *The Tree of Life: An Exploration of Biblical Wisdom Literature*, 3rd ed. (Grand Rapids, MI: Eerdmans, 2002), 34.

[32] McCann, "Wisdom's Dilemma," 19-20; emphasis original.

[33] Samuel L. Adams, *Wisdom in Transition: Act and Consequence in Second Temple Instructions* (Leiden: Brill, 2008), 85; emphasis original.

[34] Raymond C. Van Leeuwen, "Wealth and Poverty: System and Contradiction in Proverbs," *Hebrew Studies* 33 (1992): 29, 34.

[35] Katharine J. Dell, *The Book of Job as Sceptical Literature* (Berlin: de Gruyter, 1991), 80-81. See, e.g., Ps 1:5; 37:37; 49:15-20.

therefore, are grounded in and expand the understanding of retribution across the Old Testament.

4.3. The breakdown of the dialogue's third cycle. Something clearly has gone wrong in the third cycle of speeches. Bildad's speech (Job 25:1-6) is unusually brief, Zophar's is absent, and Job says things we would expect the friends to say (Job 24:18-24; 26:5-14; 27:13-23). The question facing interpreters is how to explain the breakdown of the dialogue here. Many attempt to reorganize the text in this cycle so that it conforms to the previous two in both form and content, with all the friends getting an equal say and Job continuing to complain about the injustice he faces. So, for example, the unexpected section of Job's speech in Job 26 (Job 26:5-14) is moved to the end of Bildad's short speech to fill it out, and the similar sentiments expressed in Job 27 (Job 27:13-23) are given to Zophar so that he has a speech.

Another approach, which has recently begun to gain broader scholarly acceptance, is to see the problem not in the disorder of the actual text but of the dialogue itself. Thus, Christopher Seitz claims that in the third round of the debate, Job defends the moral order, so that "the ground is effectively cut out from under the friends."[36] Whereas the friends had previously claimed that Job was being punished for his wickedness, Job conveys his confidence in his righteousness by asking God to vindicate him against evildoers, by which he means the friends. He declares, "May my enemy be like the wicked, my adversary like the unjust!" (Job 27:7). This is just the type of argumentation employed in the psalms of innocence,[37] and it drives the friends to silence.

Gerald Janzen provides a similar explanation, but goes into further detail. Pointing out that Job has quoted lines from the

---

[36]Christopher Seitz, "Job: Full-Structure, Movement, and Interpretation," *Interpretation* 43 (1989): 13.

[37]See Comment 7.4, "Appeals to Innocence in the Psalms."

friends throughout, he claims that here he "finally engages in such a stratagem wholesale."[38] Job can by now reconstruct his friends' speeches "as surely as any biblical scholar."[39] Therefore, Bildad's speech in Job 25 is short because Job interrupts him with a "sarcastic retort" in Job 26:1-4 and then mockingly completes his speech for him in Job 26:5-14. Job then makes his oath of innocence (Job 27:1-6) and an imprecation against his enemies (Job 27:7-12), raising the ante of the debate, before silencing Zophar by anticipating what he expects him to say (Job 27:13-23), picking up where Zophar left off in Job 20:29 by discussing "the fate God allots to the wicked." The narrator signals the end of the dialogue by adding a fresh introduction to Job's mimicking replacement of Zophar's speech that, distinct from previous introductions, describes it as a "taunt" (*mashal*; cf. Job 29:1; Is 14:4; Hab 2:6).[40]

4.4. Paul's citation of Eliphaz. The one explicit citation of Job in the New Testament is found in 1 Corinthians 3:19, "As it is written, 'He catches the wise in their craftiness'" (cf. Job 5:13). Paul here seems to treat a speech of the divinely discredited friends as authoritative, and most scholars believe Paul has no interest in the context of these words in the book of Job. Whether Paul intended it or not, though, there is something deliciously appropriate about citing Eliphaz's own words about the wise being caught in their craftiness, given that the book demonstrates the inadequacy of Eliphaz's own wisdom. Paul could hardly have found better support for the point he uses this citation to support: "Do not deceive yourselves. If you think that you are wise by the standards of this age, you should become 'fools' so that you may become wise. For the wisdom of this world is foolishness with God" (1 Cor 3:18-19).

---

[38] Gerald Janzen, *Job* (Atlanta: John Knox Press, 1985), 172-73.
[39] Janzen, *Job*, 171, 174.
[40] Seow, *Job*, 67.

4.5. The friends as foolish "wise men." As purported wise men, who demonstrate themselves to be fools, Job's friends conform to a pattern found throughout the Old Testament, which continues into the New. In the books of Isaiah and Jeremiah, we encounter a group of people called "the wise," but neither prophet has a very high opinion of them. Isaiah says,

> Woe to those who are wise in their own eyes
>> and clever in their own sight . . .
> for they have rejected the law of the Lord Almighty
>> and spurned the word of the Holy One of Israel. (Is 5:21, 24)

Later, Isaiah reports the Lord's judgment:

> These people come near to me with their mouth
>> and honor me with their lips,
>> but their hearts are far from me. . . .
> Therefore . . . the wisdom of the wise will perish,
>> the intelligence of the intelligent will vanish. (Is 29:13-14)

Similarly, Jeremiah declares,

> How can you say, "We are wise,
>> for we have the law of the Lord,"
> when actually the lying pen of the scribes
>> has handled it falsely?
> The wise will be put to shame;
>> they will be dismayed and trapped.
> Since they have rejected the word of the Lord,
>> what kind of wisdom do they have? (Jer 8:8-9)[41]

In the view of both prophets, a claim to wisdom apart from proper obedience to the Law of the Lord is foolishness. Similarly, in his oracle against the king of Tyre, Ezekiel recognizes the ruler's great

---

[41]See Raymond C. Van Leeuwen, "The Sage in the Prophetic Literature," in *The Sage in Israel and the Ancient Near East*, ed. Leo G. Perdue and John G. Gammie (Winona Lake, IN: Eisenbrauns, 1990), 295-306.

wisdom, by which he has amassed substantial wealth (Ezek 28:4), but, because he pridefully thought himself "as wise as a god," Ezekiel claims that wisdom will be no protection against the destruction that the Lord will bring on him (Ezek 28:6-10).

Even Solomon, whose divinely bestowed wisdom (1 Kings 3) exceeded that of all Israel's rivals (1 Kings 4:29-30) and ushered Israel into a golden age (1 Kings 10:14-22), ends his career in foolish disobedience of God's law. His acquisition of gold, horses, and foreign wives for himself leads to the worship of foreign gods (1 Kings 11:1-4), precisely what Deuteronomy 17:14-20 had commanded Israel's kings not to do. Solomon had not learned the lesson of the book attributed to him:

> Trust in the LORD with all your heart
>   and lean not on your own understanding;
> in all your ways submit to him,
>   and he will make your paths straight.
> Do not be wise in your own eyes;
>   fear the LORD and shun evil.
> This will bring health to your body
>   and nourishment to your bones. (Prov 3:5-8)

But learning Proverbs' lessons is easier said than done. At the end of the book, a man named Agur gives it its first book review, and it is not a positive one:

> I am weary, God. . . .
>   I have not learned wisdom,
> nor have I attained to the knowledge of the Holy One.
>   (Prov 30:1, 3)

Further, throughout the book, these lessons are addressed to the author's son, and yet Solomon's son, Rehoboam, is even more foolish than he is, which leads to the division of the nation. Even Hezekiah, who had his scribes copy Solomon's proverbs according to Proverbs 25:1, foolishly shows the riches of his kingdom to the Babylonians, which entices them to return, conquer Judah, and carry those riches away (2 Kings 20:12-18). The people of Israel as a whole, who preserved the book of Proverbs, and as Deuteronomy 4:6 claims, were supposed to "show [their] wisdom and understanding to the nations" by observing carefully God's commandments, disobey those commandments time and time again, leading to divine punishment: a humiliating defeat by those very nations and exile. When we consider the Old Testament as a whole, then, we might legitimately say that in its aim to impart wisdom, Proverbs is a failure. It is just like the Mosaic law, which instructs in righteousness, but could not create a righteous people.

It is little surprise, then, that Job's friends, who often say things that sound similar to Proverbs and even allude to it directly (Job 18:5; cf. Prov 13:9), are shown to be fools (Job 42:7-8). Similarly, Paul's claim that the wisdom of the world is shown to be foolishness (1 Cor 1:20-31) draws on a consistent Old Testament demonstration that wisdom divorced from obedience to the Lord—human wisdom found in one's own eyes rather than that founded on the fear of the Lord (Prov 1:9; 9:10; 15:33)—is no wisdom at all. Thus, the friends' failure to answer Job, signaled in the breakdown of the third cycle of the dialogue,[42] sets the stage for the declaration at the end of the poem to wisdom that "the fear of the LORD—that is wisdom, and to shun evil is understanding" (Job 28:28) and the Lord's fearful appearance to Job in the whirlwind.[43]

---

[42]See Comment 4.3, "The Breakdown of the Dialogue's Third Cycle."
[43]See Comment 6.4, "Wisdom and the Fear of the Lord (Job 28:28)."

five

A SUFFERER'S PROTEST

JOB 6–27

I loathe my very life;
therefore I will give free rein to my complaint
and speak out in the bitterness of my soul.

JOB 10:1

JOB IS A LONG BOOK, and the dialogue that makes up its central section goes on for twenty-four chapters. But through it all, Job doesn't move. He is stuck there—in a state of mourning, sitting on the ash heap, grieving his wretched condition.

Consider the way he describes his own miserable state:

My body is clothed with worms and scabs,
   my skin is broken and festering. (Job 7:5)

. . .

My face is red with weeping,
   dark shadows ring my eyes. (Job 16:16)

. . .

God has made me a byword to everyone,
   a man in whose face people spit.
My eyes have grown dim with grief;
   my whole frame is but a shadow. (Job 17:6-7)

Can you picture that? What a pathetic sight he is! Job is trapped in the depths of a deep, deep pit of despair. He feels that he has been totally abandoned by his God.

Job has three friends who had come from some distance to console him, and they had attempted to rescue him from his state of mourning. They wanted to return Job to the land of the living. They began well enough, but when Job gave voice to the deep pain in his soul, cursing the day of his birth, and, in the process, insinuating that God was treating him unjustly, his friends could remain silent no longer. They just could not let that kind of talk go unchallenged. They initiated three cycles of interchanges in which they each had a go at Job attempting to get him to come to his senses. By the end, as this dialogue turns into a debate and then into a savage denunciation, they explicitly accuse Job of a whole host of moral transgressions. "You have sinned, Job, just admit it, and then you can again enjoy God's blessing."

But Job is not intimidated by this onslaught. He can give it right back:

> You . . . smear me with lies;
>> you are worthless physicians, all of you!
> If only you would be altogether silent!
>> For you, that would be wisdom. (Job 13:4-5)
> . . .
>> You are miserable comforters, all of you!
> Will your long-winded speeches never end? (Job 16:2-3)
> . . .
> Have pity on me, my friends, have pity,
>> for the hand of God has struck me. (Job 19:21)

Pity is just what these friends lack. Where is their compassion, their commiseration, their condolence? They fail to enter into the depth of Job's despair; they rationalize rather than sympathize; they speak to Job's mind, but totally bypass his heart. These are the cries of a broken and despairing man, a man who had once lived in the joyous blessing of Almighty God, but who now knows nothing but pain, loss, and grief. But they treat Job as if he were a student in a theology seminar.

JOB'S RESPONSE

We now turn to look at the other side of this protracted dialogue, this time focusing not on the friends but on Job himself. You'll recall that at the instigation of Satan, and through the willing permission of God—in fact, through the suggestion of God—Job is at the center of a cosmic contest, a divine gambit. "Does Job fear God for nothing?" was the cynical question of the accuser. In other words, is there really such a thing as a true believer? Can anyone remain faithful to God even when all God's rich blessings are taken away?

And behind this question is an even deeper one—Is God really worthy of worship for his own sake and not just for the good things he gives us? Is God really worthy of all praise, honor, and glory? The honor of Almighty God himself is at stake in the behavior of this one man Job.

So how does Job do? How does he respond to the horrible calamity that has come upon him? Can he really persevere in faith? It is critical to our understanding of the book to appreciate that Job, just as much as his friends, believed both in God's sovereign rule and in the principle of retributive justice. Job believed that God is just—he gives people what they deserve; he blesses the righteous and punishes the wicked. Job's friends conclude that since God is just, Job must have sinned. But Job knows, and we the readers know, that Job hasn't sinned—or at least he hadn't sinned to the degree that merited the treatment he had received. Job's sin is not the reason for Job's suffering.

In light of his innocence, how is Job going to deal with his dreadful condition? How was his suffering going to affect his relationship with God? In light of the pain that God has afflicted on him, how could Job hold on to the notion that God is still good, while at the same time, insisting that he himself was innocent? To appreciate the central message of this book, you must feel this tension. Job feels trapped in this insoluble predicament.

HOW JOB DOESN'T RESPOND

But before we consider how Job responds to his dreadful dilemma, we should consider first how he *doesn't* respond. What are ways that he might have taken to escape this trap, but doesn't?

Job refuses a false repentance. The first road not taken is what the friends urge Job to do: he could acknowledge God's justice by admitting his own sin. If Job would simply repent and turn to God, the Lord would restore to him his former prosperity. Eliphaz says,

> If you return to the Almighty, you will be restored:
>> If you remove wickedness far from your tent. (Job 22:23)

But Job refuses to take this road because any such repentance would be false. He was innocent, and to deny that innocence would be to forfeit his own integrity.[1] To his friends he says,

> I will never admit you are in the right;
>> till I die, I will not deny my integrity.
> I will maintain my innocence and never let go of it;
>> my conscience will not reproach me as long as I live.
>> (Job 27:5-6)

To engage in some pious religious ritual with a pretense of repentance would simply be a way of manipulating God for personal gain.

---

[1]See Comment 5.1, "The Question of Integrity."

That course would have proved the cynical Satan to be right, and Job refuses to do it.

Job refuses to curse God. Second, Job does not do what Satan was sure he would do—Job does not curse God. Job does say some pretty harsh things about the way God is treating him:

> The arrows of the Almighty are in me,
>   my spirit drinks in their poison;
>   God's terrors are marshaled against me. (Job 6:4)
>
> . . .
>
> He is "multiply[ing] my wounds for no reason." (Job 9:17)
>
> . . .
>
> Does it please you to oppress me,
>   to spurn the work of your hands,
>   while you smile on the plans of the wicked? (Job 10:3)
>
> . . .
>
> Withdraw your hand far from me,
>   and stop frightening me with your terrors. . . .
> Why do you hide your face
>   and consider me your enemy? (Job 13:21, 24)
>
> . . .
>
> All was well with me, but he shattered me;
>   he seized me by the neck and crushed me.
> He has made me his target;
>   his archers surround me.
> Without pity, he pierces my kidneys
>   and spills my gall on the ground.
> Again and again he bursts upon me;
>   he rushes at me like a warrior. (Job 16:12-14)
>
> . . .

His anger burns against me;
    he counts me among his enemies.
His troops advance in force;
    they build a siege ramp against me
    and encamp around my tent. (Job 19:11-12)

. . .

God has made my heart faint;
    the Almighty has terrified me. (Job 23:16)

Some hear these words and want to condemn Job for his brazen impiety: you can't speak of God like this! Job even declares that

[God] has denied me justice,
    the Almighty . . . has made my life bitter. (Job 27:2)

But we must understand, this is the way Job *feels*. This is the way God's actions toward him appear. And we know that Job is right to feel this way. God has afflicted him for no reason. God himself has admitted that already (Job 2:3).

Job doesn't give in to those feelings; he struggles with what he is experiencing. It's true, sometimes he wants God to simply leave him alone. But there is a certain irony in that he keeps coming back to God even as he expresses that desire. His faith doesn't allow him to give in to his bitter feelings and curse God. He knows that what he is experiencing from God is not a true reflection of who he knows God to be. That is what is causing him so much distress—the fact that the God he knows to be good and just appears to be treating him in a way that seems to Job so unjust.[2]

His emotional struggle, at least as it related to God, could be over if he simply quit expecting God to act justly and reckoned him to be some evil force. That's what his wife urged him to do. But Job won't go there. He refuses to curse God.

---

[2]See Comment 5.2, "Job's Conflicted View of God."

Job refuses suicide. Third, though Job curses the day of his own birth
and wishes that he had died when he came from the womb, he resists the urge to take his own life.[3] Death seems to him as a possible
welcome relief from the intense pain he is experiencing. And he
seems to welcome the thought that God might take his life:

> Oh, that I might have my request,
>> that God would grant what I hope for,
> that God would be willing to crush me,
>> to let loose his hand and cut off my life! (Job 6:8-9)

God may kill him, but Job never considers taking his own life.

I can remember a time in my own life when I came close to doing
just that. The pain I experienced was excruciating. I entered the
emergency room doubled over, and the nurse instantly recognized
the symptoms—it was kidney stones! She immediately put me on a
morphine drip, but my heart rate dropped to a dangerous level, and
I remember urging her to just give me more morphine regardless of
the consequences. I didn't care! I knew where I was going, so just
give me more morphine and do not resuscitate! It was not quite
suicide, but it was still a desperate and perhaps reckless attempt to
escape the pain.

Job's pain seems almost unbearable: "I prefer strangling and
death," he says, "rather than this body of mine. I despise my life"
(Job 7:15-16). We could understand if he were tempted to take his
own life. But he never mentions that option. Job refuses to give up
on his own life and to give in to his despair. Job perseveres even
through the pain of his own living hell.

What restrained his desire for escape by death? Kathryn Greene-
McCreight, in her book *Darkness Is My Only Companion*, speaks of
her own battle with suicidal thoughts. "When one is plagued by

---

[3]See Comment 5.3, "Job's Death Wish."

suicidal urges," she writes, "one can feel completely isolated and imprisoned within the self. . . . There is nothing but the 'I' in pain."[4] Job never loses sight of the "other"—the God with whom he is wrestling and from whom he demands vindication. He refuses to give up hope for a restoration of relationship. In that sense, Job refuses to give up on his own life and to give in to his despair, for that would be giving up all hope in God. Job perseveres even through the pain of his own living hell.

Job refuses to abandon God. And finally, throughout the course of the book, despite his horrible suffering and intense pain, Job never abandons God. He never gives up his desire to hear from God, to meet with God, and to be vindicated by God. Though Job is arguing with his friends, his real audience throughout this dispute is God. In speech after speech, after dispensing with the friends' arguments, he turns his attention back to God. He continues to seek him, to confront him, to pray to him. It is very clear throughout the book that Job's deepest longing is not the restoration of his prosperity but the restoration of his relationship with God.

It is all too easy in the midst of deep pain and trauma to turn away from God with a feeling of betrayal and abandonment and never seek to reestablish a connection. I've seen Christian believers in times of suffering retreat from the church, and, in their pain, withdraw from Christian worship and prayer. Job doesn't do that. He wrestles with God to the end.

Job doesn't seek an easy way out. He refuses to do what many of us would be tempted to do if we were in his situation. He doesn't engage in false repentance, participating is some religious pretense, some superficial piety, as a way of seeking God's blessing. Job refuses to curse God, thereby denying God's goodness. Though he "despised his

[4]Kathryn Greene-McCreight, *Darkness Is My Only Companion: A Christian Response to Mental Illness,* 2nd ed. (Grand Rapids: Brazos Press, 2015), 32.

life," Job resists any urge to end it by his own hands. And to the end, Job never turns his back on God, abandoning him once and for all.

HOW JOB DOES RESPOND

This is what Job *doesn't* do. But now let's turn to what Job *does* do.

It's not so simple. Certainly, Job directly disputes his friends' simplistic notions of retributive justice. Job asserts that it is simply not true that the righteous are always blessed and the wicked always suffer. He asks,

> Why do the wicked live on,
>> growing old and increasing in power? (Job 21:7)

He challenges the breadth of their experience of the world: "Have you never questioned those who travel?" he asks (Job 21:29a). You need to look again at the world around you—broaden your horizons: Have you paid no regard to their accounts,

> that the wicked are spared from the day of calamity,
>> that they are delivered from the day of wrath?
>>> (Job 21:29b-30)
>
> . . .
>
> So how can you console me with your nonsense?
>> Nothing is left of your answers but falsehood! (Job 21:34)
>
> . . .
>
> Your maxims are proverbs of ashes;
>> your defenses are defenses of clay. (Job 13:12)

Job responds to the friends in various ways, but what I want to focus on is how Job relates to God in all this under two headings— lament and litigation.

Job laments. *Grieving before God.* Clearly, Job laments his miserable condition. Yes, he at first declares those most pious words of faith when he is told of the horrific calamity that has come upon him: everything comes from the hand of the Lord, and in everything his name is to be praised (Job 1:21).

Job knows that is what he should say; and he knows that is what he wants to be true in his heart. But he cannot deny the reality of what has happened, and he will not pretend that he is not in deep pain at his great loss. So he weeps, he grieves, he mourns, he cries out in his agony. His first words in response to Eliphaz in Job 6 express this:

If only my anguish could be weighed
    and all my misery be placed on the scales!
It would surely outweigh the sand of the seas—
    no wonder my words have been impetuous. (Job 6:2-3)

Yes, his words are impetuous. They are dripping with raw emotion; they are brutally honest; they express the depths of his heart.

I will give free rein to my complaint
and speak out in the bitterness of my soul. (Job 10:1)

We shouldn't be surprised by this language of lament. The Psalms are full of it. A lament is a way of pouring out one's feelings. It is a cry of real pain. And the Bible seems to endorse that practice, and in so doing, it authentically depicts human experience in this broken world.

But biblical laments have a special character. They are voiced in the presence of God. In that sense, biblical laments become a form of prayer. They contain an implicit plea for God to act, to rescue the speaker from his painful condition. This is a fallen world—a world in which we will all suffer, and the biblical laments encourage us to be honest about the pain we experience and not pretend it doesn't hurt. The Bible urges us to bring our grief, our sorrows, our suffering before God. Job certainly does.

Complaining to God. In lament we may grieve, but we may also object. In the Psalms, in the Prophets, and very much in Job, lament takes the form of complaint. In Psalm 13, David asks,

> How long, O LORD? Will you forget me forever?
>> How long will you hide your face from me?
> How long must I wrestle with my thoughts
>> and day after day have sorrow in my heart?
> How long will my enemy triumph over me? (Ps 13:1-2)

"Lord, I am hurting here—how long must I endure this? How long before you act in your love and mercy to relieve my pain? How long until you act in your justice to right what is wrong in this fallen world?" This is a question that we hear even in heaven itself. In the Revelation of John, he saw "under the altar the souls of those who had been slain because of the word of God and the testimony they had maintained. They called out in a loud voice, 'How long, Sovereign Lord, holy and true, until you judge the inhabitants of the earth and avenge our blood?'" (Rev 6:9-10)

So Job's lament includes a self-described complaint against God—

> Therefore I will not keep silent;
>> I will speak out in the anguish of my spirit,
>> I will complain in the bitterness of my soul. (Job 7:11)

Protesting against God. But Job's words go beyond complaint to real protest. Job firmly believes that he is being treated unfairly by God—and he wants God to know it.

> Does it please you to oppress me,
>> to spurn the work of your hands,
>> while you smile on the schemes of the wicked? (Job 10:3)

At one point, the encouraging and comforting words of Psalm 8, which speak of the care the Lord has for human beings, seem to be turned on their head. Job implies that we humans would be better off if God would just leave us alone:

> What is mankind that you make so much of them,
>   that you give them so much attention,
> that you examine them every morning
>   and test them every moment? (Job 7:17-18)[5]

As we said, Job feels that God stands against him as an enemy, and he doesn't like it. It's not right. He objects in protest.

Is Job being unfaithful in speaking this way? Isn't he like the Israelites in the desert after their exodus from Egypt who grumbled about their lack of food and water, and were rebuked by God and punished for it?[6] I don't think so. For one thing, unlike Job, the Israelites directed their protests against Moses and Aaron and not to God himself.[7] And then, their grumbling was not grounded in faith in God's goodness but assumed that God himself was wicked. Moses says to them, "You grumbled in your tents and said, 'The LORD hates us; so he brought us out of Egypt to deliver us into the hands of the Amorites to destroy us'" (Deut 1:27).

In contrast, Job's protest is grounded in his conviction that God is just. Job is struggling to make sense of the world around him in light of what he knows to be true about God. He is not trying to run away from God so much as run toward him. He wants to confront him, to hear from him, to be restored to him. The Israelites in the desert were rebelling against God; Job is simply in conflict with him. It's a conflict between his faith and his experience; between who he knows God to be and the way he is now being treated. His is a "defiant faith," a "pious protest," a "believing

---

[5]See Comment 5.5, "Parody."

[6]See Num 14:27-30 and 1 Cor 10:10.

[7]Cf. e.g., Ex 16:2, though God understood that ultimately he was the object of their protest (e.g., Ex 16:7).

belligerence."⁸ Job is a model of faith for us simply because in his lament he is not afraid to lay out his own inner struggles before the only one who can alleviate his suffering, heal his wounds, and dry his tears.⁹ The Israelites grumbled because they didn't believe God could provide for their needs; Job protests because he knows God can.

Job seeks litigation. This leads to one other way to describe Job's reaction: *litigation*.¹⁰ Job wants this conflict between himself and God resolved, and in his mind, there is only one way to do it: Job wants to take God to court.

Job's speeches are shot through with legal language, as he wants to take up a lawsuit against God in his effort to secure vindication. In Job 9 he begins to wonder what it might mean to stand before Almighty God in court.

> But how can mere mortals prove their innocence
> > before God?
> Though they wished to dispute with him,
> > they could not answer him one time out of a thousand.
> His wisdom is profound, his power is vast.
> > Who has resisted him and come out unscathed? (Job 9:2-4)
> . . .
> How then can I dispute with him?
> > How can I find words to argue with him? (Job 9:14)
> . . .
> If it is a matter of strength, he is mighty!
> > And if it is a matter of justice, who can challenge him?
> > > (Job 9:19)

In Job 10 he explores what he might say to God:

> I say to God: Do not declare me guilty,
>> but tell me what charges you have against me. (Job 10:2)

The litigation theme continues in Job 13:

> I desire to speak to the Almighty
>> and to argue my case with God. (Job 13:3)
> . . .
> Now that I have prepared my case,
>> I know I will be vindicated.
> Can anyone bring charges against me?
>> If so, I will be silent and die. . . .
> Summon me and I will answer,
>> or let me speak, and you reply to me.
> How many wrongs and sins have I committed?
>> Show me my offense and my sin. (Job 13:18-19, 22-23)

But such a meeting with God seems beyond his means. And in a parody of the words of Psalm 139,[11] Job says,

> If only I knew where to find him;
>> if only I could go to his dwelling!
> I would state my case before him
>> and fill my mouth with arguments.
> I would find out what he would answer me,
>> and consider what he would say to me.
> Would he vigorously oppose me?
>> No, he would not press charges against me.
> There the upright can establish their innocence
>>> before him,
>> and there I would be delivered forever from my judge.

---

[11]See Comment 5.5, "Parody."

But if I go to the east, he is not there;
> if I go to the west, I do not find him.
When he is at work in the north, I do not see him;
> when he turns to the south, I catch no glimpse of him.
>   (Job 23:3-9)

Job, in his agony of mind and body, is imagining all options. He is confident of his own righteousness, but he is frightened of the prospect of appearing before God.

My feet have closely followed his steps;
> I have kept to his way without turning aside.
I have not departed from the commands of his lips;
> I have treasured the words of his mouth more than my
>   daily bread.
But he stands alone, and who can oppose him?
> He does whatever he pleases.
He carries out his decree against me,
> and many such plans he still has in store.
That is why I am terrified before him;
> when I think of all this, I fear him.
God has made my heart faint;
> the Almighty has terrified me. (Job 23:11-16)

Job's desire for a mediator. With this we come to one of the most intriguing aspects of Job's response. He wants to meet with God, but at the same time he is terrified by the prospect. And in several places Job seems to toy with the thought of some mediator who could stand with him—some legal advocate who could state his case, some witness who could testify on his behalf, even a redeemer who would make his claim before God.

We first see this in Job 9:

[God] is not a mere mortal like me that I might answer him,
     that we might confront each other in court.
If only there were someone to mediate between us,
     someone to bring us together,
someone to remove God's rod from me,
     so that his terror would frighten me no more.
Then I would speak up without fear of him,
     but as it now stands with me, I cannot. (Job 9:32-35)

"If only," Job muses, as he longs for some way to be reconciled to God.

Then in Job 16 he imagines a similar figure, this time called his "witness," his "advocate," and his "intercessor"—a "friend" who will intercede for him.

Even now my witness is in heaven;
     my advocate is on high.
My intercessor is my friend
     as my eyes pour out tears to God;
on behalf of a man he pleads with God
     as one pleads for a friend. (Job 16:19-21)

And finally, and most famously, in Job 19—

I know that my redeemer lives,
     and that in the end he will stand on the earth.
And after my skin has been destroyed,
     yet in my flesh I will see God;
I myself will see him with my own eyes—I, and not another.
     How my heart yearns within me! (Job 19:25-27)[12]

---

[12]The proper translation of these verses is as hotly debated as their significance. The Hebrew here includes a number of difficult and unusual features, which have led to numerous proposals for emendations to correct what at points appears to many to be a corrupted text (see David Clines, *Job*, 3 vols. [Nashville: Thomas Nelson, 1989–2011], 1:433-34, 457-66). Interpreters must therefore be cautious about building arguments on specific aspects of these verses, as we have sought to do. For example, to take "in my flesh" in Job 19:26 as an Old Testament affirmation of the bodily resurrection is a possible interpretation, but a strong case may be made that Job is actually

Many will immediately recognize the first line of this passage—"I know that my redeemer lives"—as a line from Handel's *Messiah*. Perhaps because of that, they immediately conclude that this is the high point of Job's faith. He now understands that a Messiah is coming and that he will be raised with him to experience a full redemption. I can't quite go there. For one thing, if matters were that clear to Job, then why does he return to his despairing mood for another twelve chapters, never again referring to this glorious revelation? And elsewhere in the book he shows no awareness of life after death. He refers to death as "the path of no return" (Job 16:22; cf. 14:10-12).

No, Job is still wrestling with the deepest question of all. In our pain and suffering, our deepest need is to face God, but how is that possible? In his agony, Job feels that God is bearing down on him, but, at the same time, he knows that only God can rescue him. As he wrestles with the suffering he is enduring, in Job's mind, God seems to be the problem, but he also knows that only God can be the solution. How can God, who is so terrifying in his power, so overwhelming in his holiness, so vast in his knowledge, how can such a God ever relate to such an insignificant, weak, and ignorant human being like me? Do you see Job's dilemma here?[13]

If only there was a witness, an advocate, a mediator. There must be a redeemer who will stand for him. But Job is at a loss to know who this could be.

And as those on this side of the coming of Jesus Christ into the world, we can now see that what Job longed for, what he imagined as his only hope, has in fact come to pass. We do have that witness, that advocate, that redeemer. We have that one who stands both on

---

affirming that he will see God "without his flesh," and, therefore, "despite his disembodiment" (C. L. Seow, *Job 1–21: Interpretation and Commentary* [Grand Rapids, MI: Eerdmans, 2013], 826; cf. Clines, *Job*, 1:464).

[13] See Comment 5.2, "Job's Conflicted View of God."

the side of God and on our side, the one who is able to mediate, to reconcile, to arbitrate between us. We now know of that one who is both an expression of the love of God even as he in his death appeases the wrath of God. God himself has provided someone who "remove[s] God's rod from me, so that his terror would frighten me no more" (Job 9:34).

Job, in his deep pain, sees the problem, and Job, in his deep longing, points us to the only solution—the solution found in the gospel of the triune God. God in his grace provides his own Son as our mediator, our advocate, and our redeemer. In Christ, God in his love for us satisfies his own wrath against us, and he receives us as his own children. For as Paul says it—"God demonstrates his own love for in this: while we were still sinners, Christ died for us" (Rom 5:8).

In Job's darkness, we get a glimpse of glorious gospel light. And we will see that the ultimate "answer" to the problem of evil and suffering in this world is found in the cross and resurrection of Jesus Christ.[14]

AN IMPORTUNATE WOMAN

But Job is still on his ash heap, in grief and mourning, lamenting his condition, complaining about, and even protesting against, his treatment. And he is not done yet. As we close this chapter, I direct your attention to someone Jesus describes who is a lot like Job—a woman who felt she was being treated unjustly.

Jesus tells a story involving a judge "who neither feared God nor cared what people thought" and a widow "who kept coming to him with the plea, 'Grant me justice against my adversary'" (Lk 18:2-3). For some time, the judge refused her plea, but eventually he gave in, as he said to himself, "Even though I don't fear God or care what

---

[14]See Comment 5.6, "Who Is Job's 'Redeemer' (Job 19:25)?"

people think, yet because this widow keeps bothering me, I will see that she gets justice, so that she won't eventually come and attack me!" (Lk 18:5). This story is often referred to as the parable of the unjust judge, but the judge's role in the parable is just as a foil, a contrast, to the true Judge who always judges justly. The real focus of the parable is the woman. The story is more accurately named the parable of the importunate widow. She refused to give up. When things looked grim and even hopeless, she refused to give in. She kept coming; she kept asking, pleading, imploring—even to the point of being annoying.

Here Jesus assumes that in the face of the evils of this world, we will feel unjustly treated, and we must be those who persevere in a persistent faith. We must engage in what might be called *protesting* prayer—prayer of the sort Job prayed.

In commenting on this parable, David Wells makes the case that our prayer must be provoked by just such protest.

> What, then, is the nature of petitionary prayer? It is, in essence, rebellion—rebellion against the world in its fallenness, the absolute and undying refusal to accept as normal what is pervasively abnormal. It is, in this its negative aspect, the refusal of every agenda, every scheme, every interpretation that is at odds with the norm as originally established by God. . . . Nothing destroys petitionary prayer (and with it, a Christian view of God) as quickly as resignation.[15]

Jesus concludes this story, "When the Son of Man comes, will he find faith on the earth?" (Lk 18:8). Will there be those who refused to give up and to give in? Will there be those who persevered in faith, despite the pain and the hardship and the injustice and the apparent unfairness of life in this world? "Jesus told his disciples

---

[15]David Wells, "Prayer: Rebelling Against the Status Quo: Are We Angry Enough to Pray?," *Christianity Today*, November 2, 1979.

[this] parable to show them that they should always pray and not give up" (Lk 18:1).

Job refused to resign himself to the distortion of reality he experienced, and he was determined to wrestle with God until he experienced some resolution. By laying before us Job's raw experience of divine distance, his own "dark night of the soul," the book encourages us to enter into the injustice Job feels, to identify with it, and to be prepared for it when we experience it ourselves.[16] Following Job's example, glorifying God as we walk through the valley of the shadow of death means taking one's experience of God forsakenness directly to its source: God himself. It doesn't mean giving up on God's goodness or power, but it may mean holding God to those standards of his own character, and grappling in the darkness, as Jacob did (Gen 32), until the sun begins to rise. That is a real faith.

DIGGING DEEPER

5.1. The question of integrity. A primary question driving the book of Job is whether outward behavior accurately represents inward character, a correlation that the book calls "integrity" (*tummah*).[17] The Satan introduces this issue by asking, "Does Job fear God for nothing?" (Job 1:9). In so doing, the Satan does not question Job's piety, already praised by both the narrator and God (Job 1:1, 8), but the internal motivation for it. After Job maintains his piety despite the Satan's first test, God praises Job's persistence in his "integrity" (Job 2:3).

The second character to raise the question of Job's integrity is his wife (Job 2:9-10).[18] Job's response to her, in which he expresses

---

[16]See Comment 7.1, "The Hiddenness of God."

[17]Michael C. Legaspi, *Wisdom in Classical and Biblical Tradition* (New York: Oxford University Press, 2018), 90, 96-99.

[18]See "Mrs. Job and Job's Bewilderment" in chap. 3 above.

faith that his wife's external action does not conform with her true internal character, foreshadows Job's confidence that, in his justice, God must act justly toward him, which drives Job's complaints.[19] Thus, God's confidence in Job's integrity in response to the Satan's question reflects Job's confidence in God's integrity, which answers the Satan's question.

The word "integrity" is not mentioned again until Job 27:5, but Job's refusal to perform an insincere repentance ritual for personal gain despite his innocence here conforms with his dispute with both his friends and God throughout. It culminates in his lengthy self-curse in Job 31, in which Job declares, "Let me be weighed in a just balance, and let God know my integrity [*tummah*]!" (Job 31:6 NRSV). *Tummah* is only mentioned one other time in the Old Testament, Proverbs 11:3, which provides a good summary of Job's contest with his "treacherous" friends (Job 6:15 NRSV): "The integrity of the upright guides them, but the crookedness of the treacherous destroys them" (NRSV).

5.2. Job's conflicted view of God. To call Job's view of God "conflicted" is a bit of an understatement. As Roland de Pury puts it, "The amazing thing about this book is precisely the fact that Job makes no move to flee to some better kind of God but sticks it out in the direct line of fire from the divine anger. Without moving, Job, whom God treats as an enemy, in the midst of his darkness, in the midst of the abyss, appeals, not to some higher authority, not even to the God of his friends, but to the very God who is crushing him."[20] Having no higher authority, Job appeals to God against God. Job's refusal to explain his suffering as the effect of some evil power outside God thwarting his sovereign purposes reflects Israel's rejection of dualism. This belief is most succinctly expressed in Isaiah 45:7:

---

[19]Cf. Gen 18:25; see Comment 7.5, "The Biblical Tradition of Defiant Faith."

[20]Roland de Pury, *Hiob—der Mensch im Aufruhr* (Neukirchen-Vluyn: Neukirchener, 1957), 23.

I form the light and create darkness,
I bring prosperity and create disaster;
I, the LORD, do all these things.[21]

Gerhard von Rad writes that this is ultimately a comforting doctrine. He claims that all who have sought to understand how to restore order in the face of "life's great misfortune" agree, "only God is competent to deal with it. The world has no contribution of its own to make. The world is not a battlefield between God and any of the evils found in it."[22] This belief in God's ultimate sovereignty is only comforting if one also believes in God's perfect justice and goodness. Thus, though Job blames God and no other cause for his suffering, because he believes in God's justice, he also appeals to God for the vindication he craves, thereby confronting the God of his experience with the God of his faith. Job has already demonstrated this nuanced understanding of a more fundamental character that may appear to conflict with some action one may perform in his response to his wife.[23] Many of the heroes of Israelite faith respond similarly to God when they encounter apparent injustice in the world, and God frequently responds positively to their "defiant faith" as he does to Job.[24]

5.3. Job's death wish. Job (Job 7:15-21; 10:18-22), Jonah (Jon 4:3, 8-9), and several psalmists (Ps 39; 88) employ death wishes to express their displeasure with God's actions. For Job, the death wish is an expression of faith, not nihilistic despair. Job's impending death (Job 7:21; 10:21-22) is a threat, and, as such, intends to motivate changed behavior. Norman Habel is both right and wrong when he represents a widespread understanding of Job's death wish in Job 7 by saying, "Though Job does not plan suicide, he prefers

---

[21]See Comment 10.3, "God and Evil (Job 42:11)."
[22]Gerhard von Rad, *Wisdom in Israel*, trans. James D. Martin (Harrisburg, PA: Trinity Press International, 1972), 306.
[23]See "Mrs. Job and Job's Bewilderment" in chap. 3 above.
[24]See Comment 7.5, "The Biblical Tradition of Defiant Faith."

death to an endless life of oppression at the hands of an arbitrary God."[25] Yes, Job never contemplates suicide and refuses to accept his life's current status. He even, undoubtedly, prefers death to *this* life, but Job's argument does not presuppose an arbitrary God, and therefore does not intend death as an escape. Instead, he presupposes a God who will respond to the charge of unrighteousness, and thus employs the death wish as a rhetorical weapon in the struggle for life and the reestablishment of righteousness, both Job's and God's.[26] Job has no advantage in death, but God has a disadvantage, the lost opportunity to provide justice to Job and prove divine righteousness. The psalmist similarly claims that if God allows him to die, he will no longer be able to praise God (Ps 88:10-12).

5.4. Job as lawsuit. Noting that legal forms far outnumber wisdom forms in the book and legal language (444 verses) far outweighs that of wisdom (346 verses), Heinz Richter argued that Job is better understood as a lawsuit than a "Wisdom" book.[27] But to conform the entire book, with its narrative frame, to this genre, these legal connections must be dramatized to make the book a "lawsuit drama"[28] or "trial narrative" made up of conflicting "legal stories" patterned on ancient Near Eastern models.[29] Further, the roles of the characters, nature of the charges, and numbers of suits, countersuits, and even parallel suits are debated.[30]

Though the book, therefore, is more than simply a lawsuit, noticing its similarities with ancient legal proceedings highlights its use of legal genres and motifs, which "make the reader aware of

---

[25]Norman Habel, *The Book of Job* (London: SCM, 1985), 299.

[26]See Comment 3.2, "Job's Countercosmic Curse."

[27]Heinz Richter, *Studien zu Hiob: Der Aufbau des Hiobbuches, dargestellt an den Gattungen des Rechtslebens* (Berlin: Evangelische Verlagsanstat, 1959), 13, 16.

[28]Sylvia Huberman Scholnick, "Lawsuit Drama in the Book of Job" (PhD diss., Brandeis, 1975).

[29]F. Rachel Magdalene, *On the Scales of Righteousness: Neo-Babylonian Trial Law and the Book of Job* (Providence, RI: Brown University Press, 2007), 263, 50.

[30]Magdalene, *On the Scales*, 6-8.

the strong claims made by Job."[31] Job uses the lawsuit metaphor to convey his "case" against God as yet another rhetorical means to compel God to respond.[32] This technique reaches its climax in Job's final monologue (Job 29–31). Here, Job lays out his case, following ancient judicial precedent.[33] He describes his past prosperity (Job 29), how God has taken everything from him (Job 30, esp. Job 30:11, 20-31), and concludes with a self-curse to declare his innocence (Job 31).[34] He then signs his complaint (Job 31:35b) and dares God to respond (Job 31:35c). Recognizing this provocation, the Lord uses legal language in his response. Using the legal term *rib*, which refers to contesting a lawsuit, pleading a legal cause, lodging a complaint, or attacking within a dispute,[35] God asks, "Will the one who contends [*rib*] with the Almighty correct him? Let him who accuses God answer him!" (Job 40:2). Even after Job withdraws his complaint by covering his mouth (Job 40:4), God continues, "Would you discredit my justice? Would you condemn me to justify yourself?" (Job 40:8).[36] Some, however, see God's double compensation for Job's losses (Job 42:12) as a concession of fault on God's part, since a double repayment is the punishment for theft (Ex 22:4).[37] Some also see the harsh punishment God levies on Job's friends—a burnt offering of seven bulls and seven rams (Job 42:8)—as retribution for their false testimony against Job.

Habel claims the lawsuit metaphor "is a major literary device which integrates narrative progression and theological motif" and gives the book a chiastic pattern, centered on Job's oath of innocence in Job 29–31, and culminating in Job's exculpation of guilt

---

[31]Roland E. Murphy, *Wisdom Literature: Job, Proverbs, Ruth, Canticles, Ecclesiastes, and Esther* (Grand Rapids, MI: Eerdmans, 1981), 17.

[32]See Comment 5.3, "Job's Death Wish."

[33]Seow, *Job*, 60-61.

[34]See Comment 7.4, "Appeals to Innocence in the Psalms."

[35]*The Hebrew and Aramaic Lexicon of the Old Testament*, ed. Ludwig Köhler, Walter Baumgartner, and Johann Jakob Stamm, trans. Mervyn E. J. Richardson (Leiden: Koninklijke Brill, 1994–1999), s.v. רִיב.

[36]See Comment 9.3, "Discounting a Dichotomous Theology (Job 40:8)."

[37]E.g., Clines, *Job*, 3:1237.

by God (Job 42:7-8), which corresponds to God's original declarations of his piety (Job 1:6-11; 2:1-6).[38] And yet, Habel concludes that the divine speeches throw the legal metaphor into question by declaring "Yahweh is bigger than the law or any legal metaphor."[39] Though the lawsuit genre contributes to our understanding of the book, no single genre can comprehend its meaning.[40]

5.5. Parody. The author of Job appears to be well acquainted with Israel's Scriptures. Throughout, he alludes to texts across the Hebrew Bible.[41] One of his favorite allusive techniques, especially in Job's speeches, is parody. The clearest and most well-known example of Job's parody is his reversal of Psalm 8. In the midst of his hymn praising God for the honor the deity bestows on comparatively insignificant human beings, the psalmist asks, "What are human beings that [*mah 'enosh ki*] you are mindful of them, mortals that you care [*paqad*] for them?" In his lament, Job repeats the first phrase of this question and imitates its basic structure but reverses the significance of the ambivalent term *paqad* to twist praise into protest: "What are human beings, that [*mah 'enosh ki*] you make so much of them, that you set your mind on them, visit [*paqad*] them every morning, test them every moment?"

Parody is commonly understood to ridicule its target. Thus, Job's parody of Psalm 8 is often considered an indication of his, or even the book's, skepticism.[42] However, though ridicule and humor are common in parodies, the essence of parody is simply antithetical allusion, as an author connects his or her work to an earlier text, but reverses it in some way.[43] That reversal may be intended as a mocking rejection or humorous send-up of the

---

[38]Habel, *Job*, 54-57.

[39]Habel, *Job*, 57.

[40]See Comment 1.2, "The Genre(s) of Job."

[41]See Comment 1.4, "Allusion and Intertextuality."

[42]See Katharine J. Dell, *The Book of Job as Sceptical Literature* (Berlin: de Gruyter, 1991), 126.

[43]See Will Kynes, "Beat Your Parodies into Swords, and Your Parodied Books into Spears: A New Paradigm for Parody in the Hebrew Bible," *Biblical Interpretation* 19 (2011): 276-310.

authority of an earlier text, but it could also employ the earlier text to attack some aspect of the world of the text in which the parody appears. As it does so, the parody could appeal to the respect that readers have for that earlier text in a deadly serious way. For example, Job 1–2 is a mirror image of Genesis 2–3.[44] It has the same cast of characters—God, a man and wife, and a supernatural adversary—but it reverses the story; the man resists his wife's temptation to question God and instead maintains his integrity, even at great loss. It is a parody, but not one that intends to ridicule the Eden narrative. Similarly, the question in Job 21:17, "How often is the lamp of the wicked snuffed out?" is clearly an attempt to question the confident assertion of Proverbs 13:9: "The light of the righteous shines brightly, but the lamp of the wicked is snuffed out." However, Job does not intend to reject the proverb but to employ it to urge God to act justly.

Understanding parody to include respectful allusions to the authority of earlier texts provides a more compelling understanding of how the poet intends us to understand Job's parodies in Job 7 and elsewhere. Rhetorically, Job stands to gain nothing if he rejects the astounding concern God shows for lowly humanity in Psalm 8. However, if he can appeal to that vision of God to express just how far the treatment he is currently receiving from God falls short of that standard, he may be able to coax God into rectifying his situation. Thus, the contrast he creates between his experience of God and that of the psalmist does not ridicule the psalm but appeals to its authority to call God to account.[45]

The same goes for the parody of Psalm 139:7-9 in Job 23:8-9. The psalmist describes God's inescapable presence, which would accompany him even if he ascended to the heavens, descended to the depths, fled to the dawn in the east or across the sea to the west of Israel. But when Job longs to find God, so that he can

---

[44]See Comment 2.2, "The Prologue and Genesis 2–3."
[45]See Comment 7.5, "The Biblical Tradition of Defiant Faith."

receive an answer to his cry for justice, he cannot find him in the east, west, north, or south. Job's point is not to reject the psalmist's experience of God's presence but to call God to act similarly toward him.

5.6. Who is Job's "redeemer" (Job 19:25)? Job's enigmatic appeal to a "redeemer" (*go'el*) is one of the book's greatest conundrums. In the Old Testament, *goel* is a term that was commonly used to describe the kinsman-redeemer, a family member who would provide help in times of struggle. This figure would rescue his relative out of debt or slavery, marry his widow to provide an heir, or even avenge his blood. However, in the verses leading up to Job's desperate cry (Job 19:13-19), he describes how all his family and friends have forsaken him, so it seems unlikely that he has a human *go'el* in mind, at least not one currently willing to play this role. At least eleven different possibilities have been proposed for who or what Job may have in mind.[46] In addition to God, a variety of third parties have been suggested, including the arbiter of Job 9:33-34 and witness in heaven of Job 16:19, a member of the divine council, Job's own cry (Job 16:18-20), another accuser alongside Job, another human who will eventually believe in Job's innocence, another deity, whether a pseudodivine counterdeity or the god Ba'al, or even nobody in particular, because Job is merely testing a hypothesis.

Though God is repeatedly called a redeemer elsewhere in the Old Testament (e.g., Is 41:14; Jer 50:34; Ps 78:35), many interpreters struggle to see Job expressing his faith in God here in light of the enmity Job perceives in God throughout the dialogue, which is particularly intense in the immediately preceding verses, as Job claims that God has "wronged" him (Job 19:6), counted him as an enemy (Job 19:11), and alienated him from family and friends (Job 19:13-19). Marvin Pope scoffs, "The heavenly witness, guarantor,

---

[46]See the list in Seow, *Job*, 823. He includes Christ with God as one entry in his list, but I prefer to separate them, at least initially, because some interpreters argue for one rather than the other.

friend can scarcely be God who is already Accuser, Judge, and Executioner."[47] Others claim it stretches the logic of the book for God to appear as a witness against himself in his dispute with Job. Such action would present God as a "schizophrenic deity."[48] It would be "a complete reversal in the pattern of Job's thought to date," as he consistently refers to God as his enemy and adversary before this moment (Job 13:24; 16:9; 19:11), and "as his accuser and adversary at law to the very end (31:35-37)."[49] As it would not make sense for God, who is accusing Job, to act as a witness against himself, it would make less sense for Job, who sees God as his adversary, to put any hope in such a witness.

Job seems to recognize this, which is why he expresses a longing for a third party, an arbiter (Job 9:33-35) or witness (Job 16:19-21), to intervene on his behalf with God. In the end, however, Job appears to recognize that God has, in fact, played this role. His words, "I know" and "my eyes have seen," echoing Job 19:25, in Job's response to the divine speeches (Job 42:2-6) followed by God's vindication of Job (Job 42:7-8) suggest that God is indeed the redeemer for which Job hoped.[50] The book does not explain how to make sense of this, but Christian readers since at least Jerome have seen the text as a prophecy of Christ. Though there is no indication in the text that Job completely understood what he was grasping at here (hence the validity of the view that he is testing a hypothesis), Christ unites in himself the aspects of the longing Job expresses that lead to the various views mentioned above. He is God, and yet is also an intermediary between God and humanity, who intercedes for his people in heaven (Heb 7:25).

---

[47]Marvin H. Pope, *Job* (Garden City, NY: Doubleday, 1965), 118.
[48]Habel, *Job*, 275.
[49]Habel, *Job*, 306.
[50]Seow, *Job*, 810.

six

A DRAMATIC ASIDE

JOB 28

Where then does wisdom come from?
Where does understanding dwell?

JOB 28:20

THE WINDS ARE HOWLING, the trees bending, the rains
pounding. Then suddenly, all is still. Just for a few brief minutes.
Then the fury resumes all over again. "If it's at night, the sky is clear,
the wind is calm, and the stars are out! It's a little spooky if you
have not been there before. . . . It's calming but frightening at the
same time. . . . You think it's over but the worst is yet to come." So
writes Mike Connelly, self-described inventor, problem solver, and
student of nature, recounting what it is like to pass through the eye
of a hurricane.[1]

Job 28 comes as the eye of the storm, a calm reprieve from a tu-
multuous clash. In contrast both to the passionate and combative
dialogue of the previous chapters and to Job's continuing protes-
tation that follows, this chapter seems peaceful and untroubled. And
it seems to have no clear connection with what comes before or after.
We are at first disoriented by its place in the book.

---

[1]Connelly claims to have been through at least twenty hurricanes and tropical storms ("What
Does It Feel Like to Be in the Eye of a Hurricane?," Quora, www.quora.com/What-does-it
-feel-like-to-be-in-the-eye-of-a-hurricane).

These could well be the words of Job, continuing from the previous chapter, though there's no reference to Job as the speaker as we find at the beginning of Job 26, 27, and 29.[2] Whatever the reason for this chapter's distinctive character, its reflection on wisdom provides a kind of parenthesis in the drama's progress. It offers some "breathing space" for us as readers, a thought-provoking "interlude," as the NIV11 chapter title puts it, to reflect on where the story has gone. There are plenty more fireworks to come; here we are given some space for some quiet reflection.

Whether Job is speaking or not, it is helpful to think of this chapter as a dramatic aside. It's as if the playwright himself pauses the action and comes on stage to address the audience. The biblical author takes a moment to reframe the book's central struggle without resolving it, while pointing us in the direction from which the resolution must come.

THE QUEST FOR WISDOM

Since Job began his lament in Job 3, he has been asking, Why? Why is this happening to me? Why have I lost everything that I valued, everything that brought joy into my life. It's all gone. My life is a wreck! I am miserable! Why, Lord? Why should this be?

Why, Lord? That's a question that we all deal with when disaster strikes, whether it be a school shooting, a terrorist bombing, or even a global pandemic. We want answers. We want to know how to manage life in this world full of trouble and heartache.

The "why?" question is really a search for some meaning and purpose. It's a desire to discover some underlying order in the world. How are we to live so that we might flourish and not flounder? We want wisdom for living.

---

[2] See Comment 6.1, "The Speaker in Job 28."

I define wisdom as the best way to the best end.[3] It involves both means and ends. A person may be a very effective thief, but we'd hardly call that person wise. Or a person could have the best intentions in the world but have no clue as to how to fulfill them. That person is not wise either. No, it must include both means and ends. In that sense, wisdom is more than knowledge, for wisdom involves value judgments about what is worth pursuing, and it includes the will to pursue it. Wisdom understands the way things work; it entails a practical knowledge; it is the skill of living well.

Job is wrestling with what it could mean to live well when his world is in ruins. Shouldn't his righteous way of life have led to prosperity? What does it mean to live wisely in a world of pain and hardship?

Where can wisdom be found? But where can such wisdom be found? Who can answer Job's most perplexing questions? Who has the wisdom to address his agonizing circumstances?

Job's friends think they do. They come to console him with the hope of drawing him out of his state of mourning. They begin well, but after Job moves from pious praise to honest lament and even protest, they cannot help but try to provide the wisdom that Job so desperately needs. They think they know the answer to Job's calamity: "Job, you must have sinned, so repent and your prosperity will be restored." But Job knows, and we too know, that they are wrong. He mocks their presumptuous claim to know what God is up to in his case:

> Doubtless you are the only people who matter,
>   and wisdom will die with you! (Job 12:2)
>
> . . .
>
> If only you would be altogether silent!
>   For you, that would be wisdom. (Job 13:5)
>
> . . .

---

[3]See Comment 6.2, "Defining Wisdom."

> Do you listen in on God's council?
>
> Do you have a monopoly on wisdom? (Job 15:8)

Job scoffs at their claim to have the wisdom that would comfort him in his pain. Job ends his fiery response to his friends in Job 27, and he will offer a final and dramatic challenge to God in Job 29–31. In between, in Job 28, we find this poem focused on wisdom. Its emphasis on the elusiveness of wisdom captures the narrative of the book thus far. Its conclusion regarding the source of wisdom points us to what is to come.

The hiddenness of wisdom. The first eleven verses speak of *the hiddenness of wisdom*. To make that point, the author first extols human ingenuity and courage in discovering and recovering the hidden treasures of the earth.

> There is a mine for silver
>
> and a place where gold is refined.
>
> Iron is taken from the earth,
>
> and copper is smelted from ore.
>
> Mortals put an end to the darkness;
>
> they search out the farthest recesses
>
> for ore in the blackest darkness.
>
> Far from human dwellings they cut a shaft,
>
> in places untouched by human feet;
>
> far from other people they dangle and sway. (Job 28:1-4)

Job 28:4 seems to be a reference to people being lowered down on ropes through vertical mining shafts deep into the heart of the earth. These ancient engineers did what no animal could ever be capable of, not even the sharp-eyed falcon or proud, prowling lion (Job 28:7-8).

No, this excavation of the earth is a magnificent human achievement—chiseling through rock, tunneling into the mountains "to bring hidden things to light" (Job 28:9-11).

Even today we can be amazed at mining and drilling techniques, ways that have been devised to acquire coal, precious stones, and metals. But our author tells us, there is one thing human technology can never uncover in this world—and that is wisdom.

> But where can wisdom be found?
> Where does understanding dwell? (Job 28:12)

As we read in Job 28:21,

> It is hidden from the eyes of every living thing,
>   concealed even from the birds in the sky.

Wisdom and science and technology. We live in a scientific age. Science has enabled us to understand the material world around us, to control it, and to harness it for our welfare. This has made scientific knowledge the gold standard, or, for many, even the only standard, when it comes to claiming to know anything. The methods of science—its empirical research, observation, quantifiable measurements, testing of hypotheses, peer review, objective assessment of evidence—and the technology that flows out of that scientific discovery have brought tremendous benefits to our lives. Would any of us really want to go back in time before aspirin and anesthesia, smartphones and GPS?

But what we sometimes forget is that science and technology—despite their success, still have nothing to say about what is good or bad, right or wrong, what is valuable and what is worthless. Science can only observe and predict. It cannot make judgments of value. The scientific method cannot demonstrate that "torturing babies is wrong." Renowned atheist Richard Dawkins states it starkly when he says, "Science has no methods for deciding what is ethical."[4]

---

[4]Richard Dawkins, *A Devil's Chaplain: A Reflection on Lies, Science, and Love* (Boston: Houghton Mifflin, 2003), 34.

Science is a wonderful tool, but it is only one tool among others by which we come to know things. And in fact, science is incapable of knowing the most important things—the most personal things. And this chapter in Job tells us that one of the things that science and technology cannot discover is wisdom. It cannot fathom the deepest questions of our hearts—questions of meaning and purpose. It cannot move from what is to what ought to be.

Science can be of great help with finding the best means, but it is of little value in determining the best ends. If I know where I want to go, my GPS can tell me how to get there—but it can't tell me whether my destination should be Sunday school or a strip club.

You see, science can never tell us what human beings are for, or what constitutes a good human life, or what makes for real human happiness. A recent article describing the growing disillusionment with internet dating sites illustrates this limitation:

> The singles of Silicon Valley, the heart of America's techno-logical ambition, spend much of their lives in quiet devotion to the power of the almighty algorithm, driven by the belief that technology can solve the world's most troubling ills. But when it comes to the algorithms of love, many say they are losing faith. They wonder whether Silicon Valley . . . has proved too vexing for even its own dating apps. But they're also left with a more fundamental doubt: Maybe the human mysteries of chemistry and attraction aren't problems big data can solve.[5]

I think of the lines of a poem by Edna St. Vincent Millay:

Upon this gifted age, in its dark hour,
Rains from the sky a meteoric shower

---

[5]Drew Harwell, "Why Silicon Valley Singles Are Giving Up on the Algorithms of Love," *Washington Post*, February 14, 2018, www.washingtonpost.com/business/economy/why-silicon-valley-singles-are-giving-up-on-the-algorithms-of-love/2018/02/14/6cbd74ee-1041-11e8-8ea1-c1d91fcec3fe_story.html.

Of facts . . . they lie unquestioned, uncombined.
Wisdom enough to leech us of our ill
Is daily spun; but there exists no loom
To weave it into fabric.[6]

We are inundated daily with a veritable meteoric shower of facts—
information abounds, but there exists no loom to weave the facts into
a fabric of wisdom. Despite its great power, science, and the human
ingenuity it demonstrates, fails us.[7] We are left with the question,

But where can wisdom be found?
Where does understanding dwell? (Job 28:12)

Wisdom and wealth. Our author moves from the hiddenness of
wisdom to its supreme value. The most precious metals—gold and
silver—and the most expensive jewels—onyx, sapphires, or the beautiful blue stone lapis lazuli—none of them are its equal (Job 28:15-17).
"No mortal comprehends its worth" (Job 28:13).

Not only is wisdom not the kind of thing that can be bought, its
value is far beyond any price that anyone could pay. And intuitively
we know this to be true. Are the one hundred richest people in the
world the one hundred wisest? Are they the happiest? If they could
buy what wisdom offers, surely they would, but they can't. Wisdom
can't be bought.

The Proverbs makes this connection:

Blessed are those who find wisdom,
    those who gain understanding,
for she is more profitable than silver
    and yields better returns than gold.
She is more precious than rubies;
    nothing you desire can compare with her. (Prov 3:13-15)

---

[6]From the sonnet "Huntsman, What Quarry?" (1939).
[7]See Comment 6.3, "Wisdom and Science."

How much better to get wisdom than gold,
  to get insight rather than silver! (Prov 16:16)

Jesus certainly confronted us with this truth. The rich young man who came to him desperately wanted the wisdom that Jesus had, but his wealth was not only irrelevant; it was, in fact, a hindrance. It blinded him to the one thing he lacked. "What good will it be for someone to gain the whole world, yet forfeit their soul?" Jesus asked. "Or what can anyone give in exchange for their soul?" (Mt 16:26).

God alone holds the key to wisdom. The author moves in the final section to his central point—the source of wisdom.

[Wisdom] is hidden from the eyes of every living thing,
  concealed even from the birds in the sky.
Destruction and Death say,
  "Only a rumor of it has reached our ears."
God understands the way to it
  and he alone knows where it dwells. (Job 28:21-23)

There are some things only God can know—and wisdom is one of them. Only God knows the best way to the best end in human life.

That shouldn't surprise us. We are finite creatures, limited in space and time. We live in the present, with some knowledge of the past, but we are totally ignorant about the future. We are caught up in the ebb and flow of life on this horizontal frame. We can only see bits and pieces. Our vision is narrow; we need someone who can see the whole. It's as if we sit in the airport terminal at the gate waiting for our plane to take us where we want to go. But we want to be in the control tower with the air traffic controllers knowing where all the planes are, where they've come from, and where they are going. And that's what God alone can do.

[God] alone knows where [wisdom] dwells,
for he views the ends of the earth
and sees everything under the heavens. (Job 28:23-24)

Wisdom and creation. God is the Creator, the divine Architect of the cosmos. He is the one who knows how we are designed to live and what we were made to live for. Who else could tell us the way to true human flourishing? The Bible declares that God created the world with wisdom at his side. This is the theme of Proverbs 8. There Lady Wisdom declares,

I was there when he set the heavens in place,
when he marked out the horizon on the face of the deep,
when he established the clouds above
and fixed securely the fountains of the deep. . . .
Then I was constantly at his side. (Prov 8:27-30)

This world was created with a divine order, and it was the biblical expectation of that order that gave rise to modern science. Natural laws embedded by God in the cosmos lay waiting to be discovered by human observation. And in our passage this connection between wisdom and the natural world is affirmed, but with an interesting twist:

When [God] established the force of the wind
and measured out the waters,
when he made a decree for the rain
and a path for the thunderstorm,
then he looked at wisdom and appraised it;
he confirmed it and tested it. (Job 28:25-27)

God in his wisdom is the guiding force ordering the winds that blow here and there, the waters of the seas that ebb and flow, the rains that come in their seasons, and even the paths of the thunderstorms with their lightning bolts that strike with apparent randomness. All these unpredictable and sometimes wild forces of the weather, God in his wisdom has "established," "measured," and "decreed." God created them, and God rules over them all. They all submit to his divine will.

This is comforting to us. We can live with the conviction that this is not a chaotic universe, "but one built upon a fundamental underlying and majestic order."[8] We can expect the sun to rise tomorrow, just like today. And we can look with great anticipation for spring to bring its flowers in abundance.

But what is striking in this passage is that those manifestations of God's wisdom—the wind, the waters, the rain, and the thunderstorm—are all ambiguous when it comes to human well-being. Yes, they all can be forces for good—providing, among other things, a fruitful environment in which to produce crops for food. But these forces can also pose a threat. After all, it was "a mighty wind" that caused the house to collapse, resulting in the death of Job's sons and daughters (Job 1:19). And it was "fire . . . from the heavens"—lightning from a thunderstorm—that consumed his sheep and servants (Job 1:16). Is that, too, a demonstration of God's wisdom?

"The fear of the Lord—that is wisdom." This poem has led us on a search for wisdom from the depths of a mine within the earth to the realm of death and destruction. But that search is in vain. Wisdom remains a treasure hidden and inaccessible. The question haunts us: "But where can wisdom be found?"

The answer to that question is necessarily beyond the grasp of the human mind; God alone knows where wisdom dwells. This leads to the poem's decisive conclusion in Job 28:28—

> And [God] said to the human race,
>> "The fear of the Lord—that is wisdom,
>> and to shun evil is understanding."[9]

---

[8] Christopher Ash, *Job: The Wisdom of the Cross* (Wheaton, IL: Crossway, 2014), 280.
[9] See Comment 6.4, "Wisdom and the Fear of the Lord (Job 28:28)."

Many will recognize this as a familiar theme in Proverbs, though there it is worded slightly differently—"The fear of the LORD is the beginning of wisdom" (Prov 9:10).[10] Here it is stated even more strongly—"The fear of the Lord—that is wisdom."

Wisdom as a relationship. Wisdom here is essentially relational. It is found in "fearing" God. That is, it comes in relating to God in reverent awe, recognizing him as the God that he is—holy and majestic, full of glory. And because he is righteous, this relationship necessarily has a moral dimension. It includes turning away from evil. Having this relationship with God—fearing God—that is wisdom. The knowledge that comes through this relationship is not scientific; it is personal.

You see, this is what science can never comprehend. The ultimate reality underlying this cosmos and us as humans is personal. We are not just material objects, and the world we live in does not simply exist as an autonomous material entity—self-existing, self-contained, and self-sufficient. This universe and we ourselves have a personal source—the mind of God.

All of creation has been created for a divine purpose, and it will, in one way or another, display a divine glory. For that reason, we can only gain wisdom—that understanding of the meaning of things, the purpose of things, the ultimate value of things—through a relationship with the personal God who created us.

Wisdom is not a thing to be discovered; it is a relationship to be lived.

The fear of the Lord—that is wisdom,
    and to shun evil is understanding.

That relationship with God our Creator is the only way to discover true wisdom, for God himself is the best way to the best end in our

---

[10]Cf. also Prov 15:33; Ps 111:10.

lives. In the end, wisdom is not so much a "knowing how," but a "knowing who." Wisdom is found in fearing God, and trusting him, for he alone knows the underlying order that governs his creation.

THE PLACE OF THIS CHAPTER IN JOB'S STORY

Some see this chapter as the final answer to Job's plight and the grand climax to the book. Job just needs to fear God, and he will have the wisdom to deal with his tragic circumstances. But that interpretation runs into two obstacles. First, in the flow of the book, this chapter doesn't conclude; it interrupts. Job's dispute with God will continue in the next three chapters with a renewed vehemence. And second, we were told in the very first verse and repeatedly in the opening chapters that Job already feared God and shunned evil (Job 1:1, 8; 2:3). If this is wisdom, it seems that he already had it. No, the story is not over; Job's struggle is still on; there must be more. The resolution is yet to come.

So what purpose does this chapter have in this drama? As a break in the action, we can reflect for a moment on where we are in the story. The debate is done, but nothing has been settled—no answers have been found, and God is still silent. The question of this chapter is natural at this point—"Where then is wisdom to be found?"

What we find in this chapter also reinforces the failure of the friends. They have searched the world for wisdom, and failed. True wisdom is not found in this world. It is hidden from our view. It must come from God himself.

In addition, the emphasis of this chapter on the value of wisdom encourages us to think well of Job, for he is refusing to give up his quest for it. Most people would have quit long ago and taken one of those easy ways out we discussed in the previous chapter—either giving in to despair or to anger, or giving up on one's integrity or on God. Job doesn't do that. He presses his case, because nothing is as precious to him as wisdom. He wants it desperately. And I think the conclusion of this chapter in Job 28:28 is an encouragement to Job—for this description of wisdom is a description of Job himself (Job 1:1). Job does fear God, and he does shun evil, which means that he is on the right track.

Wisdom can only be found in a relationship with God, and that is what Job wants more than anything else. This chapter in many ways anticipates the divine speeches at the end, and it gives us hope that if Job continues to fear God and shun evil, some resolution is possible.

THE PLACE OF WISDOM IN OUR LIVES

But what does this chapter teach us about wisdom in our lives? For one thing, it reminds us that the quest for wisdom is a universal human occupation, but that seeking it apart from God is a primal human sin. Doesn't Genesis 3 point to that? Doesn't the serpent tempt the woman to take for herself what God had prohibited with the prospect that her eyes would be opened and she would obtain wisdom? But that is the way of death, for wisdom is the fear of God. It comes in a relationship with God. Seeking our own wisdom apart from God destroys that relationship, and cuts us off from the very source of wisdom. That's foolishness. And it is the opposite of faith.

Listen again to voice of Lady Wisdom in Proverb 8:

The LORD brought me forth as the first of his works, . . .
   Then I was constantly at his side. (Prov 8:22, 30)

. . .

Blessed are those who listen to me,
   watching daily at my doors,
   waiting at my doorway.
For those who find me find life
   and receive favor from the LORD.

But those who fail to find me harm themselves;
　　all who hate me love death. (Prov 8:34-36)

Wisdom is a description of the way God has ordered the world from the beginning. It is the way we were meant to live as human beings, the best means to the best ends. Wisdom is the guiding principle of all of life, and God alone is the source of wisdom.

Now listen to what the apostle Paul writes in his letter to the Colossians—

> The Son is the image of the invisible God, the firstborn over all creation. For in him all things were created: things in heaven and on earth, visible and invisible, whether thrones or powers or rulers or authorities; all things have been created through him and for him. He is before all things, and in him all things hold together. (Col 1:15-17)

Jesus Christ stands in the place of God's wisdom. This divine wisdom, this guiding principle of creation, this final cause of all things, has become embodied in Jesus Christ. He is the center of the cosmos. Jesus Christ is the one man who lived all that wisdom is—living in a relationship of faith with his Father in heaven, fearing God and shunning evil, fully and completely.

It is Jesus who says, like wisdom, "everyone who hears these words of mine and puts them into practice is like a wise man who built his house on the rock" (Mt 7:24). It is Jesus who says, like wisdom, "I have come that they may have life, and have it to the full" (Jn 10:10).

And that same understanding of Jesus is expressed in another way in that opening passage from the Gospel of John. Instead of wisdom, John speaks of the Word—"In the beginning was the Word, and the Word was with God, and the Word was God. He was with God in the beginning. Through him all things were made; without him nothing was made that has been made. In him was life, and that life was the light of all mankind" (Jn 1:1-4).

In describing Jesus as the "Word," John uses the Greek word *logos* that had wide use in philosophical circles in the Greek world. It referred to that rational principle through which the world was created. The *logos* referred to the design, the purpose, the meaning of it all.

But John drops a bombshell in John 1:14 when he says, "The Word became flesh and made his dwelling among us." This Word, this rational principle, this wisdom of God—who was with God from the beginning, and through whom and for whom all things were created—has entered into our world as a human being. Do you want to know what life is all about? Do you want to discover the meaning of life? Do you want to know how we are to live and to what end? Here we have it—the key to understanding the whole creation; the one who shows us what God had in mind when he created human beings in the first place. Here is the one who shows us how we are to live; here is the one who shows us what we're here for; here is the one who embodies the wisdom of God.

And in the foolishness of the cross of Christ we find the supreme expression of the wisdom of God. Wisdom is found in a relationship with him—with Jesus Christ. "For those who find me find life and receive favor from the LORD" (Prov 8:35). These are the words of the wisdom of God, and these are the words of Jesus Christ. As Paul affirms, it is "Christ, in whom are hidden all the treasures of wisdom and knowledge" (Col 2:2-3).

Where are you looking for wisdom? There are lots of voices crying out, claiming to offer us wisdom. Do you look to Hollywood and the emotive messages of its movies? Do you look to Madison Avenue and the images of the good life that bombard us in its advertising? Do your social media screens full of Facebook, Instagram, or TikTok stir up longings for a life you don't have? Do you listen to the voices of our culture to guide you—popular voices, whether from Oprah Winfrey or Joel Osteen, Kanye West or Jordan Peterson? Where is wisdom to be found?

As we wrestle with Job, we must keep looking to Jesus—for the answers Job keeps seeking are ultimately found in a relationship with a person, that person who brings God's wisdom into our world.

DIGGING DEEPER

6.1. The speaker in Job 28. The speaker in Job 28 is not clearly indicated. The poem praising wisdom fits somewhat uncomfortably with the tone and content of Job's speeches, so some have attributed it to the narrator or one of the friends, such as Zophar or Elihu, or even to a "disembodied voice."[11] Alison Lo, however, has made an extensive case for reading the chapter, as it is presented, as Job's speech.[12] She acknowledges the radical shift in mood between Job 28 and Job's vehement oaths of innocence on either side of it (Job 27:2-6; 29–31), but she argues that such contradictory juxtaposition is a major rhetorical device throughout the book, most notably in the juxtaposition between Job's initial piety in the prologue and the protests that characterize his response in the dialogues. With this speech, she claims that Job declares the friends' failure to provide insight into his suffering. Similarly, Choon-Leong Seow notes how two monologues bookend the dialogue, with the wisdom poem ending the dialogue that Job's curse on the day of his birth had begun.[13]

If Job is speaking this monologue, he appears to step momentarily out of the drama, perhaps even addressing the audience

---

[11]See Michael V. Fox, "The Speaker in Job 28," in *"When the Morning Stars Sang": Essays in Honor of Choon Leong Seow on the Occasion of His Sixty-Fifth Birthday,* ed. Scott C. Jones and Christine Roy Yoder (Berlin: De Gruyter, 2018), 21-38.

[12]Alison Lo, *Job 28 as Rhetoric: An Analysis of Job 28 in the Context of Job 22–31* (Leiden: Brill, 2003).

[13]C. L. Seow, *Job 1–21: Interpretation and Commentary* (Grand Rapids, MI: Eerdmans, 2013), 68.

directly, to reflect on the nature of wisdom. The poem reveals the friends' efforts at wisdom to be lacking, but implies that Job continues to embody wisdom (Job 28:28; cf. 1:1).

6.2. Defining wisdom. *Khokhmah*, the main Hebrew word for wisdom, refers broadly to "a high-degree of knowledge and skill in any domain."[14] Ultimately, "wisdom aims at a successful life and proves itself to be a life skill."[15] The concept of wisdom in the Bible is presented as one of God's defining characteristics (Is 31:2; Job 12:13; cf. Rom 16:27), present with him at creation (Prov 3:19; 8:27-31), the product of obedience to the Torah (Deut 4:6; Ps 119:98), and a divine gift (Prov 2:6; Jas 1:5). It is identified with the fear of the Lord (Prov 1:7; 9:10; Job 28:28; Ps 111:10), righteousness (e.g., Prov 10:31), and life (Prov 13:14), as well as with skill in practical matters, such as spinning yarn (Ex 35:25), sailing ships (Ezek 27:8), proper speech (Prov 12:18; 29:11), and amassing wealth (Ezek 28:4; Prov 8:18). The wise, those who possess wisdom in special measure, are respected for their just judgments (1 Kings 3:28) and insightful counsel (Jer 18:18). In the New Testament, wisdom is associated with Christ (1 Cor 1:24, 30) and is one of the attributes for which he receives eternal worship (Rev 5:12). The Christian community is expected to be characterized by its own distinctive wisdom (Jas 3:13, 17), different from that of the Greeks (1 Cor 1:22-25).

Within biblical scholarship, the discussion of wisdom and the Bible has been primarily oriented around Wisdom Literature. However, this focus leaves features of the biblical conception of wisdom in the blurry periphery of our vision. This issue is exacerbated by the tendency throughout history to conform the definition of wisdom to what people most value at the time, so that definitions of wisdom commonly "mirrored man's conception of

---

[14]Fox, *Proverbs 1–9* (New York: Doubleday, 2000), 32. For further discussion, see Will Kynes, "Wisdom and Wisdom Literature: Past, Present, and Future," in *The Oxford Handbook of Wisdom and the Bible*, ed. Will Kynes (New York: Oxford University Press, 2021), 1-14.

[15]Markus Witte, "Literary Genres of Old Testament Wisdom," in Kynes, *Oxford Handbook of Wisdom and the Bible*, 359.

himself, of the world, and of God."[16] The post-Enlightenment period in which the "Wisdom Literature" category was developed was no different, and it imported the highest values of that time, such as secularism, rationalism, universalism, and naturalism into the common understanding of the term in the Bible.[17] But this obscures the inescapably theological, emotional, specific, and revelational nature of biblical wisdom. After all, the closest thing we have to a definition of wisdom in the Bible, repeated multiple times with minor modifications, is, "The fear of the Lord—that is wisdom, and to shun evil is understanding" (Job 28:28; cf. Prov 1:7; 9:10; 15:33; Ps 111:10).

6.3 Wisdom and science. In an insightful theological reflection on Job 28, Craig Bartholomew and Ryan O'Dowd argue that the poem "seem[s] at first to be a celebration of human wisdom but then catch[es] us unawares with a critique of human self-confidence."[18] They argue that the hymn to wisdom is an implicit rebuke of the friends' attempt to address Job's struggles with proverbial truisms, which also chastises "the secular turn of recent centuries[, which] has replaced religion with new idols like progress, education, technology and imperialism."[19] Contributing to this pride is the common modern view, surprisingly similar to ancient pagan belief, that the fundamental understanding of the world is immanently available in nature. The faith some put in science is akin to deifying nature. But in Job 28, "Job reinforces the Hebrew teaching that nature's purpose is to testify to God's glory in, before and beyond nature (Ps 19:1-6; 24:1-2; 104:1-35)."[20] Like Adam and Eve's disobedient grasping for the fruit of the tree of

---

[16]Eugene Rice Jr., *The Renaissance Idea of Wisdom* (Cambridge, MA: Harvard University Press, 1958), 2.

[17]See Comment 1.1, "The Demise of 'Wisdom Literature.'"

[18]Craig G. Bartholomew and Ryan O'Dowd, *Old Testament Wisdom Literature: A Theological Introduction* (Downers Grove, IL: IVP Academic, 2011), 184.

[19]Bartholomew and O'Dowd, *Old Testament Wisdom Literature*, 185.

[20]Bartholomew and O'Dowd, *Old Testament Wisdom Literature*, 183.

the knowledge of good and evil (Gen 3:6) or the Corinthians' puffed-up pride in their knowledge (1 Cor 8:1-3), Job 28 reminds us that being wise in one's eyes is not to be wise at all (Prov 3:5-7).[21]

6.4. Wisdom and the fear of the Lord (Job 28:28). Throughout the Bible, wisdom is consistently associated with the fear of the Lord (Job 28:28; cf. Prov 1:7; 9:10; 15:33; Ps 111:10). Biblical scholars, and ordinary readers of the Bible, too, often treat the book of Job as simply wise reflections about life—not unlike what you find in other ancient literature—cut off from Israel's law and history. But separating Job from Israel's special revelation makes it difficult to understand what the "fear of the Lord" actually means. Without God's self-revelation in the rest of the Bible, how can one know who this Lord is? And without God's revelation of his commands and character, how and why should one fear him? Job, like the other so-called Wisdom books, declares that the fear of the Lord is the foundation of true wisdom, and yet cordoning these books off from the rest of the Bible evacuates the fear of the Lord of any concrete meaning and leaves it merely an abstract respect for a higher power. This is not the way the Old Testament as a whole presents the fear of the Lord. As Michael Fox writes, "The importance Israelite Wisdom assigns to the fear of God in motivating behavior is not paralleled in foreign Wisdom [where] . . . it is one virtue among many. . . . Its importance in Wisdom literature is an Israelite innovation and shows the rootedness of Israelite Wisdom in Israelite thought generally."[22]

Just as wisdom is repeatedly connected with the fear of the Lord, the fear of the Lord is consistently linked with obeying God. Ecclesiastes concludes,

Now all has been heard;
here is the conclusion of the matter:

---

[21]See Comment 4.5, "The Friends as Foolish 'Wise Men.'"
[22]Fox, *Proverbs 1–9*, 71.

> Fear God and keep his commandments,
>> for this is the duty of all mankind. (Eccles 12:13; cf. Deut 5:29;
>>> 6:2; 8:6; 13:4; 17:19; 28:58; 31:12; 2 Kings 17:37; Jer 44:10)

When God appeared in cloud and fire on Mount Sinai to give his people the law, Moses declared to Israel, "Do not be afraid. God has come to test you, so that the fear of God will be with you to keep you from sinning" (Ex 20:20). The fear of the Lord is a fear that should inspire obedience, not terror. Later, Moses tells the people how they should respond to their Lord: "And now, Israel, what does the LORD your God ask of you but to fear the LORD your God, to walk in obedience to him, to love him, to serve the LORD your God with all your heart and with all your soul, and to observe the LORD's commandments and decrees that I am giving you today for your own good?" (Deut 10:12-13).

This fear can be joined with love. But it is something deeper than honor or respect. It is a filial fear, the emotion that motivates a son to obey a father, who will, when necessary, demonstrate his fatherly love through discipline. So Proverbs instructs,

> My son, do not despise the LORD's discipline,
>> and do not resent his rebuke,
> for the LORD disciplines those he loves,
>> as a father the son he delights in. (Prov 3:11-12)

This cord of three strands—fear of the Lord, wisdom, and obedience to God's law—is strongest in Deuteronomy 4:6-8:

> Observe them carefully, for this will show your wisdom and understanding to the nations, who will hear about all these decrees and say, "Surely this great nation is a wise and understanding people. "What other nation is so great as to have their gods near them the way the LORD our God is near us whenever we pray to him? And what other nation is so great as to have such righteous decrees and laws as this body of laws I am setting before you today?

Though the word *fear* is not explicitly mentioned here, both the wisdom of the Israelites and the close relationship they have with their God is demonstrated to the world through their obedience to his law. Proverbs 3:5-8 interweaves the same three strands:

> Trust in the LORD with all your heart
>> and lean not on your own understanding;
> in all your ways submit to him,
>> and he will make your paths straight.
> Do not be wise in your own eyes;
>> fear the LORD and shun evil.
> This will bring health to your body
>> and nourishment to your bones.

The fear of the Lord is a fear oriented toward trust, and it leads to true health and nourishment. One of the primary questions in Job, then, is whether Job's wisdom will be expressed in a continued fear of God when doing so leads instead to the crooked path of illness and loss.

seven

JOB'S CLOSING ARGUMENT

JOB 29–31

I will not let you go unless you bless me.

JACOB (GEN 32:26)

I DON'T KNOW WHAT IT'S LIKE in a real courtroom, but in
legal dramas on television, the closing argument is always the
gripping climax of the trial. The lawyers get one final opportunity to
deliver an emotional plea for justice to be done. They seek to tell a
compelling story—a story that allows the evidence to shine on their
client in the best light possible, a story that draws the jury onto their
side. I've never witnessed a real trial in person, but I can think of the
conclusion to the most famous murder trial of the last fifty years, in
which defense lawyer Johnny Cochran makes his final plea in defense of O. J. Simpson—"If the glove doesn't fit, you must acquit."
And it worked!

Our study of the book of Job isn't nearly as long as the O. J. Simpson
trial, but after the opening narrative that creates the conflict, the
twenty-five chapters of heated debate, and the interlude reflecting on
divine wisdom in Job 28, we come, at last, to Job's final argument.
Here we see the culmination not only of his lament, but also of his desire
for litigation—as Job is desperate to take God to court and set his case
before him.[1] In this section of the book, Job gives a passionate appeal

---

[1]See Comment 5.4, "Job as Lawsuit."

for personal vindication, for his own honor is at stake. But more than anything else, he longs for a renewed relationship with God.

A NOSTALGIC LOOK BACK

Job 29 begins with a nostalgic look back on his past life. It's nostalgia mixed with grief about what has been lost—"How I long for the months gone by" (Job 29:2).

Life had been good for Job, very good. He could look back on a life of health and prosperity with vast property, a loving family, and high social position. Those were the good old days. If only he could recapture their delight. But what Job most longs for is his lost connection with God, for in those days he felt he was enjoying God's blessing on his life:

How I long for the months gone by,
  for the days when God watched over me. (Job 29:2)

How he yearned for that assurance that he lived under God's loving care. How Job wished he could return to that time

when [God's] lamp shone upon my head
  and by his light I walked through darkness! (Job 29:3)

Yes, there was darkness, but God was always there to show the way forward.

Oh, for the days when I was in my prime,
  when God's intimate friendship blessed my house.
    (Job 29:4)

"God's intimate friendship"—the word used here is one of warmth and strength, suggesting a relationship in which one confidently confides in another. It is found in Psalm 25:14—"The LORD confides in those who fear him"—and in Proverbs 3:32—the Lord "takes the upright into his confidence."

Job, like Abraham, had been a friend of God. How much more painful it was for him now to feel as if God were treating him as his enemy, hiding his ways from him.[2]

How Job longed for those days "when the Almighty was still with me" (Job 29:5). God had been with him; God had been for him; and Job had experienced that blessing of God in very material ways—

> my children were around me,
> when my path was drenched with cream
> and the rock poured out for me streams of olive oil.
> (Job 29:5-6)

"Paths drenched with cream" and "streams of olive oil"—not exactly the way I would put it, but we get the idea. He was blessed with an abundance that more than met his every need.

But Job was no hedonist. He wasn't simply longing for all-you-can-eat banquet tables. This material blessing seems to be surpassed in his mind by his longing for the place of dignity and respect he once enjoyed in society. He held an honored seat in the public square, young men deferred to him, old men looked up to him, and all held him in high esteem (Job 29:7-11).

And his status was not based on his wealth, or his power, or frivolous celebrity. It was grounded in his character—he was considered a great man because he was a good man. People spoke well of him, they blessed him, because he listened to the cry of the poor, the fatherless, and the widow. In his public role, he showed no favorites; he was impartial and incorruptible; he was a righteous judge who brought the blessing of justice to others (Job 29:11-14). We'll talk more about Job's righteous character later, but there's one more thing that Job longed for as he looked back on his past—the expectation that his blessed state would last:

---

[2]See Comment 7.1, "The Hiddenness of God."

I thought, "I will die in my own house,
　　my days as numerous as the grains of sand."
My roots will reach to the water,
　　and the dew will lie all night on my branches.
My glory will not fade;
　　the bow will be ever new in my hand. (Job 29:18-20)

A "nostalgia for paradise." Isn't this the way life is supposed to work? Walking with God, experiencing the blessing of God, joy, glory, and honor, world without end. Job had tasted that life, and he longed to experience it. Something of that longing is in all of us—a longing for a joy once experienced but now lost. It's been called a "nostalgia for paradise."[3] It's a longing grounded in creation itself—when Adam and Eve, as God's image in the world, were put in the garden to live in God's presence and to rule as God's vice-regents over his good world. In that good world, they were crowned with glory and honor, with access to the tree of life that would enable them to live in the blessedness of God forever. When sin entered the world, that paradise was lost.

But deep within us all is a distant memory of that divine status, that heavenly delight. And every joy in this life points us back to what once was. When we taste it, we long to hold on to it forever. But it always fades, leaving us, like Job, longing once again.

That deep longing can only be satisfied in Christ, who is the second Adam.[4] For, as the author of Hebrews tells us, we now see Jesus "who was made lower than the angels for a little while, now crowned with glory and honor" (Heb 2:9). He suffered death so that he might "bring many sons and daughters to glory" (Heb 2:10). Only in Christ can we have an enduring destiny, a lasting human dignity, and be forever crowned with glory and honor.

---

[3]Christopher Ash, *Job: The Wisdom of the Cross* (Wheaton, IL: Crossway, 2014), 289.
[4]See Comment 7.2, "Allusions to Adam."

A PATHETIC PRESENT

As we turn to Job 30, we see that as Job moves from a nostalgia for the past to an assessment of his present condition, it is his lost dignity that he most grieves.

> But now they mock me,
>   men younger than I,
> whose fathers I would have disdained
>   to put with my sheep dogs. . . .
> And now those young men mock me in song;
>   I have become a byword among them.
> They detest me and keep their distance;
>   they do not hesitate to spit in my face. (Job 30:1, 9-10)

As one commentator put it: "Job has exchanged the respect of the most respectable for the contempt of the most contemptible."[5]

Job seems overwhelmed by a deep sense of shame at his sorry condition.

> Terrors overwhelm me;
>   my dignity is driven away as by the wind,
>   my safety[6] vanishes like a cloud. (Job 30:15)

His sufferings seem to brand him as a sinner in the eyes of all those around him. He feels isolated and alone:

> I have become a brother of jackals,[7]
>   a companion of owls.[8]
> My skin grows black and peels;
>   my body burns with fever. (Job 30:29-30)

---

[5]Francis Anderson, *Job* (London: Inter-Varsity Press, 1976), 235.
[6]Hebrew: *yeshu'ati.* Cf. ESV: "my prosperity."
[7]Those disgusting wild dogs that feed on decaying flesh.
[8]This refers to those creatures known to inhabit ruins.

A dirge, a requiem, a funeral march—that is the only music Job's ears
can hear (Job 30:31).

And what is most hurtful in Job's mind is that God himself is the
source of his hardship:

> In his great power [God] becomes like clothing to me;
>> he binds me like the neck of my garment.
> He throws me into the mud,
>> and I am reduced to dust and ashes.
> I cry out to you, O God, but you do not answer;
>> I stand up, but you merely look at me.
> You turn on me ruthlessly;
>> with the might of your hand you attack me.
> You snatch me up and drive me before the wind;
>> you toss me about in the storm. (Job 30:18-22)

"This is not the way you are supposed to act, Lord. Isn't it true that,
as the psalmist says, 'To the faithful you show yourself faithful, to
the blameless you show yourself blameless' (Ps 18:25)? Haven't I
been blameless before you? So when I am in distress, aren't you
supposed to be my deliverer, my Rock, and my Refuge. And when
I call to you, aren't you supposed to hear my voice and answer?
And when my enemies surround me, aren't you supposed to attack
them, not me (cf. Ps 18)? Is this how you treat your servants,
your friends?"

> Surely no one lays a hand on a broken man
>> when he cries for help in his distress.
> Have I not wept for those in trouble?
>> Has not my soul grieved for the poor?
> Yet when I hoped for good, evil came;
>> when I looked for light, then came darkness. (Job 30:24-26)

Why, Lord? Why would you treat me this way?

Here Job is making his emotional closing argument. He tells his tragic story—from enjoying God's blessing to experiencing what seems to him to be God's curse. Job had declared earlier, "But I desire to speak to the Almighty and to argue my case with God" (Job 13:3). In this final speech, he appeals to God's compassion as he relates his horrible fall from honor into shame.

A FINAL CHALLENGE

Now, in Job 31, Job engages in his most daring ploy. He makes a final appeal to God's justice in the form of a negative confession and a self-curse. It's a *negative* confession because it affirms what he *hasn't* done. Here he refutes the charges of his friends that he was, in fact, a guilty sinner. The list in these denials is extensive, describing, between ten and sixteen misdeeds, depending how you number them. Job denies them all.

This negative confession takes the form of a self-curse. The form Job uses (though not complete in every case) is "If I have done X, then let Y happen to me!" where X is the crime, and Y is the penalty. For example, look at Job 31:7-8:

> If my steps have turned from the path,
>> if my heart has been led by my eyes,
>> or if my hands have been defiled,
> then may others eat what I have sown,
>> and may my crops be uprooted.

And again in Job 31:9-10:

> If my heart has been enticed by a woman,
>> or if I have lurked at my neighbor's door,
> then may my wife grind another man's grain,
>> and may other men sleep with her.

And yet again in Job 31:21-22:

If I have raised my hand against the fatherless,
knowing that I had influence in court,
then let my arm fall from the shoulder,
let it be broken off at the joint.

An ancient legal procedure lies behind this chapter.[9] This self-curse is a kind of oath, sometimes called an "oath of clearance," forcing a verdict by calling down on oneself the wrath of God if what one is swearing is false.[10] This oath forces the issue—God must either clear him or activate the curse. It's Job's last desperate attempt to get God's attention, a final appeal to God's justice.[11]

That desperation comes out in Job 31:35:

Oh, that I had someone to hear me!
I sign now my defense—let the Almighty answer me;
let my accuser put his indictment in writing.

Earlier Job had said to God, "Summon me and I will answer, or let me speak, and you reply to me" (Job 13:22). But since God had not replied, he now seeks to compel God to respond—to file his complaint in writing—to make a formal indictment against him. In fact, Job is so sure of his right standing with God that he is confident that any indictment must result in an acquittal and become a written statement of his innocence.

Job would be so proud of that document, that he says in Job 31:36,

Surely I would wear it on my shoulder,
I would put it on like a crown.

Like a military insignia worn on the sleeve or a royal crown of honor, Job would want to declare to the world his blameless,

---

[9]See Comment 5.4, "Job as Lawsuit."
[10]See Comment 7.4, "Appeals to Innocence in the Psalms."
[11]See Comment 7.3, "Allusions to Deuteronomy."

upright character. "Having been humiliated publicly, Job would be vindicated publicly."[12]

Again, notice that Job's preeminent concern is not with the restoration of his wealth or even his family. It is his right relationship with God and his own sense of dignity that comes with it. Job now puts his own life on the line, as he seems to say, "O God, if I am guilty, pour out your wrath upon me; but if not, just speak to me. Bring me out of this deep darkness into your light. Vindicate me before the world!"

After this final declaration, we read in Job 31:40, "The words of Job are ended."

The defense rests. All Job can do is await the verdict of the court. All that is left is the declaration of the Judge. We as readers are on the edge of our seats, anxious to hear God's ruling.

JOB'S LIFE AND OURS

By way of application, let's step back and look at two issues that stand out in this passage. First, what does this passage tell us about human virtue? What does it mean to live a good life, a godly life?

Remember, it was Job's righteous life that got him into this mess in the first place. When he was approached by the satanic accuser, God himself put Job forward—"Have you considered my servant Job? There is no one on earth like him; he is blameless and upright, a man who fears God and shuns evil" (Job 1:8).

In this passage, we get a fuller description of Job's life than in any other place in the book. So what do we find? What does Job's godliness—his holiness before God, his blameless and upright life—look like?

A description of a righteous man. Exercising justice. Job first sets forth what set him apart in the beginning of his defense. He was commended by the respected men at the city gates because of his concern for the vulnerable and the marginal, his protection of the weak, the disabled, and the defenseless.

> I rescued the poor who cried for help,
>> and the fatherless who had none to assist them.
> The one who was dying blessed me;
>> I made the widow's heart sing.
> I put on righteousness as my clothing;
>> justice was my robe and my turban.
> I was eyes to the blind
>> and feet to the lame.
> I was a father to the needy;
>> I took up the case of the stranger.
> I broke the fangs of the wicked
>> and snatched the victims from their teeth. (Job 29:12-17)

Here Job depicts the qualities that are distinctive of biblical justice, which is a reflection of the righteousness and justice of God. God contends for the poor, and he will plunder those who plunder them (Prov 22:22-23). God is the defender of the fatherless, who takes up the case of those who encroach on their property (Prov 23:10-11). As the psalmist declares,

> The LORD secures justice for the poor
>> and upholds the cause of the needy. (Ps 140:12)

Job asserts that he has done the same.

Guarding sexual purity. In Job 31 the description of his holy life is filled out even further. He begins there with a statement of his sexual purity—

> I made a covenant with my eyes
>> not to look lustfully at a young woman. (Job 31:1)

Now there's a verse that every man should commit to memory! The eyes are the gateway to the heart, and here Job has resolved to guard that gateway, and to avoid the lustful gaze.

Since the introduction of the internet and now the smartphone, we are experiencing an epidemic of pornography.[13] It is estimated that 30 percent of all data transferred across the internet is porn. Porn sites receive more regular traffic per month than Netflix, Amazon, and Twitter put together.[14] One of the world's largest porn sites reported that it had 21.2 billion visitors last year, who viewed over 87 billion videos. In one survey it was reported that 64 percent of young people, ages thirteen to twenty-four, actively seek out pornography weekly or more often.

But we know it's not just a problem for young people—or even just for men. And it's not just internet pornography that will get you. Now it's what's on television and in the movies, what's in the shopping mall, and what comes in the mail. Pornography is a plague in our culture. It acts like an addictive drug, wreaking havoc among us. And it is crippling marriages, distorting our minds, perverting the good gift of our God-given sexuality, and using human beings made in God's image as objects for one's pleasure.

Job says, "I made a covenant with my eyes not to look lustfully at a young woman." He says this, for he knows that it is wrong in God's sight, and our God sees everything—"Does he not see my ways and count my every step?" (Job 31:4). He certainly knows everything that you put before your eyes. A life of sexual purity before God demands constant vigilance.

---

[13]Cf. "20 Must-Know Stats About the Porn Industry and Its Underage Consumers," Fight the New Drug, October 8, 2021, https://fightthenewdrug.org/10-porn-stats-that-will-blow-your-mind/.

[14]Cf. Alexis Kleinman, "Porn Sites Get More Visitors Each Month Than Netflix, Amazon and Twitter Combined," *Huffpost*, updated December 6, 2017, www.huffingtonpost.com/2013/05/03/internet-porn-stats_n_3187682.html.

Living in honesty. From lust, Job moves to *honesty.*

> If I have walked with falsehood
>> or my foot has hurried after deceit—
> let God weigh me in honest scales
>> and he will know that I am blameless. (Job 31:5-6)

The word for "falsehood" is especially used of lying speech, a perversion of the truth. Job didn't equivocate, prevaricate, or obfuscate to deceive and deflect. He was a man of his word. Period.

"Honest scales" signify integrity in one's business dealings—not cheating a customer, or using deceit to gain an advantage. Job is willing to be judged by the same standard that he has used with others.

Rejecting adultery. Then Job rejects *adultery*:

> If my heart has been enticed by a woman,
>> or if I have lurked at my neighbor's door,
> then may my wife grind another man's grain,
>> and may other men sleep with her. (Job 31:9-10)

Notice that Job would count himself guilty if he *allowed* himself to be enticed. He knew that he was responsible for the inclinations of his heart. Adultery is a treacherous act, violating the trust of his neighbor, of his own wife, and supremely of God himself—

> For that would have been wicked,
>> a sin to be judged.
> It is a fire that burns to Destruction. (Job 31:11-12)

Giving fair wages for workers: Grounded in human dignity. Then Job moves to the treatment of his servants.

> If I have denied justice to any of my servants,
>> whether male or female,
>> when they had a grievance against me,

what will I do when God confronts me?

What will I answer when called to account? (Job 31:13-14)

You must treat others as you would want to be treated—by God! And the rationale for this standard of fair treatment of his servants is critical:

Did not he who made me in the womb make them?

Did not the same one form us both within our mothers?
(Job 31:15)

Job is pointing to the intrinsic dignity of every human being that is grounded in their creation by God. Every person is created in his image and therefore is deserving of being treated with respect. Proverbs makes this same connection—"Rich and poor have this in common: The LORD is the Maker of them all" (Prov 22:2).

This is a central moral principle, for Job goes on to talk about his treatment of the poor, the widow, and the fatherless. All are deserving of care. We all share a common humanity—which means we share a certain sacredness as persons created in God's image.

You see, meaning and value are personal qualities—we instinctively value persons. Respect for others is almost demanded of us when we see their personhood—and we identify ourselves with them. Think of what happens when we personify our dogs—we give our dogs names, we talk to them, we attribute to them personal qualities. That's very easy to do, because dogs seem to have a sort of empathy and can seem to be very expressive of emotion. That's what makes them such great pets.

When we attribute personhood to our dogs, we give them dignity, and we care for them. But too often we treat our dogs like people, and treat people like dogs. They become less than human—brute beasts. Ultimately by dehumanizing them, we are enabled to mistreat them and even to kill them. Consider Dylann Roof, who was convicted of the gruesome racist killing of nine church members at a prayer meeting at a church in Charleston, South Carolina, in 2015. The prosecutor Nathan Williams said in his closing argument at the trial, "He executed them because he believes they are nothing but animals."[15]

All human beings are persons created in the image of God and so are to be treated with dignity. And isn't that what we all want? Isn't this what the #MeToo movement is all about—women wanting to be treated with respect and dignity as human beings, real persons, and not as mere sexual objects? In listening to some of my African American brothers I have found that this is what is most needed for real racial reconciliation to take place. Black Americans want to be afforded real dignity in this dominant-White culture, a dignity of which they have been so long deprived.

> Did not he who made me in the womb make them?
>> Did not the same one form us both within our mothers?
>>> (Job 31:15)

Job respected that dignity in all his relationships in society. And so must we.

A rejection of greed. Job goes on to speak in Job 31:24 of his refusal to put his faith in gold, instead of in God. Holiness, godliness, cannot coexist with greed. And generosity is the necessary evidence of a freedom from such idolatry. It is appropriate then that in Job 31:26 Job next denies that he had been drawn to worship other idols in the form of the sun or the moon. These would

> be sins to be judged,
>> for I would have been unfaithful to God on high.
>>> (Job 31:28)

Then he says he didn't gloat over the misfortune of his enemies, or fail to show hospitality to strangers (Job 31:29).

---

[15]Dustin Waters and Kevin Sullivan, "Dylann Roof Guilty on 33 Counts of Federal Hate Crimes for Charleston Church Shooting," *Washington Post*, December 15, 2016, www.washingtonpost .com/national/dylann-roof-guilty-on-33-counts-of-federal-hate-crimes-for-charleston-church -shooting/2016/12/15/0bfad9e4-c2ea-11e6-9578-0054287507db_story.html.

All this is what it looks like to fear God and to shun evil. Necessarily, it involves how you treat people—people who are created in the image of God. Godliness is a life of compassion, kindness, humility, gentleness, and patience (cf. Col 3:12) and one that seeks righteousness and justice in the world (Is 1:17; Zech 7:9-10; Mic 6:8). Let Job, in his righteousness, be a model to us, as he points us to the holiness we are called to as followers of Christ.

Presumptuous protest or a tenacious faith? But hasn't Job rather overplayed his hand? Hasn't he overstepped the bounds of what is appropriate in this rather pompous protest of his innocence? What one might describe as "an unparalleled volley of vehement vituperation at the Almighty."[16] Doesn't he border on blasphemy when he questions God's justice? Hasn't he demonstrated a loss of faith in voicing his complaints and even declaring God to be acting like his enemy? Some think so. There is a strong Christian tradition that questions whether the protesting Job of the poetic middle chapters is quite up to the pious Job of the prose prologue, and wonders whether he should be considered a model of piety at all.

We should reject that assessment—first, because, as we will see, God never calls for Job to repent of any sin,[17] and instead commends the way Job has spoken about him.

Second, we should reject it because Job is not alone among the heroes of faith in the Bible who engage in this kind of struggle with God. We noted earlier how often the psalmists cry out in anguish, "How long, O Lord?"[18] And what about Abraham who contends with God and almost bargains with him when he announces his plans to judge Sodom and Gomorrah? "Will you sweep away the righteous with the wicked? What if there are fifty righteous people in the

---

[16]Will Kynes, "The Trials of Job: Relitigating Job's 'Good Case' in Christian Interpretation," *Scottish Journal of Theology* 66 (2013): 176.

[17]Job 38:2 comes close, but the affirmations of Job 42:7-8 speak otherwise.

[18]See Comment 7.4, "Appeals to Innocence in the Psalms."

city? . . . Far be it from you to do such a thing . . . Far be it from you! Shall not the Judge of all the earth do right?" (Gen 18:23-25). Moses similarly dissuades God from wiping out Israel after the sin of the golden calf by reminding him of his promises to their forefathers, his mighty acts on their behalf, and how the Egyptians would respond (Ex 32:11-13). And I could mention the psalmists who dare to cry "Why?" and "How long?" and prophets, such as Jeremiah (e.g., Jer 20:7-20), and Amos (Amos 7:1-9), and Habakkuk (Hab 1:2-4, 12-17)—all of whom also confronted God with their demands.

And then there is Jacob—from whom the people of Israel derive their name. In Genesis 32 Jacob wrestles with the angelic stranger, who represents God himself. And he says, "I will not let you go unless you bless me" (Gen 32:26). Then the man said to him, "Your name will no longer be Jacob, but Israel, because you have struggled with God and with humans and have overcome" (Gen 32:28). That's what the name Israel means: "struggles with God." And that's what Job does—he struggles with God. He struggles with God precisely because he believes that God is just and that he will in some way vindicate him. That's why he is so confident in this final appeal—so confident that he is willing to place his own life on the line with this self-curse, demanding that God reply.[19]

It is Job's faith that keeps him coming back to God even when God's current actions toward him seem so harsh. Job won't give up; he won't give in. He won't let go of God until God blesses him with his presence. Job is struggling with the conflict between his faith *in* God and his experience *of* God—between who he knows God to be and the way he is now being treated. His is, as I've said, a "defiant faith," a "pious protest," a "believing belligerence."

To wrestle with God takes courage few can muster. Most would rather adjust their theological perceptions by minimizing either

---

[19]See Comment 7.5, "The Biblical Tradition of Defiant Faith."

God's goodness or his power, settling for a tamed and domesticated God who can fit into our experience. Job's courage is grounded ultimately in a vision of God so great that he is to be feared above all else. As one commentator puts it, "To Job . . . people who are afraid of confronting the tough, faith-shattering questions are not fearers of God. Rather, they are simply fearers, theological cowards, for they fear the truth."[20] I appreciate Will's assessment: "If Job has a vision of God which he deems worth fighting God for, the friends have a much smaller understanding of God which they are only willing to fight Job for."[21] In the end, it will be Job's fear of God that will be true wisdom.

DIGGING DEEPER

7.1. The hiddenness of God. Job repeatedly complains of God's hiddenness. He asks God, "Why do you hide your face and consider me your enemy?" (Job 13:24). He complains,

> But if I go to the east, he is not there;
> > if I go to the west, I do not find him.
> When he is at work in the north, I do not see him;
> > when he turns to the south, I catch no glimpse of him.
> > > (Job 23:8-9)[22]

The psalmists express similar experiences of the hidden God: "How long, LORD? Will you forget me forever? How long will you hide your face from me?" (Ps 13:1; cf. 30:7; 44:24; 88:14; 89:46). Isaiah even declares this elusiveness an aspect of God's character: "Truly, you are a God who has been hiding himself, the God and Savior of Israel" (Is 45:15).

In the Old Testament, God's hiddenness is frequently associated with his judgment against sin (Deut 31:17-18; 32:20; Is 57:17;

---

[20]C. L. Seow, "Job," in *Dictionary of Scripture and Ethics,* ed. J. B Green (Grand Rapids, MI: Baker Academic, 2011), 421.

[21]Kynes, "The Trials of Job," 190.

[22]See Comment 5.5, "Parody."

59:2; 64:7; Ezek 39:23-24, 29; Mic 3:4). However, the innocent Job's experience of God's hiddenness indicates that sin is not its only source. In fact, the sixteenth-century Carmelite mystic John of the Cross argued that a "dark night of the soul," such as Job endured, may be a means through which the spirit is purged for a deeper communion with God. As he describes it, "The soul feels itself to be perishing and melting away, in the presence and sight of its miseries, in a cruel spiritual death, even as if it had been swallowed by a beast and felt itself being devoured in the darkness of its belly, suffering such anguish as was enduring by Jonas in the belly of that beast of the sea."[23] John argued that in the dark night when God felt absent, he was in fact unbearably present, digging at the very roots of the weeds that threaten to choke our spirit. Thus, even as Job complains of God's hiddenness, he also expresses a longing to hide himself from God (Job 14:13) and for God to leave him alone (Job 7:17-20; 10:20-21).

With the help of John of the Cross, we can see Job's inner conflict with God's hiddenness, his dark night of the soul, as an expression of his faith. As Samuel Terrien argues, "In man's extremity, God's presence is elusive and cannot be ordained, yet Job's ancient trust remained the underground source of his hope. He still expected that at some unspecified future an intervention from above would not fail him."[24] And, when God does finally reveal himself, Job receives that revelation, and perhaps even his entire experience of suffering, as an act of grace, which gave him a more intimate understanding of God (Job 42:5). Therefore, Bartholomew and O'Dowd argue that Job testifies to the value of recognizing that God can be at work, deeply, in suffering: "We do not need to know what he is doing or when it will end or how it will work out—that is all entirely out of our control, but that

---

[23]St. John of the Cross, *Dark Night of the Soul*, trans. E. Allison Peers (Garden City, NT: Doubleday, 1959), 111.

[24]Samuel L. Terrien, *The Elusive Presence: Toward a New Biblical Theology* (San Francisco: Harper & Row, 1978), 365.

he is at work deeply and graciously, we need to cling to, as we are able."[25]

7.2. Allusions to Adam. Having already alluded to Genesis elsewhere,[26] the author of Job is more likely to do so again and expect his readers to recognize it. Because the Hebrew word for "humanity," *'adam*, is also the name of the first human, a number of potential allusions to Adam appear through the book.[27] This would include Eliphaz's claim that "man [Adam?] is born to trouble as surely as sparks fly upward" (Job 5:7), particularly in light of the labor God gives Adam in the garden (Gen 2:15), which is made more toilsome after the fall (Gen 3:17; cf. Job 7:1). It might also include Eliphaz's question to Job, "Are you the first man [Adam] ever born?" (Job 15:7). Adam had a special intimacy with God, which gave him special access to wisdom, so Eliphaz may be accusing Job of claiming something similar for himself. Zophar appears to make a similar sarcastic jab at Job in Job 20:4: "Surely you know how it has been from of old, ever since mankind [Adam] was placed on the earth" (Job 20:4). Finally, Job appears to take on the friends' comparison of him with Adam, but does so to make an important contrast: "If I have concealed my sin as [Adam], by hiding my guilt in my heart" (Job 31:33). In light of the mirror image of the fall in the prologue, in which Job resists the Satan's testing,[28] he declares that he, as the second Adam, has not disobeyed God, and therefore has no need to hide (cf. Gen 3:8). As Manfred Oeming concludes, "Job sees himself as the perfect Adam. Is the will of God realized in any creature more fully than in Job?"[29]

---

[25]Craig G. Bartholomew and Ryan O'Dowd, *Old Testament Wisdom Literature: A Theological Introduction* (Downers Grove, IL: IVP Academic, 2011), 321.
[26]See Comments 2.2, "The Prologue and Genesis 2–3" and 3.2, "Job's Countercosmic Curse."
[27]Manfred Oeming, "To Be Adam or Not to Be Adam: The Hidden Fundamental Anthropological Discourse Revealed in an Intertextual Reading of אדם in Job and Genesis," in *Reading Job Intertextually*, ed. Katharine Dell and Will Kynes (New York: Bloomsbury T&T Clark, 2013), 19-29.
[28]See Comment 2.2, "The Prologue and Genesis 2–3."
[29]Oeming, "To Be Adam," 28.

7.3. Allusions to Deuteronomy. Deuteronomy teaches clearly that obedience to God brings blessing, while disobedience earns divine punishment (e.g., Deut 30:19). The book of Job draws heavily both on that logic and on the book of Deuteronomy itself.[30] However, as with the book's engagement with other biblical texts,[31] Job reflects Deuteronomy in an upside-down fun-house mirror. Though Job obeys God's law punctiliously (Job 1:1, 5) and has received the blessings corresponding to his righteousness (Job 1:2-3, 10; cf. Deut 28:12; 30:9-10), he is forced to endure the type of sufferings with which Deuteronomy threatens those who disobey God's law, including a skin disease that afflicts him from head to foot (Job 2:7), mentioned in Deuteronomy 28:35. He rightfully expresses agonized dismay that he has received precisely what he "dreaded" (Job 3:25-26), using a word that appears several times in Deuteronomy's curses on the disobedient (Deut. 28:60, 65-67). In his self-curse in Job 31, Job echoes the Ten Commandments in Deuteronomy several times in order to affirm his innocence. He has not worshiped idols or the sun and moon (Job 31:24-28; cf. Deut 5:8; 4:19; 17:2-3) or misused God's name (Job 31:5; cf. Deut 5:11). He has honored his parents (Job 31:18; cf. Deut 5:16).[32] He has not even committed murder with his mouth through angry words (Job 31:30; cf. Deut 5:17; Mt 5:21-24) or adultery with his eyes through lust (Job 31:1, 7-10; cf. Deut 5:18; Mt 5:27-30). Rather than stealing or coveting (Deut 5:19, 21), he has been generous with his property (Job 31:13-18, 29-32), and rather than lying (Deut 5:20), he has listened to the claims of slaves and the poor (Job 31:13-14, 21-22, 30). Even the reference to his land crying out against him (Job 31:38-40) may be a reference to the Sabbath (Deut 5:12-15), in which the land should be allowed to rest

---

[30] Markus Witte, "Does the Torah Keep Its Promise? Job's Critical Intertextual Dialogue with Deuteronomy," in Dell and Kynes, *Reading Job Intertextually*, 54-65.

[31] See Comment 1.4, "Allusion and Intertextuality."

[32] Witte translates Job 31:18, "Because from my adolescence onwards he [i.e. the fatherless] was great like my father and from the womb onwards I conducted her [i.e. the widow] like a mother" (cf. Job 31:16-17).

(Lev 25:4-5). Thus, Job builds his argument on the basis of the Deuteronomic Covenant (cf. Ps 89). God responds favorably and "restored his fortunes" (Job 42:10), using a phrase similar to Deuteronomy 30:3. The blessing Job finally receives, long life surrounded by four generations of his family, is what Deuteronomy repeatedly promises to those who obey God (Deut 5:16, 29, 33; 6:2).

7.4. Appeals to innocence in the Psalms. Appeals of innocence are common in the Psalms (e.g., Ps 5; 7; 17; 26; 35; 41; 44; 59; 66; 68; 69; 73; 86; 101). In Psalm 7, for example, the psalmist affirms his innocence with a self-curse similar to those in Job 31:

> If I have repaid my ally with evil
>   or without cause have robbed my foe—
> then let my enemy pursue and overtake me;
>   let him trample my life to the ground
>   and make me sleep in the dust. (Ps 7:4-5)

The psalmist then proceeds, it appears, to put his faith in his own righteousness: "Vindicate me, LORD, according to my righteousness, according to my integrity, O Most High" (Ps 7:8). Dietrich Bonhoeffer acknowledges that these psalms may cause readers some discomfort, since they seem to reflect "a vestige of the so-called Old Testament works righteousness."[33] However, he claims both testaments agree: "It is thoroughly unbiblical and destructive to think that we can never suffer innocently as long as some error still lies hidden within us."[34] The interpretive error behind this discomfort is totalizing a claim of innocence from a particular sin of which the psalmist is accused into a self-righteous proclamation of perfect blamelessness. Job admits that he has committed some sins (Job 7:21; 13:26; 14:16-17), just none that would merit the suffering he has received or his friends' accusations (e.g., Job 22:5). In the end, as in the psalms of innocence (Ps 7:17; 26:1-3), Job's appeal

---

[33]Dietrich Bonhoeffer, *Psalms: The Prayer Book of the Bible* (Minneapolis: Augsburg, 1970), 52.
[34]Bonhoeffer, *Psalms*, 54.

to his innocence is an expression of faith in God's justice, a belief that God will make things right. For both, this ultimate trust in God makes their appeals of innocence a celebration of God's righteousness, not their own.[35] And, like Job's friends, "if anyone is self-righteous in Psalm 7, it is the enemies who presumptuously usurp the prerogative of God by condemning the psalmist."[36] Finally, with the psalmists in the psalms of innocence, Job's complaint wins him a divine justificatory verdict, and, thus, in his complaints, the lament tradition itself is vindicated.[37]

7.5. The biblical tradition of defiant faith. Job's perplexing appeal to God against God,[38] the practice of a type of pious protest or defiant faith, actually reflects a common response to suffering and injustice across the Hebrew Bible. Job joins the heroes of Israelite faith, Abraham, Jacob, Moses, the psalmists, and prophets, in demanding that God make things right.[39] They struggle with God, but never let him go, because of their faith in his justice, goodness, and power. And God repeatedly responds favorably to their protests (e.g., Gen 18:26-32; 32:28; Ex 32:14; Job 42:7). Reflecting this biblical tradition, Jesus tells a parable of a widow whose persistent pleading convinces an unjust judge to intervene on her behalf, thereby teaching his followers to express their faith through pleading with God to rectify injustice rather than submissively accepting it (Lk 18:1-8).[40]

Job's complaints should be understood in this same tradition of defiant faith. When he asks God whether oppressing his creation and bestowing favor on the wicked seems good to him (Job 10:3), Job fully believes that God does not approve of such injustice; his

---

[35]J. Clinton McCann Jr., "The Book of Psalms," in *1 & 2 Maccabees, Introduction to Hebrew Poetry, Job, Psalms,* The New Interpreter's Bible 4 (Nashville: Abingdon, 1996), 709.
[36]McCann, "Psalms," 709.
[37]C. L. Seow, *Job 1–21: Interpretation and Commentary* (Grand Rapids, MI: Eerdmans, 2013), 92.
[38]See Comment 5.2, "Job's Conflicted View of God."
[39]See "Presumptuous Protest or a Tenacious Faith?" above.
[40]See "An Importunate Woman" in chap. 5.

argument with God depends on God agreeing with him on this point. Like the arguments of those other heroes of Israelite faith, Job's accusatory question, like Abraham's "Shall not the Judge of all the earth do what is just?" (Gen 18:25) is an expression of his faith, which is intended to remind God of who he has revealed himself to be—just, good, powerful, and committed to his people. Job expresses the depth of his faith by clinging to God's goodness even when his experience of God would suggest just the opposite.

Beyond the Bible, this tradition appears, for example, in the spirituals sung by enslaved African Americans. For instance, the spiritual "Wrestle On, Jacob" presents "a paean of hopeful strife," as W. E. B. Du Bois puts it, in which enslaved people sang, "I will not let you go, my Lord" and explicitly associated their spiritual struggles with the Israelite patriarch in the moment he earned the name "wrestles with God" for his people.[41] Their cries are echoed in those of Jews who faced suffering, including the horror of the Holocaust, with what Anson Laytner calls "faithful defiance" and Dov Weiss labels "pious irreverence."[42] Some in both of these communities undoubtedly stifled their protests under piety and others defiantly discarded their faith. But, for those who saw protest as an expression of faith, their defiant faith reflected the comfort they found in a God good and great enough to make things right, and therefore to deserve complaint when they were not.

---

[41]W. E. B. Du Bois, *The Souls of Black Folk* (New York: Penguin, 1989 [1903]), 208. For further examples, see Will Kynes, "Wrestle On, Jacob: Antebellum Spirituals and the Defiant Faith of the Hebrew Bible," *Journal of Biblical Literature* 140 (2021): 291-307.

[42]Anson Laytner, *Arguing with God: A Jewish Tradition* (Northvale, NJ: Aronson, 1990); Dov Weiss, *Pious Irreverence: Confronting God in Rabbinic Judaism* (Philadelphia: University of Pennsylvania Press, 2017).

eight

THE MYSTERIOUS ELIHU

Job 32–37

I am full of words,
and the wind in my belly compels me.

Job 32:18 AT

WHEN I WAS A KID, one of the highlights of the week was watching Batman on television. Now, this Batman was not the menacing Dark Knight of more recent days. The Batman that appeared on TV in my youth was much more the friendly comic book variety, who battled bad guys in Gotham City in fistfights with words like "Bam!" and "Smash!" actually superimposed on the screen.

What I remember most about that show was the ending. Instead of resolving the conflict at the conclusion of each episode with Batman and his sidekick Robin riding into the sunset, the show would inevitably build to a climax in which Batman was put in some precarious position, about to be overcome by the Joker or the Riddler or whomever else was menacing the city that week, and suddenly the screen would freeze and a voice would announce: "Is Batman about to meet his match? To find out, see you next week. Same bat time; same bat channel." We were left hanging in suspense for a whole week.

That's how it has been with our hero Job. At the end of thirty-one chapters of agonizing dialogue, Job, in a sense, lays it all on the line in his final words. He issues a "self-curse," virtually challenging God to make himself known—either to vindicate him if he is innocent or to curse him if he is guilty. The chapter concludes with "The words of Job are ended" (Job 31:40). And we are left in suspense.

And here we are—same bat time, same bat channel—anxious to see how God responds. We expect the exciting conclusion to our drama. But alas! Our hopes are dashed.

Instead of that long-anticipated divine response to Job's protests, we are introduced to a totally new character, one who appears out of nowhere—the mysterious Elihu. This young man evidently had been there all along, following the debate, but holding his tongue. Now he speaks, and he ends up giving the longest monologue of the entire book—six whole chapters! We are left waiting once again for Job's fate to be resolved.

So who is this Elihu, and what role does he play in this story?

ELIHU: PROPHET OR PRETENDER?

I call this Elihu character "mysterious" because he enters the story suddenly, says his piece, and then disappears without a trace. The epilogue of the book ignores him completely—not a word, either of praise or rebuke. Because of this, some biblical critics wonder if he was even a part of the original book at all.[1] Whether added to the dialogue by the original author or a later editor, Elihu's speeches must have a purpose, but what is it?

Scholarly opinion is divided.[2] Some see the prominence given to him at this critical juncture in the book as a pointer to his role as a prophet of God. They argue that Elihu, unlike the friends, is given a very distinguished genealogical introduction: he is "Elihu son of Barakel the Buzite, of the family of Ram" (Job 32:2). And he seems

---

[1] See Comment 8.1, "Elihu as a Later Addition?"
[2] See Comment 8.2, "Elihu as Intentionally Ambiguous."

to claim that his knowledge, again unlike the friends, comes not from age or experience, but from "the breath of the Almighty" (Job 32:8). He presents himself as a divinely inspired speaker of the truth. He even speaks about Job's need for an angel—a mediator— one who can speak what is true and who can graciously guide him to restoration (Job 33:23-28). Elihu seems to think that he might even be that angelic mediator who is going to set everything right.[3] Finally, the conclusion of Elihu's speech, with its majestic descriptions of God's unfathomable glory in creation, sounds much like what God will say in the divine speeches that follow.

I can see the attraction of this view, and it has been held by some respectable interpreters. And I will say a bit more about what Elihu says that *is* true in a moment. But in the end, I can't buy it. Elihu may aspire to be a prophet, but I judge him to be a pretender to that title for two main reasons.

First, our view of Elihu has to be influenced by the way that he is portrayed by the biblical writer. Immediately, we see that Elihu is angry. We read in Job 32:1 that Job's three friends had stopped answering Job. They have said, in effect, "Job, we give up! There's nothing more we can say. You win."[4] And that surrender leaves Elihu incensed. The narrator tells us he is "angry" with Job for "justifying himself rather than God" (Job 32:2), "angry" with the friends failing to refute Job (Job 32:3), and "his anger was aroused" that they stopped trying (Job 32:5). His anger is mentioned three times in just four verses. We get the decided impression that Elihu may be *too* angry.[5]

Elihu is angry because Job justified himself, but then this young man Elihu spends an entire chapter and a half justifying his own entrance into this debate. He begins by speaking to Job's friends, defending his right as a young man to enter this debate.

---

[3] See Comment 8.3, "Elihu as a Mediator."
[4] In Is 41:21-29 it is implied that whoever fails to answer in a legal dispute loses.
[5] Lindsay Wilson, *Job* (Grand Rapids, MI: Eerdmans, 2015), 158.

But it is the spirit in a person,
> the breath of the Almighty, that gives them understanding.
It is not only the old who are wise,
> not only the aged who understand what is right.
Therefore I say: Listen to me;
> I too will tell you what I know. (Job 32:8-10)

And Elihu claims to know quite a lot. He refers to "what he knows" four times in his opening speech (Job 32:6, 10, 17; 33:3). Elihu may be young, but he is anything but reserved, reticent, or self-effacing. On the contrary, Elihu seems full of himself, even pompous, and his attitude toward Job is downright patronizing—

But now, Job, listen to my words;
> pay attention to everything I say. (Job 33:1)
. . .
Answer me then, if you can;
> stand up and argue your case before me. (Job 33:5)
. . .
Pay attention, Job, and listen to me;
> be silent, and I will speak.
If you have anything to say, answer me;
> speak up, for I want to vindicate you.
But if not, then listen to me;
> be silent, and I will teach you wisdom. (Job 33:31-33)

Not exactly what you would expect from a young man addressing a man who was once "the greatest man among all the people in the East" (Job 1:3).[6]

His brash arrogance comes to a head in Job 36:2-4, where he assumes an almost God-like posture:

---

[6]Wilson, *Job*, 161.

> Bear with me a little longer and I will show you
>> that there is more to be said in God's behalf.
> I get my knowledge from afar. . . .
> Be assured that my words are not false;
>> one who has perfect knowledge is with you.

In a moment we'll see that his knowledge was not so perfect after all.

But there's one more aspect to the way Elihu is portrayed in the book. All along, there's been a dispute between Job and his friends as to who speaks truth. Job complains that they treat his words as mere "wind" (Job 6:26). Then Bildad describes Job's words as "a blustering wind" (Job 8:2). And Eliphaz asks,

> Should a wise man answer with windy knowledge,
>> and fill his belly with the east wind? (Job 15:2 ESV)

Then Job responds to them, "Will your long-winded speeches never end?" (Job 16:3).

"Windiness" is not a good thing in this book, so we should take that into account when we hear Elihu boast about his own "windiness":

> I am full of words,
>> and the spirit within me [literally, "the wind in my belly"]
>>> compels me;
> inside I am like bottled-up wine,
>> like new wineskins ready to burst.
> I must speak and find relief;
>> I must open my lips and reply. (Job 32:18-20)

I hesitate to say it, but there is a rather crude, comic image here. Elihu is the one who is "full of wind," and he says that that wind is about to burst forth. You get the idea. As one commentator puts it,

"Elihu is flatulent with words."[7] Elihu, of course, intends this in one way, but it comes across in quite another.

In the end, Elihu turns out to be the most long-winded of all the speakers in the book. He can't stop talking about his words (Job 33:1-3). His self-confident words flow like a flood, as he goes on without stopping for six whole chapters! Nobody multiplies words like Elihu! Our author clearly does not portray Elihu with the dignity that a prophet of God would deserve.

Second, and most importantly, Elihu shouldn't be seen as a prophet of God simply because his conclusion about Job's words is contradicted by God himself. Elihu says,

> Job speaks without knowledge;
>> his words lack insight.
> Oh, that Job might be tested to the utmost
>> for answering like a wicked man!
> To his sin he adds rebellion;
>> scornfully he claps his hands among us
>> and multiplies his words against God. (Job 34:35-37)

But, as we shall see, God will judge otherwise. For though God will challenge Job, in the end, God exonerates him. Job is vindicated, and Job, not the friends, is declared to be the one who has spoken rightly about God.

Despite his pretenses, Elihu is not the prophet of God who speaks God's truth into the story. We are, in the words of one commentator, "tantalized by the torrent of [his] talk which promises enlightenment but offers in the event little more than eloquence."[8] He ends up more on the friends' side than on God's side. The fact that Elihu is totally ignored in the end may suggest that he really has nothing new

---

[7]Marvin Pope, *Job*, 3rd. ed. (New York: Doubleday, 1973), 213.

[8]Derek Kidner, *Wisdom to Live By: An Introduction to the Old Testament's Wisdom Books of Proverbs, Job and Ecclesiastes* (Leicester, UK: Inter-Varsity Press, 1985), 70.

to offer. We've heard it all before. He doesn't even qualify for condemnation.[9] "The effect of this," concludes Derek Kidner, "is to
imply that God has already heard more than enough of well-meaning
arguments, even before Elihu offers his opinions, and that any
further contributions are simply not invited, from us or from
anyone else."[10]

WHAT ELIHU GETS RIGHT

To be sure, as with Job's friends, Elihu does get some things right. For
one, he strongly affirms that God is just. That is certainly true, and
this provides the grounds for his harshest criticisms of Job. He is
angry that Job seems to be justifying himself at God's expense, when
he hears Job say, for example, "I am innocent, but God denies me
justice" (Job 34:5). Such talk offends Elihu, and he declares it in no
uncertain terms:

> Far be it from God to do evil,
>   from the Almighty to do wrong.
> He repays everyone for what they have done;
>   he brings on them what their conduct deserves.
> It is unthinkable that God would do wrong,
>   that the Almighty would pervert justice. (Job 34:10-12)

But let's look more closely at this statement. First, I don't think
Elihu has listened to Job well enough. He accuses Job of declaring
his own sinlessness:

> But you have said in my hearing—
>   I heard the very words—
> "I am pure, I have done no wrong;
>   I am clean and free from sin.

[9]Kidner, *Wisdom*, 70.
[10]Kidner, *Wisdom*, 70.

Yet God has found fault with me;

he considers me his enemy." (Job 33:8-10)

In fact, Job has never claimed to be without sin. He admits some sin (Job 7:21; 13:26; 14:16-17) and was very conscious of his need to make sacrificial offerings for his children, so we can assume that he made them for himself. He was blameless before God only in the sense that he feared God and shunned evil. As was evident from his final defense, Job's life was characterized by a godly morality. He maintained a repentant heart, habitually turning away from evil in his thoughts, words, and deeds. This doesn't mean that Job was a perfectly sinless man. Only one man who ever lived fits that description.

Further, in his affirmation of God's justice, Elihu says, "[God] repays everyone for what they have done; he brings on them what their conduct deserves" (Job 34:11). But we know that that is simply not true in Job's case. Job does not deserve the treatment he is getting. Both Elihu and Job believe that God is just, and neither has any idea why Job is in his current predicament.

Finally, Elihu criticizes Job for complaining that God does not speak to him:

Why do you complain to him

that he responds to no one's words?

For God does speak—now one way, now another—

though no one perceives it. (Job 33:13-14)

Again, this is true. Elihu tells how God speaks to human beings through revelation—dreams and visions (Job 33:15-18) and how God speaks to us through suffering (Job 33:19-22). I think of the famous words of C. S. Lewis—"God whispers to us in our pleasures, speaks in our conscience, but shouts in our pains: [pain] is His megaphone to rouse a deaf world."[11] Elihu asserts, helpfully, that God

---

[11]C. S. Lewis, *The Problem of Pain* (London: Collins, 1940), 81.

can use pain to teach us, to warn us, to shape our souls.[12] But again, that is not why Job is suffering now.

Whatever the assessment of the speech as a whole, beginning in the second half of Job 36, Elihu eloquently prepares the way for God's own speech that follows. He points to the majesty of God in creation, and how God works through the rain and the thunderstorm and the snow to execute his purposes in the world.

[God] brings the clouds to punish men,
or to water his earth and show his love. (Job 37:13)

But these purposes are unfathomable; they are inscrutable, he says.

How great is God—beyond our understanding!
The number of his years is past finding out. (Job 36:26)
. . .
Who can understand how he spreads out the clouds,
how he thunders from his pavilion? (Job 36:29)
. . .
Listen to this, Job;
stop and consider God's wonders.
Do you know how God controls the clouds
and makes his lightning flash?
Do you know how the clouds hang poised,
those wonders of him who has perfect knowledge?
(Job 37:14-16)

These are just the questions God will ask of Job. Elihu concludes:

Out of the north he comes in golden splendor;
God comes in awesome majesty.
The Almighty is beyond our reach and exalted in power;
in his justice and great righteousness, he does not oppress.

---

[12]But Eliphaz had already made that point in Job 5:17-22. See Comment 8.4, "Suffering as Educational."

Therefore, people revere him,

   for does he not have regard for all the wise in heart?
      (Job 37:22-24)

Yes, all this is true; and it seems to reflect the conclusion of Job 28 on wisdom. Wisdom is the fear of God. Elihu is right here; God's works are wonderful, beyond our understanding. But Elihu is wrong in thinking that he has the wisdom to know what is unknowable—that is, that he can discern the mysterious ways of God in the world, and the reason that Job is suffering as he is.

WHERE ELIHU (AND WE) GO WRONG

And isn't this where we can often go wrong? We want answers. We want to know, Why? This is Job's burning question, isn't it—"Why, Lord? Why are you treating me like this?" Elihu gives his answer even while he confesses the impenetrable mystery of God's ways. He thought he had some sort of charismatic endowment, enabling him to speak for God (cf. Job 32:8), but he was wrong!

And don't Christians sometimes give answers when they shouldn't? When a hurricane strikes New Orleans, some Christian will declare it to be the judgment of God. Or when an earthquake hits Haiti, it's because God hates voodoo and witchcraft. Or when a deadly virus attacks, it is seen as an expression of divine wrath. It could be true, but we don't know that—and besides, the purposes of God in any single event may be as diverse as the people who experience it.

We don't know. So beware of people who think they do. When confronted by a man born blind, Jesus had to correct his disciples' assumption that some sin had to lie behind his condition: "Neither this man nor his parents sinned," said Jesus, "but this happened so that the works of God might be displayed in him" (Jn 9:3). Often that is all that can be said or should be said. Things happen so that somehow the work of God may be displayed. What that may mean in any given circumstance is quite often beyond our comprehension. Beware of pat answers—answers that sound pious but may be empty wind.

WHAT JOB (AND WE) MOST NEED

So beyond that, what purpose does Elihu have in this story and what should we learn from his appearance? Coming as he does after Job's final appeal to God, Elihu's long-winded speeches leave us wondering if God will ever show up. We as readers grow weary of reading six more chapters rehearsing yet again most of what we've heard before.[13] Elihu tries to do what the friends fail to do—he tries to bring resolution to Job's perplexity. But, he too, fails. We are left with only one hope—only God can meet Job's need. More human arguments just won't do it.

Job's problem is not an intellectual one. He doesn't need a course in theology. Job's problem is personal. He needs to know if God can be trusted. Is he really worthy of our worship, even when we aren't showered with his blessings, even when we aren't privy to his ways in our lives? That's the question. If God is the ultimate source of his problem, then only God can be the solution. For that, Job must have a personal encounter with God himself—nothing else will do.

In a sense, this makes me, as a preacher (or writer), a little like Elihu. I can try to expound biblical truth. I can clarify and amplify. I can theologize and seek to evangelize. But all I can offer you are words. And you can listen and learn; you can grasp the concepts and ideas. Perhaps you will be persuaded by them, and you will affirm the truth of the Christian message and of the God who is revealed there. You can think right thoughts about God—but that will never

---

[13]This is yet another mimetic feature of the book. See Comment 1.5, "Mimesis."

be enough. God must be more than a concept, an idea, a proposition. He must become a person to you—a person you are willing to trust with your very life. Elihu and all his words won't do it. God must still draw near to you personally.

"Would that that would happen!" you might say. "If only God would reveal himself to me personally!" But, you see, he has. In the opening words of the letter to the Hebrews we read, "In the past God spoke to our ancestors through the prophets at many times and in various ways, but in these last days he has spoken to us by his Son" (Heb 1:1-2). John, in his Gospel, tells us that the Word who was in the beginning with God and who was God—that Word has become flesh and has dwelt among us. The eternal Word of God has become a human person. John writes, "No one has ever seen God, but the one and only Son, who is himself God and is in closest relationship with the Father, has made him known" (Jn 1:18).

The almighty God—the God who created the universe in all its majesty—this great and wonderful God has revealed himself as a baby in a manger, as a carpenter's son in the village of Nazareth, as an itinerant preacher who declared the coming of the kingdom of God, and as one who demonstrated the presence of that very kingdom by healing the sick, giving sight to the blind, and even raising the dead. Yes, God was in Jesus Christ when he died on a cross as a sacrifice for sin, and God was in Christ when he conquered death on that first Easter morning. God has come personally into our world.

And in a mysterious way, this Jesus Christ—who is God with us—makes himself known personally today by his Spirit whom he sends into the world to unite us to himself. God sends his Son, and the Son sends the Spirit, so that we might experience God's personal presence. I can't make that happen in your life—I can only point you to it. And this, in a sense, is what Elihu does in his final words.

Don't be content to hear the words of those who think themselves wise, claim to have all the answers, or aspire to prophetic status. Like Job, you must seek God's own presence until he appears.

Encountering God personally begins in a simple act of faith—a faith that God is there, and that he is worth pursuing—for he is God and he is to be honored as God in your life. You must begin with a desire for the wisdom that comes in fearing God and shunning evil.

Is that what you want? Then be like Job, who didn't give up in his pursuit of God—"Ask and it will be given to you; seek and you will find; knock and the door will be opened to you" (Mt 7:7).

DIGGING DEEPER

8.1. Elihu as a later addition? It has become a scholarly common-place that the Elihu speeches are a later addition to Job. The reasons provided for this conclusion include his (1) distinct language and style, (2) absence from the rest of the book, including the references to Job's *three* friends in the prologue and epilogue (Job 2:11-13; 42:7-9), (3) general repetition of arguments from the friends, (4) interruption of the progression from Job's final words to the Lord's response; and, relatedly, (5) the minimal effect removing these chapters from the book would have on its meaning.[14]

However, in recent scholarship, this firm scholarly edifice has begun to crumble. Seow, for example, disputes each of these points, and makes a strong argument for the value of the Elihu speeches within the book's design. He observes that mentioning Elihu in the prologue would have been "infelicitous," given that he does not appear for another thirty chapters, and even then, not to console Job as the friends do. Further, he notes that God may not include Elihu in his final verdict because Elihu was not wrong as the friends were, which was a view popular among medieval

---

[14]See C. L. Seow, *Job 1–21: Interpretation and Commentary* (Grand Rapids, MI: Eerdmans, 2013), 31-33.

Jewish commentators, who consistently thought Elihu's discourses to be the book's most profound and therefore absolutely critical for properly understanding its message. Elihu also may not have been included with Job's friends because of differences between him and them. He is not an important visitor but a young resident of Job's own town.[15] Even those modern scholars who claim Elihu's speeches to be later additions thereby concede that the author or editor who added them saw them contributing something to the book that it was deficient without.[16]

8.2. Elihu as intentionally ambiguous. The debate over the meaning of Elihu's speeches extends from the earliest witnesses, such as the negative portrayals of Elihu in the Old Greek translation and the Testament of Job from the Second Temple period, to Chrysostom's approval and Gregory the Great's criticism in the early church, to the universal praise of Elihu among medieval Jewish interpreters and Calvin's approbation of the speeches as providing the book's answer to Job's suffering, to the continuing debate in current scholarship, which ranges from characterizing him as a "buffoon" to "the mouthpiece of God."[17]

In his recent study, Cooper Smith argues that the interpretive ambivalence Elihu has inspired results from the ambiguity with which the author has intentionally imbued his speeches.[18] In other words, the difficulty of determining their meaning within the book is a feature, not a bug. He compares the speeches to case studies, frequently used in business schools, which tell an open-ended, true-to-life story of a dilemma and require students to apply what they're learning to determine the course of

---

[15]David Clines, *Job*, 3 vols. (Nashville: Thomas Nelson, 1989–2011), 3:1231.
[16]E.g., Carol Newsom's claim that the speeches are the product of a "dissatisfied reader" (*The Book of Job: A Contest of Moral Imaginations* [Oxford: Oxford University Press, 2003], 200-33).
[17]See Cooper Smith, *Allusive and Elusive: Allusion and the Elihu Speeches of Job 32–37*. Leiden: Brill, 2022. Quotations from William Whedbee, "The Comedy of Job," *Semeia* 7 (1977): 20 and Al Wolters, "Job 32–37: Elihu as the Mouthpiece of God," in *Reading and Hearing the Word: From Text to Sermon*, ed. Arie Leder (Grand Rapids, MI: CRC Publications, 1998), 108, respectively.
[18]Smith, *Allusive and Elusive*.

action. The Dialogue of Pessimism provides an ancient Near Eastern example of a similar technique.[19] Elihu is neither clearly right nor clearly wrong, and God refrains from passing a judgment on his words at the end of the book as he does for Job and the friends (Job 42:7-8), which requires readers to do so themselves, thereby testing their understanding of the book's message.

8.3. Elihu as a mediator. Elihu appears in the book in precisely the position that he sees himself fulfilling, between the human quest for wisdom led by Job's friends (Job 3–31) and the direct divine address from the whirlwind (Job 38–41). As he declares, "Do not say, 'We have found wisdom; let God, not a man, refute him'" (Job 32:13). Elihu declares the friends' search for wisdom a failure (Job 32:7, 9; 34:2; cf. Job 28), while concurrently rejecting a reliance on divine intervention. What is needed, he argues, is a mediator, "a messenger, one out of a thousand, sent to tell [sufferers] how to be upright," intervening on their behalf with God (Job 33:23-25), and filled with the divine spirit (Job 32:8). Job had requested just such a figure, a *mokhiakh*, "someone to mediate between us" (Job 9:33), but Elihu criticizes the friends, because none has been a *mokhiakh* for Job (Job 32:12).[20] He presents himself as playing this "necessary intermediary role between humanity's intellectual quest and direct divine communication" (Job 32:18; 33:4).[21]

Biblical precedents exist for this role. Joseph and Daniel were young men whose divinely bestowed wisdom succeeded where the wisdom of foreign wise men had failed (Gen 41:38; Dan 2:1-23; 4:8-9, 18; 5:11-12, 15).[22] Ezekiel 3:26 similarly speaks of the prophets performing the *mokhiakh* function of mediating between God

---

[19]See Comment 4.1, "Dialogues in the Ancient Near East."

[20]The NIV translates this, "not one of you has proved Job wrong." See Comment 5.6, "Who Is Job's 'Redeemer' (19:25)?"

[21]Seow, *Job*, 34.

[22]Seow, *Job*, 35.

and humanity.[23] However, even those with divinely inspired wisdom, such as Solomon, may act foolishly (1 Kings 11:1-4) and prophets who claim divine inspiration may be unreliable (1 Kings 22).[24] Discerning the reliability of claims to wisdom and inspiration itself requires wisdom. Just as the friends claim to be wise men, Elihu claims to be a divinely inspired mediator between God and humanity in the tradition of Joseph, Daniel, and the prophets, but the book presents them all failing to provide Job the consolation he needs. This only the Lord can provide.

8.4. Suffering as educational. How interpreters perceive Elihu's argument that suffering can serve a pedagogical purpose is at the heart of the debate over the value of his contribution to the book. Newsom finds this idea "repugnant."[25] She quotes a long passage from C. S. Lewis, in which, she claims, he "captures not only the essence of Elihu's argument but also the smugness of tone and the abstract quality of his reasoning," as he suggests that God may purposefully "make 'our own life' less agreeable to us, and take away the plausible sources of false happiness" to encourage us to seek the happiness that may only be found in God.[26] She compares this to "a parent who would break a child's arm or kill a child's dog to draw the child's attention to some moral lesson or to remind the child of its absolute dependence," and claims such a parent would not be loving but "a sadist who takes a perverted pleasure in cruelty."[27] However, arguments based on analogy are only as strong as the analogy chosen. If the parent were a brain surgeon, then there would be nothing sadistic about him even cutting his child's head open if his purpose were to remove a cancerous tumor. Newsom, Lewis

---

[23]Susannah Ticciati, *Job and the Disruption of Identity: Reading Beyond Barth* (London: T&T Clark International, 2005), 130-31.

[24]See Gerald Janzen, *Job* (Atlanta: John Knox Press, 1985), 215.

[25]Newsom, *Job*, 571.

[26]Citing Lewis, *Problem of Pain*, 84-85.

[27]Newsom, *Job*, 572.

would likely argue, has underestimated the danger facing those who suffer and God's skill in applying suffering to deliver them from it. Even so, as Newsom observes, when Lewis faced the intense suffering of his wife's death to cancer, he did not fall back on trite explanations, but genuinely grappled with pain and bewilderment, which she sees as an expression of deep, Job-like faith.[28]

Seow, however, argues that Elihu's clearly flawed character hardly distinguishes him within the biblical corpus, particularly among other prophetic figures, "who are typically angry, frequently eccentric, and always claiming to bring that truth that comes to them by divine revelation."[29] Elihu's primary theological contribution to the book, in Seow's view, is an alternative understanding of Job's suffering that escapes the false dichotomy driving the dialogue, in which the friends reason from God's justice to Job's guilt and Job reasons from his innocence to God's injustice.[30] Instead, Elihu argues, God may use suffering to educate, to shape the future of a sufferer rather than simply punish them for past deeds, as Eliphaz had suggested (e.g., Job 4:7-9; 5:2-18). Seow compares Elihu's contribution to Jesus' response to his disciples, who asked if a man's blindness was due to his sin or that of his parents.[31] "Neither," Jesus responds, "but this happened so that the works of God might be displayed in him" (Jn 9:2-3). Suffering may be intended, not to punish, but "to uncover human ears" to God's revelation and, thus, "those who suffer he delivers in their suffering; he speaks to them in their affliction" (Job 36:15).

When the book is considered as a whole, the truth of both these interpretations emerges. God does not repeat Elihu's pedantic pedagogical explanation for Job's suffering. Instead, he

---

[28]Newsom, *Job*, 572.
[29]Seow, *Job*, 97.
[30]Seow, *Job*, 98.
[31]Seow, *Job*, 99.

approves of the way Job wrestled with questions of divine justice (Job 42:7-8). And yet, it appears that Job has learned something, both from his suffering and from the answer God gives him, such that he can declare, "My ears had heard of you but now my eyes have seen you" (Job 42:5).

nine

GOD SPEAKS

JOB 38:1–42:6

My ears had heard of you
but now my eyes have seen you.

JOB 42:5

IMAGINE FOR A MOMENT that you're a part of the French resistance movement during the Nazi occupation of France in WWII. Every day you face life and death situations as you engage in covert operations against the German army. Secrecy is of the utmost importance; one case of misplaced trust could be fatal. One night you meet a stranger, whom you had heard about from a friend. This man deeply impresses you, and you spend the entire night in conversation. He claims that he is on your side. In fact, he claims that he is in command of the entire resistance movement, and his knowledge of it certainly backs up his words. He urges you to trust him, to have faith in him, no matter what happens.

You emerge from that encounter utterly convinced, and in sincerity and constancy you undertake to trust him. As it happens, you and the stranger never meet in conditions of intimacy again. Often you see this stranger helping the resistance fighters, and you are encouraged; but sometimes he is seen in the uniform of the German SS, apparently doing their work and even handing patriots over to the enemy. Still, in spite of appearances, you continue to believe that the stranger did not deceive you.

Sometimes you ask him for help and receive it, and you're thankful. Other times your messages get no response, but you say, "The stranger, he knows best." But lately it seems that you've had to say that more and more. In fact, you can't remember one time in the last ten months when he has done anything for the resistance. Besides, the deaths of two friends appear to be related to the actions of the stranger. You wonder, you doubt.

Then one day, there's a knock at your door. It's the German secret police with the stranger leading them. Does the stranger still know best? Has he deceived you? Will you let him in?

THE RISK OF FAITH

This parable of the stranger, made famous by Oxford philosophy professor Basil Mitchell,[1] illustrates the difficulty that is sometimes involved in faith and trust. It dramatically portrays the risk that is involved in every close relationship, particularly, I would say, in our relationship with God.

Certainly, our faith in God is not a blind faith. We have good reasons for believing what we do. But those beliefs will be buffeted by life's complications and complexities. As with the stranger, we sometimes find it difficult to understand the mysterious ways of God in the world and in our lives.

All the things that seem to count against God in our world can seem overwhelming: babies born addicted to drugs because of the actions of their mothers; mass shootings at an elementary school; or a global pandemic killing hundreds of thousands. Not exactly what you expect in a world in the control of a good and gracious heavenly Father.

---

[1]Basil Mitchell, "Theology and Falsification," in *The Philosophy of Religion: Oxford Readings in Philosophy* (Oxford: University Press, 1971), 13-22. See Os Guinness, *Doubt: Faith in Two Minds* (Berkhamsted, UK: Lion Publishing, 1976), 200-201.

Or in our own lives, we struggle through circumstances beyond our control. We seek guidance about our future and get no answer from above and only closed doors here below. Or we see loved ones suffer. As I was writing this, I received news from a friend that his daughter, who recently gave birth to a child, was diagnosed with a cancer that could result in blindness or even death.

It's perplexing. "God, are you really there?" And even more often we ask, "Lord, do you really care?" God's ways are mysterious in our sight, and we wonder—Does the stranger really know what is best? Can he really be trusted? Is he still on my side?

Faith involves risk, and even a healthy faith will not be without questions, doubts, and struggles in its relationship with God. I believe our Lord would have it no other way—God uses trials to refine faith (1 Pet 1:6-7). As Annie Dillard puts it, "You do not have to sit outside in the dark. If, however, you want to look at the stars, you will find that darkness is required."[2]

JOB'S LONELY DARKNESS

Our hero Job is certainly sitting in darkness—deep darkness. He is devastated in every area of his life.

> Though I cry, "Violence!," I get no response,
>   though I call for help, there is no justice.
> [God] has blocked my way so I cannot pass;
>   he has shrouded my paths in darkness. (Job 19:7-8)

Job had trusted God, had basked in the warm light of his love. Now he feels abandoned.

As a man of faith, Job expected God to act on his behalf, and so he made his appeal. He called on God to come to him, to make himself known, either to vindicate his righteous standing or to

---

[2]Annie Dillard, *Teaching a Stone to Talk: Expeditions and Encounters* (New York: Harper Perennial, 1992), 43.

show him where he has gone wrong. But what happened? Nothing. That silence can be the most difficult aspect of suffering. Job wants to find answers, but in the end, his problem is not intellectual, it is personal. He feels let down by someone he had trusted. "Why, Lord? Why are you treating me this way? Why are you allowing this to happen to me?"

The agnostic and even the atheist will, in a moment of pain, say, "God, why me?" (which is in itself interesting). But their distress is just not the same. Theirs is not a cry of betrayal but of mere desperation. But for the believer the issue can create a crisis of faith. Only the one who has trusted the stranger has questions when he appears to be helping the enemy. Your closest friends can hurt you the most; only someone you're committed to can let you down.

Job had put his trust in a living, personal God, and that trust involved risk, for it caused him to expect that God would act justly toward him, and would respond to him when he called on him. Now, he feels abandoned in senseless suffering.[3]

Consider the experience of C. S. Lewis.[4] Earlier in his career Lewis had written a book called *The Problem of Pain*, in which he sought to address some of the intellectual issues related to believing in a good God in a world of suffering. Many have found that book quite helpful. But later in his life, Lewis encountered his own pain, and the reality of affliction struck him in a new way. He married late in life, and after only a couple of years, his wife died of bone cancer. Her death plunged Lewis into the depths of despairing grief, and during that travail of his soul he kept a brutally honest record of his thoughts and feelings, which he later published in a book titled *A Grief Observed*.

---

[3]See Comment 7.1, "The Hiddenness of God."
[4]This connection between the two books is referred to by Philip Yancey, *Where Is God When It Hurts?* (Grand Rapids, MI: Zondervan, 1990), 20.

At one point Lewis wrote these words:

Meanwhile, where is God? This is one of the most disquieting
symptoms [of grief]. When you are happy, so happy that you
have no sense of needing Him, so happy that you are tempted
to feel His claims upon you as an interruption, if you remember
yourself and turn to Him with gratitude and praise, you will—
or so it feels—be welcomed with open arms. But go to Him
when your need is desperate, when all other help is vain, and
what do you find? A door slammed in your face, and a sound
of bolting and double-bolting on the inside. After that,
silence. . . . Why is He so present a commander in our time of
prosperity and so very absent a help in time of trouble?[5]

That's Job—and maybe that's you; or maybe it will be you. But
somehow Job perseveres. His is not the acquiescence of the Stoic,
denying the very real pain that he feels. Job perseveres, though he is
never passive, simply submitting to some impersonal fate. No, he
continues to cry out to the personal God who he knows is behind it
all. So he laments, he complains, he protests, he even seeks to
litigate—to bring God to court to explain himself. But Job never
gives up—he never curses God.

Os Guinness in his book on doubt suggests that "a sure mark of
Christian vision is its godly impatience and holy restlessness."[6]
That's Job. It is this very activity of seeking him that God wants to
stir up within us. Perhaps this is what Jesus was referring to when
he told that parable of the persistent widow before the unjust judge,
who won't leave him alone until he acts on her behalf. Jesus wanted
to show that at all times we ought to pray and not to lose heart—
"Will not God bring about justice for his chosen ones, who cry out
to him day and night?" he asks (Lk 18:7).

[5]C. S. Lewis, *A Grief Observed* (New York: Seabury, 1961), 9.
[6]Guinness, *Doubt*, 229.

GOD SPEAKS OUT OF THE STORM

We return to our story, and Job is right where we left him six chapters before—waiting for God to respond to his desperate, even demanding, plea. Will Job ever be delivered from his grief and despair? Will he ever rise from the ash heap and resume his life in the world? Who can comfort him? His three friends tried, but only seemed to make things worse. The young, brash Elihu entered the picture, and though he said some good things, he failed, as well. In the end, Job's consolation relies on something far beyond Elihu's grasp. And we must not miss it either: if God himself is the ultimate source of Job's problem, then only God can be its solution. And now, after thirty-five chapters of dialogue and debate, of Job's cries of lamentation and calls for litigation, God finally makes his appearance.

We first need to appreciate the fact that God appears at all. Certainly, God is under no obligation to respond to any demand we may put on him. As he says to Job,

> Who has a claim against me that I must pay?
>   Everything under heaven belongs to me. (Job 41:11)

He is God Almighty, the Creator of heaven and earth. He is, by no means, subject to our beck and call. And some suggest that the long-winded speeches of Elihu, separating Job's demand that God appear and God's actual appearance, are meant to make that very point. God will speak when God wants to speak.

But God does appear—he "responds" to Job (Job 38:2). In an act of humble grace, God condescends to interact with him. Elihu thought it impossible that God would do such a thing:

> God does not listen to the empty plea [of the wicked];
>   the Almighty pays no attention to it.
> How much less, then, will he listen [to you, Job,]
>   when you say that you do not see him,

that your case is before him

and you must wait for him. (Job 35:13-14)

But God has listened to Job's lament, and now he responds to it. And he doesn't send an emissary—an angel or a prophet. God cares enough to respond in person. What an affirmation of Job's value in God's sight!

More than that, here we find God's personal name Yahweh (translated as "the LORD" in small capitals). That name has almost been absent since Job 2.[7] It's the name he revealed especially to his people Israel as his covenant name, expressing his personal commitment to them as their God.

The LORD, Yahweh, answers Job, and he does it "out of the storm" (Job 38:1). Nothing is more terrifying than a hurricane-force windstorm. Job's children had been destroyed by one (Job 1:19). And Job himself was afraid that if God actually did appear to him, "he would crush me with a storm" (Job 9:17). The "storm" can be a sign of God's anger and wrath,[8] and if Elihu and the friends were right about Job, we might have expected God to destroy him—to condemn him and crush him for all his rebellious talk about God being unjust toward him. But that doesn't happen.

Yes, the Lord speaks "out of the storm." And it is right that he should do so. He is no tame god; he is great and awesome and beyond our comprehension, and Job needs to know that.

But instead of denouncing Job, the Lord challenges him with questions.[9] He engages him, probing and prodding. There is almost a gentle, some even say, a "playful tone"[10] to God's words to Job.

---

[7] It appears only in Job 12:9.

[8] Cf., e.g., Jer. 23:19: "See, the storm of the LORD will burst out in wrath, a whirlwind swirling down on the heads of the wicked."

[9] See Comment 9.1, "Rhetorical Questions."

[10] Anderson, Job, 271; followed by Lindsay Wilson, Job (Grand Rapids, MI: Eerdmans, 2015), 180, and Derek Kidner, Wisdom to Live By: An Introduction to the Old Testament's Wisdom Books of Proverbs, Job and Ecclesiastes (Leicester, UK: Inter-Varsity Press, 1985), 70.

One commentator says that God's response "puts Job in his place more as a father might do it to a dogmatic adolescent than as a judge to an offender."[11]

God's grace. The Lord God affords Job the dignity of addressing him personally. The Lord's appearance to Job is surely a demonstration of God's grace. Here we see the great and awesome God of the universe—and he is that, as he makes clear—in his grace making himself known personally to Job. The paradox here should not be missed. As Tim Keller observes, "God comes both as a gracious, personal God and as an infinite, overwhelming force—at the same time."[12] Shouldn't this point us to Christ? In Jesus we can see how the "untamable" and infinite God can be born as a baby and give his life as a loving Savior. In Christ on the cross, God's wrath and mercy meet as nowhere else.[13]

More than anything, in his suffering, Job wanted his relationship with God restored. It was God's absence that most disturbed him.[14] Now, in his appearance to Job, God responds in his grace to Job's cry.

But when he appears, he does not respond as Job expected. Job wanted an explanation for his suffering. He expected God either to vindicate him or to condemn him. But God does neither.

Consider what else God might have done. God could have explained to Job that he had nothing to do with his sufferings; they were the work of the satanic accuser—"Blame him, not me." Or God could have denied that he had the power to stop such awful things from happening—that's just the way things are in a fallen world.

He says neither of those things; nor could he. Instead of giving answers, God asks questions.[15] And in fact, he completely changes

[11]Kidner, *Wisdom*, 71.
[12]Timothy Keller, *Walking with God Through Pain and Suffering* (New York: Dutton, 2013), 282.
[13]Keller, *Walking with God*, 282.
[14]See Comment 7.1, "The Hiddenness of God."
[15]See Comment 9.2, "Why Doesn't God Explain?"

the subject. The all-consuming talk of Job's suffering is entirely left behind. Instead, God intends to change the way Job looks at his own situation by changing the way he looks at the world. He wants to broaden Job's horizons, so that he might see that his perspective is far too narrow to understand what God is up to in his life—"his ash-heap is not the centre or circumference of the world."[16]

Questions of cosmogony. In his first address to Job, God peppers him with all sorts of questions—unanswerable questions—in an interrogation meant to remind Job of the kinds of things he cannot do, which only God can.[17] In Job 38:4-21 the questions all concern the creation of the universe—what we call "cosmogony": laying the earth's foundation, marking off its dimensions, setting its foundation, and laying its cornerstone (Job 38:4-7).

Questions of meteorology. Then in Job 38:22-38 the Lord speaks of the workings of the sky and the weather. He questions Job about meteorology:

> Have you entered the storehouses of the snow
> or seen the storehouses of the hail,
> which I reserve for times of trouble,
>   for days of war and battle? (Job 38:22-23)
>
> . . .
>
> Do you know the laws of the heavens? (Job 38:33)
>
> . . .
>
> Do you send the lightning bolts on their way?
> Do they report to you, "Here we are"? (Job 38:35)

Questions of zoology. And then beginning in Job 38:39, God depicts the ways of the animals. He gives Job a lesson in zoology. For example,

---

[16]Kidner, *Wisdom,* 70. See Comment 9.3, "Discounting a Dichotomous Theology (Job 40:8)."

[17]So D. A. Carson, *How Long, O Lord? Reflections on Suffering and Evil,* 2nd ed. (Grand Rapids, MI: Baker Academic, 2006), 150.

Do you hunt the prey for the lioness
    and satisfy the hunger of the lions
when they crouch in their dens
    or lie in wait in a thicket?
Who provides food for the raven
    when its young cry out to God
    and wander about for lack of food?
Do you know when the mountain goats give birth?
    Do you watch when the doe bears her fawn?
      (Job 38:39-39:1)

He proceeds to question Job about the wild donkey, the wild ox, the war horse, the hawk, and the eagle—all of them beyond the power of humans to domesticate and control; each endowed with its own habitat, and its own ways of living that human beings have nothing to do with. God's care extends even to animals that were considered "unclean."[18]

There's even the delightful description of the ostrich—who has silly wings and foolish ways, but what it lacks in sagacity, it makes up for in speed (Job 39:13-18).

Job, were you the one who designed all this? Are you the one who controls the workings of these things?

God is portrayed as an architect, a surveyor, an engineer, and perhaps most interestingly, as a parent, in language reflecting parents caring for their children—swaddling the seas in a garment (Job 38:9), acting as a father to the rain (Job 38:28), giving birth to the frost (Job 38:29), providing food for the ravens (Job 38:41). God is at work in his creation in multifarious ways, and he seems to be posing the question, "Job, if you can't understand how I govern the physical universe, do you think you can understand how I govern the moral universe?"

---

[18]The hawk and eagle are "unclean" animals (Lev 11:13, 16). In Job this uncleanness is alluded to by their contact with blood and dead corpses (Job 39:30).

Think of the way Jesus speaks in the Sermon on the Mount, as he points to the birds of the air and the lilies of the field—if God cares for them, won't he also care for you (Mt 6:26)? So here, God points to his care for his creatures in the natural world as a sign of his care for Job: "If I care for a wild donkey in the desert, do you not think that I can care for you, Job?"

The Lord presses his case:

> Will the one who contends with the Almighty correct him?
>   Let him who accuses God answer him! (Job 40:1-2)

And Job does answer—in a way:

> I am unworthy—how can I reply to you?
>   I put my hand over my mouth.
> I spoke once, but I have no answer—
>   twice, but I will say no more. (Job 40:3-5)

Job is humbled in his response to the Lord's first speech. He is rendered speechless, but there is as yet no resolution.

But God is not through. God again speaks, confronting Job's belief that he stands in a position to assess God's justice.

> Do you have an arm like God's,
>   and can your voice thunder like his?
> Then adorn yourself with glory and splendor,
>   and clothe yourself in honor and majesty.
> Unleash the fury of your wrath,
>   look at all who are proud and bring them low.
>   (Job 40:9-11)[19]

. . .

> Then I myself will admit to you
>   that your own right hand can save you. (Job 40:14)

---

[19]See Comment 9.3, "Discounting a Dichotomous Theology (Job 40:8)."

God's power and control: Behemoth and Leviathan. At this point God speaks of two mysterious and frightening creatures, Behemoth and Leviathan. Some have scorned God's response to Job here. George Bernard Shaw, noting the description of the Behemoth in terms of a massive semi-aquatic African mammal, scoffed, "If I complain that I am suffering unjustly, it is no answer to say, 'Can you make a hippopotamus?'"[20]

But such critics have missed the point. These frightening creatures become symbols of God's mysterious power, even over the chaotic forces of his creation.

> Look at Behemoth,
>> which I made along with you
>> and which feeds on grass like an ox.
> What strength it has in its loins,
>> what power in the muscles of its belly! (Job 40:15-16)

This creature hides among the reeds in the marsh and makes the raging river his home.

Then all of Job 41 speaks of Leviathan, with its menacing mouth full of fearsome teeth (Job 41:14), back laced with rows of shields tightly sealed together (Job 41:15), and underside that slices a trail in the mud (Job 41:30). This creature "stirs up the seas" and "makes the depths churn like a boiling caldron" (Job 41:31); one can "fill its hide with harpoons" to no effect (Job 41:7).

> Smoke pours from its nostrils . . .
> Its breath sets coals ablaze,
>> and flames dart from his mouth. (Job 41:20-21)
> . . .
> Nothing on earth is its equal—
>> a creature without fear.

---

[20]J. A. Baker, "The Book of Job: Unity and Meaning," in *Papers on Old Testament and Related Themes*, vol. 1 of *Studia Biblica,* ed. E. A Livingstone (Sheffield: JSOT Press, 1979), 17.

It looks down on all that are haughty;

   it is king over all that are proud. (Job 41:33-34)

There are two ways of understanding what is going on here. Either the Behemoth and the Leviathan are literal animals—animals like the hippopotamus and the crocodile—described in highly mythical language. Or they are mythical creatures,[21] described in language related to literal animals, such as the hippopotamus and the crocodile. The fact that both the ESV and the NIV capitalize their names suggests that they prefer the latter view.[22]

In the end, the view you take doesn't matter, because either way, these two mysterious creatures are symbols of the forces of chaos in the cosmos, forces that are frightening and beyond human control. These menacing creatures represent hostile powers in the world which God alone can subdue.

Of Behemoth, the Lord asks,

Can anyone capture it by the eyes,

   or trap it and pierce its nose? (Job 40:24)

And of Leviathan, he says,

If you lay a hand on it,

   you will remember the struggle and never do it again!

Any hope of subduing it is false;

   the mere sight of it is overpowering.

No one is fierce enough to rouse it. (Job 41:8-10)

. . .

When it rises up, the mighty are terrified;

   they retreat before its thrashing. (Job 41:25)

---

[21]In Is 27:1 Leviathan symbolizes moral chaos in the world—"The LORD will punish with his sword . . . the gliding serpent, Leviathan the coiling serpent; he will slay the monster of the sea."
[22]See Comment 9.4, "What Are Behemoth and Leviathan?"

These are ferocious and fearsome beasts, yet the Lord created them and the Lord controls them. They are embodiments of the human fear of chaos, of the unknown, which cannot be slain with sword or spear or restrained with rope or chain. By describing them to Job, God acknowledges the very real threat of fear. But God is not intimidated by these terrors. He created them. He can put Leviathan on a leash if he likes (Job 41:5). Therefore, he asks,

> Who then is able to stand against me?
> Who has a claim against me that I must pay?
> Everything under heaven belongs to me. (Job 41:10-11)

"Don't you understand, Job?" the Lord seems to be saying. "If I can control these terrifying creatures, can't you trust me to manage the affairs of your life?" And isn't this the same message we get from Jesus himself, when he says, "In this world you will have trouble. But take heart! I have overcome the world" (Jn 16:33). Jesus, in his glorious resurrection, has overcome the forces of sin and death. He has been declared victorious over "the powers and authorities"—those spiritual forces of darkness that threaten us and that we cannot control (Col 2:10, 15). Peter says that Jesus "has gone into heaven and is at God's right hand—with angels, authorities and powers in submission to him" (1 Pet 3:22). Can't we then trust him, even when we feel overwhelmed by the forces of evil in our world? For what can separate us from God's love (Rom 8:38-39)?

These speeches of God are meant to put Job, and us, in our proper place—and that's not a bad thing. In fact, it's good and right. As Derek Kidner puts it, God's speeches "cut us down to size, treating us not as philosophers but as children—limited in mind, puny in body—whose first and fundamental grasp of truth must be to know the difference between our place and God's, and to accept it."[23]

---

[23]Kidner, *Wisdom*, 72.

The divine speeches don't attempt to explain why a good and powerful God allows evil to exist, or why God ever created Behemoth and Leviathan in the first place (see Job 40:15). But that's also part of what makes these divine speeches so masterfully applicable to any sufferer. God redirects our question from why God allows suffering to persist, the answer to which is different in each situation and beyond our comprehension in most. Instead he directs our attention to whom we must trust in every situation, and why this God can sustain our hopes.

He is the Creator of heaven and earth—and we are not. He rules over all; and we don't. He is wise beyond our ability to comprehend; he knows what we could never know. His ways transcend our understanding, and we have to accept that fact and trust him, even when it's hard. Isn't this what our worship week after week is meant to teach us? God is God, and we are not, and that's a good thing!

JOB'S RESPONSE

A deepened fear of God. Finally, Job seems to get it. His first response was insufficient; now he seems satisfied as his vision of the greatness of God has expanded.

Then Job replied to the LORD:

"I know that you can do all things;
    no purpose of yours can be thwarted.
You asked, 'Who is this that obscures my plans
        without knowledge?'
    Surely I spoke of things I did not understand,
    things too wonderful for me to know.
"You said, 'Listen now, and I will speak;
    I will question you,
    and you shall answer me.'
My ears had heard of you
    but now my eyes have seen you." (Job 42:1-5)

Job's faith had always been real. Remember his initial profession:

> The LORD gave and the LORD has taken away;
>> may the name of the LORD be praised. (Job 1:21)

Now, after this long struggle with God, his faith has been deepened; it has been refined; and it is now as precious as pure gold.

Elisabeth Elliot, the wife of a martyred missionary, thinking back over her life of tragedies and troubles, puts it well: "God is God. If He is God, he is worthy of my worship and my service. I will find rest nowhere but in His will, and that will is infinitely, immeasurably, unspeakably beyond my largest notions of what He is up to."[24] This is where Job has arrived in his long journey of faith. The God he had feared is now seen to be more fearful than he had imagined, and, for that reason, more worthy of his trust. As Goethe writes in his play *Torquato Tasso*, "At last the sailor lays firm hold, Upon the rock on which he had been dashed."[25]

Job is "comforted." So we come to the critical Job 42:6—"Therefore I despise myself and repent in dust and ashes." This, at least, is how the English versions traditionally translate the Hebrew. The sense is that now Job recognizes that in his lament he had spoken wrongly against God. His complaints were too harsh, his questions were too pointed, his attitude too full of pride, and he needed to confess his sin and turn from it. John Calvin, for example, in his sermons on Job, spoke of Job's "excessive and outrageous talk" for which he needed to repent.[26]

There are strong voices supporting this way of translating this verse. But this is one of those very rare cases when I will go against

[24]Elisabeth Elliot, "Epilogue II," in *Through the Gates of Splendor*, 40th anniversary ed. (Tyndale, 1996), 267.
[25]Johann Wolfgang von Goethe, *Torquato Tasso* (United Kingdom: Manchester University Press, 1979), cited in Karl Barth, *Church Dogmatics: The Doctrine of Reconciliation*, vol. 4, part 3.1, trans. G. W. Bromiley (New York: T&T Clark International, 1961), 424.
[26]Sermons on Job, 1.

the majority and disagree with the English translations and offer an alternative that makes better sense of this verse's context in the book.

The Hebrew verb *nakham*, translated as "repent" in most English versions of this verse, is generally translated "comfort" every other time it appears in the book.[27] If it is translated as "comfort" here, then we see how the divine speeches address a main issue of the book—Job's search for comfort and his friends' failure to provide it. Though Job's friends come to "comfort" Job (2:11), they fail, leading him to call them "miserable comforters" (Job 16:2; cf. Job 21:34). What Job now "despises" or "rejects" is not "himself" (the Hebrew verb has no object) but his condition of mourning. After God speaks, Job can now say, "therefore I reject [my mourning], and I am comforted regarding dust and ashes"—"dust and ashes" being the ritual symbol of Job's state of mourning and grief.[28] Job now turns from his state of mourning and can re-enter normal relationships in society, which is just what we see him do in what follows.[29]

What comforts Job? As Job 42:5 says, it's a new vision of God, a direct experience of God that exceeds the previous knowledge he had heard about God. And, as Job 42:2-4 indicates, that experience of God revealed to him his vast ignorance of God's wonders, his wisdom or "counsel," and his power, by which he carries out all his purposes. In other words, though Job is described as fearing the

---

[27]See Job 2:11; 6:10; 7:13; 15:11; 16:2; 21:2; 21:34; 29:25; 42:11.

[28]For a thorough analysis of the interpretive options and the Hebrew semantics involved to make a compelling case for the translation: "Therefore, I reject and am comforted regarding dust and ashes," see Heath A. Thomas, "Job's Rejection and Liminal Traverse," in *The Unfolding of Your Words Gives Light: Studies on Biblical Hebrew in Honor of George L. Klein*, ed. Ethan C. Jones (University Park, PA: Eisenbrauns, 2018), 155-74. Some interpreters translate the verb *naham* with the preposition in this verse as "turn away (from)" or "change one's mind (concerning)" dust and ashes. Since being comforted in one's grief entails a turning from the ritual symbols of mourning, this amounts to the same basic meaning as we have suggested. Cf., e.g., Wilson, *Job*, 204-7.

[29]A close parallel occurs in Gen 37:34-35, where Jacob assumed the ritual of mourning (tearing his clothes and putting on sackcloth) and refused to be comforted (using the verb *nakham*) by his children. Job had been in a similar state, but now emerges from it.

Lord in the book's first verse, he now fears him in a deeper way. His vision of God is now much clearer, and thus his wisdom far greater.

Job's questions have not been answered, but he is now satisfied that God—who seemed to him to be a stranger—is still on his side. Job is comforted with the conviction that God knows what he's doing, even if Job doesn't.

And Job never learns what had transpired in the heavenly courts, how God had commended him, nor how the accuser had challenged God by cynically asserting that Job only feared God because God blessed him. And it has to be that way if his faith is to be proved genuine, for real faith trusts even in the dark. This is what makes Job's faith so powerful.

FROM JOB TO US

So I ask, Is your faith real? Is it authentic? Or is it just mercenary and conditional? That is, will you trust God only so long as he blesses you, and only so long as you can understand what he's doing in your life?

This is not to say you won't struggle to trust God when you encounter hardships. You may indeed ask "Why, Lord? How long, Lord? What are you doing? Why are you allowing this to happen in my life?" It can be hard to trust the stranger. But you must keep reminding yourself why you ever trusted him in the first place. Even those questions can be an expression of that trust, as they were for Job. You wouldn't ask them of the stranger if you no longer believed him to be on your side.

And for us, living in this new covenant age, there is no clearer, no stronger ground for trusting God, for believing that despite all appearances, he really is on our side, than what is found in the gospel of Jesus Christ. In sending his own Son into the world, God himself enters into our suffering; on the cross of Christ he shares our pain.

You could even say, with Dorothy Sayers, that on the cross, "[God] had the honesty and courage to take His own medicine."[30]

In Christ, God not only shares our pain on the cross, he also bears our sin, and he takes it away. And in Christ's glorious resurrection from the dead we have assurance that nothing can separate us from his love—nothing at all!—for he now reigns forever. I appreciate the words of Cornelius Plantinga: "We do not refer each other to the cross of Christ to explain evil. It is not as if in pondering Calvary we will at last understand throat cancer. We rather lift our eyes to the cross, whence comes our help, in order to see that God shares our lot and can therefore be trusted."[31]

My ears had heard of you
but now my eyes have seen you.

Have your eyes seen something of what Job saw—the Lord God in all his majesty, the One who rules his cosmos with his own unfathomable wisdom? And I ask you, have your eyes seen what Job never could see—that same God in love hanging on a cross for you?

In closing, consider the challenging prayer of Blaise Pascal:

I ask you, Lord, neither for health nor for sickness, for life nor for death; but that you may dispose of my health and my sickness, my life and my death, for your glory. . . . You alone know what is expedient for me; you are the sovereign master; do with me according to your will. Give to me, or take away from me, only conform my will to yours. I know but one thing, Lord, that it is good to follow you, and bad to offend you. Apart from that, I know not what is good or bad in anything. I know not which is most profitable to me—health or sickness, wealth or poverty, nor anything else in the world. That discernment is beyond the

---

[30]Dorothy L. Sayers, *Christian Letters to a Post-Christian World* (Grand Rapids, MI: Eerdmans, 1969), 14.

[31]Cornelius Plantinga Jr., "A Love So Fierce," *The Reformed Journal*, November 1986, 6.

power of men or angels, and is hidden among the secrets of your Providence, which I adore, but do not seek to fathom.[32]

To that prayer, add the apostle Paul's glorious benediction:

> Oh, the depth of the riches of the wisdom and knowledge
>   of God!
>   How unsearchable his judgments,
>   and his paths beyond tracing out!
> "Who has known the mind of the Lord?
>   Or who has been his counselor?"
> "Who has ever given to God,
>   that God should repay him?"
> For from him and through him and to him are all things.
>   To him be the glory forever! Amen. (Rom 11:33-36)

DIGGING DEEPER

9.1. Rhetorical questions. As a rhetorical device, rhetorical questions emphasize the intimacy between speaker and audience. They do not expect an answer because they ask "something which both the questioner and his auditor [listener] know, and which the questioner knows that his auditor knows, and which the auditor knows that the questioner knows he knows."[33] The awkwardness of an audience member yelling out the response to a rhetorical question results from the violation of this intimacy. Either the speaker or the listener misjudged the other's knowledge. Building on their intimacy, rhetorical questions draw the listener into a speaker's message by encouraging the listener to perceive the speaker's claims as already the listener's own rather than as externally imposed.

---

[32]Blaise Pascal, "Prayer, To Ask of God the Proper Use of Sickness," in *Thoughts, Letters, and Minor Works of Blaise Pascal* (P. F. Collier and Son, 1910), 372-73.

[33]Michael V. Fox, "Job 38 and God's Rhetoric," *Semeia* 19 (1981): 58.

In the divine speeches, God's heavy reliance on rhetorical questions creates this intimacy both between God and Job and between the author and the reader, as we, with Job, are expected to know the answers to God's questions. Most, like, "Who marked off [the earth's] dimensions?" (Job 38:5), expect the answer, "You, God." Others, such as "Have you ever given orders to the morning?" (Job 38:12), compel the response, "No, but you do." Together, the questions aim to convey to Job both his limitations and God's greatness, but with a "stern gentleness" that humbles Job without humiliating him.[34] If God were simply to declare the wonders for which he takes credit in contrast with the ignorance and weakness of Job, the charge of bullying some interpreters level at his speeches might better apply. However, by using rhetorical questions, God expresses throughout a respect for the relationship he has with Job and the wisdom Job already has about God's ways in the world while deepening both. The questions say to Job, "You know very well that I and I alone created order and maintain it in the world, and I know that you know, and you know that I know that you know."[35] Naturally, then, Job's response emphasizes the new intimacy that now accompanies his knowledge of God (Job 42:5).

9.2. Why doesn't God explain? When God finally appears to Job, his lack of explicit explanation for Job's suffering has left the divine speeches one of the most mysterious aspects of this enigmatic book. Some take this lack of justification as God's abdication of moral responsibility for Job's plight, an "implicit assertion that he has not undertaken to act justly, that the world is not ordered according to principles of justice."[36]

---

[34]Fox, "Job 38," 59.

[35]Fox, "Job 38," 60.

[36]David Clines, "Does the Book of Job Suggest That Suffering Is Not a Problem?," in *Weisheit in Israel: Beiträge des Symposiums, "Das Alte Testament und die Kultur der Moderne," anlässlich des 100. Geburtstags Gerhard von Rads (1901–1971), Heidelberg, 18–21. Oktober 2001*, ed. David J. A. Clines, Hermann Lichtenberger, and Hans-Peter Müller (Münster: LIT, 2003), 104–5.

God's reticence here must be understood, however, in the context of the entire book. The author of Job has set for himself a daunting challenge. For God to win the wager with the Satan, Job must express his faith *khinnam*, "for nothing" (Job 1:9); receiving a reward for faithful suffering would seem to invalidate that. However, a God who would allow such unjust suffering to go un-requited is hardly worthy of faith. The solution the author pro-vides is to have Job express his faith, first, explicitly in his initial confessions, then through calling God to act according to God's just character in his protests, and, finally, through setting aside his mourning after encountering God in the divine speeches but before his restoration (Job 42:6).[37] This vindicates the faith God put in Job, and allows God to restore Job, thereby vindicating the faith Job put in God's justice, without invalidating the wager. This is why God cannot explicitly address Job's situation in the divine speeches—not because God is denying that God is, in fact, just, but because either to explain the wager or to promise to restore Job if he will remain faithful would be to make Job's faith con-tingent on God's reward and invalidate the wager altogether. All God can communicate to Job is that he is worthy of Job's trust. The author has sought to vindicate both Job's credibility and God's, rather than forcing the reader or the characters themselves to side with one over the other.[38]

By employing poetic description rather than rational expla-nation, the divine speeches also serve an important rhetorical purpose. They affirm what anyone who has truly suffered already knows: logical comprehension is only one way of knowing, one that is often inadequate to the devastation affliction wreaks on one's psyche. As Alvin Plantinga observes,

> When God does come to Job in the whirlwind, it is not to convince him that God really does have reasons (although it

---

[37]See "Job Is 'Comforted'" in chap. 9.
[38]See Comment 9.3, "Discounting a Dichotomous Theology (Job 40:8)."

may, in fact, do this); it is instead to still the tempest in his soul, to quiet him, to restore his trust for God. The Lord gives Job a glimpse of his greatness, his beauty, his splendid goodness; the doubts and turmoil disappear and are replaced, once more, by love and trust.[39]

Therefore, if God were to address Job's arguments clearly he would not address them fully. As Bartholomew and O'Dowd write, "God is indeed good, and his purposes will be accomplished in the end; but this journey must be lived by embracing the mystery and wonder of human life in this world."[40]

9.3. Discounting a dichotomous theology (Job 40:8). Job 40:8 is a prime example of how God attempts to broaden Job's horizons in the divine speeches. God asks Job, "Would you discredit my justice? Would you condemn me to justify yourself?" Here, God warns Job that his use of the legal metaphor is drawing him into a dichotomous, win-lose understanding of his relationship with God. This undercuts the trust necessary for Job to cope with his suffering. He risks moving his relationship with God from fights behind closed doors to public divorce proceedings, which will transform it irrevocably. A way exists in which Job can be in the right without God being in the wrong, for God to allow the innocent Job to suffer without being ultimately unjust, but it will require Job to acknowledge the mysterious freedom of God. Whether or not God has allowed Job's suffering for a pedagogical purpose,[41] he will have to trust without understanding. As von Rad puts it, for the wise, "the presupposition for coping with life was trust in Yahweh and in the orders put into operation by him."[42] For them, reason "is surrounded by the insurmountable wall of the

---

[39]Alvin Plantinga, *Warranted Christian Belief* (New York: Oxford University Press, 2000), 497-98.

[40]Craig G. Bartholomew and Ryan O'Dowd, *Old Testament Wisdom Literature: A Theological Introduction* (Downers Grove, IL: IVP Academic, 2011), 155.

[41]See Comment 8.4, "Suffering as Educational."

[42]Gerhard von Rad, *Wisdom in Israel*, trans. James D. Martin (Harrisburg, PA: Trinity Press International, 1972), 307.

inexplicable," as they describe both what can be known and what cannot.[43] In Job's words,

And these are but the outer fringe of his works;
how faint the whisper we hear of him!
Who then can understand the thunder of his power?
(Job 26:14)

The divine speeches, then, coax Job to run headlong into that wall of mystery. His response, as elsewhere in the Hebrew Bible, is adoration (Job 42:2-5). He declares, "Surely I spoke of things I did not understand, things too wonderful for me to know" (Job 42:3).

9.4. What are Behemoth and Leviathan? The mysterious creatures Behemoth and Leviathan have defied scholarly comprehension just as they resist human capture (Job 40:24; 41:8-10). Interpreters have variously characterized them as supernatural, mythological, imaginary, or symbolic.[44] Though Clines claims the association of Behemoth and Leviathan with the hippopotamus and the crocodile, respectively, currently enjoy a majority consensus, the debate, in fact, continues.[45] Though his view that these two creatures culminate God's tour of creation as prime examples of the divine zoological creativity that dominated most of the first speech (Job 38:39–39:30) has literary appeal, and the evidence of hippos and crocodiles in Palestine between the twelfth and fourth centuries BCE gives it historical credibility,[46] unlike Leviathan (Job 41:15-17), there are chinks in its armor. Clines admits that "it would be wrong to say that Behemoth and Leviathan have no symbolic value"; that features of the creatures are "heightened, if not exaggerated," such as the depiction of Leviathan breathing fire (Job 41:19-20); that elsewhere in the Old Testament Leviathan appears as a "violent

---

[43]Von Rad, *Wisdom in Israel*, 293.
[44]See David Clines, *Job*, 3 vols. (Nashville: Thomas Nelson, 1989–2011), 3:1191.
[45]Clines, *Job*, 3:1178; cf. 1186.
[46]Clines, *Job*, 3:1179, 1185, 1187.

seven-headed sea-monster, personifying the waters of chaos, which was subdued in primeval times" (cf. Ps 74:14; Is 21:1) similar to primeval chaos monsters in other ancient Near Eastern myths; and that both figures are clearly mythological in postbiblical literature, such as 2 Esdras 6:49-52 and 2 Baruch 29:4, where Leviathan and Behemoth are devoured at the eschatological messianic banquet.[47] Even earlier in Job Leviathan appears to have a mythological referent when Job requests in his opening speech, "May those who curse days curse that day, those who are ready to rouse Leviathan" (Job 3:8). Job's curse loses much of its rhetorical force if it refers to crocodile trainers.

Some, therefore, emphasize these supernatural features of the descriptions to argue that these creatures are far more than animals. Robert Fyall takes this interpretation furthest, claiming that these creatures draw on imagery from ancient Near Eastern mythology and ultimately represent death and Satan.[48] Yet even he must acknowledge that their poetic depictions incorporate features of actual natural creatures, though he claims this suggests that "evil is rooted in the natural world."[49] However, read in the context of the divine speeches, rather than in the broader theological context of Canaanite mythology before them and the fully developed picture of Satan, which only came after them (e.g., Rev 12:3, 9), it is not clear that Behemoth and Leviathan are presented as evil. God claims to have made Behemoth (Job 40:15), ranking it first among his works (Job 40:19), and compares Leviathan's power with his own (Job 41:10-11), while praising its strength and graceful form (Job 41:12). Rather than divine condemnation, both creatures are described with a certain pride, even fascination, which recalls the psalmist's description of God's creation of Leviathan to frolic in the sea (Ps 104:26) and the divine approbation of

[47]Clines, *Job*, 3:1186, 1191-92.
[48]Robert S. Fyall, *Now My Eyes Have Seen You: Images of Creation and Evil in the Book of Job* (Downers Grove, IL: InterVarsity Press, 2002), 18. See Comment 2.1, "'The Satan' and the Heavenly Council."
[49]Fyall, *Now My Eyes*, 27.

even his creation of "sea monsters," using a parallel term, as "good" (Gen 1:21). Therefore, William Brown argues, "Whatever they are, these larger-than-life beasts are the quintessential embodiments of the wild; they are highly esteemed rather than deeply loathed by God."[50]

As with so much else in Job, the ambivalence of the depictions of Behemoth and Leviathan supports, rather than undercuts, their rhetorical role in the book. The author of Job masterfully combines the two strains of biblical representation of Leviathan elsewhere in the Old Testament. At points, Leviathan is presented as a terrifying chaos monster akin to those in other ancient Near Eastern myths,[51] but at other points, to demonstrate God's superiority, Leviathan is reduced to a lowly creature, a divine plaything. In the divine speeches, both traditions mutually reinforce one another. From Job's perspective, Leviathan is terrifying, but from God's, it is a harmless pet (Job 41:5). Though Behemoth does not appear elsewhere in the Bible, his description here reflects a similar dynamic. The mixture of natural and mythological elements reflect these dual perspectives. The natural elements also make these creatures more concrete, and therefore imaginable and real to Job, but the throbbing exaggeration and hyperbole of their descriptions communicates the fear they create. Together, whether natural or supernatural, they personify the terror of a world beyond human control, while communicating the peace that comes with realizing that even chaos is not beyond divine sovereignty.

---

[50]William P. Brown, *Wisdom's Wonder: Character, Creation, and Crisis in the Bible's Wisdom Literature* (Grand Rapids, MI: Eerdmans, 2014), 116.

[51]See also the closely associated creatures Rahab (Job 9:13; 26:12; Ps 89:10; Is 51:9) and *tannin* (Job 7:12; Ps 74:13; Is 27:1; Ezek 29:3; 32:2).

ten

JUSTICE AFTER ALL?

JOB 42:7-22

After Job had prayed for his friends, the LORD restored his fortunes
and gave him twice as much as he had before.

JOB 42:10

So, THIS IS IT—the final stop in our long journey through the book of Job. We've come a long way. We were first introduced to Job forty-two chapters ago as a man who "was blameless and upright; he feared God and shunned evil" (Job 1:1). As was fitting for such a righteous man, he was blessed in every way with abundant wealth, a thriving family, and high social standing. Job was, we were told, "the greatest man among all the people of the East" (Job 1:3).

But then we were taken into the heavenly courts, where the satanic accuser presents "the cynic's taunt," posing the central question posed by the book of Job—"Does Job fear God for nothing?"—which is really the question, Is there a God who is worthy of our worship, our love, and our trust—regardless of our circumstances?

Job's faith is put to the test, and he wrestles with God with a defiant persistence. And he does not let go until he receives a blessing—when God himself reveals himself as a God whose wise rule of the cosmos is way beyond human understanding. Job finally gets the point:

> Surely I spoke of things I did not understand,
>> things too wonderful for me to know. (Job 42:3)
>
> . . .
>
> My ears had heard of you
>> but now my eyes have seen you. (Job 42:5)

This new vision of the greatness of God—this deepened fear of God—is enough. Job is humbled. He relents. He protests no more. God does what the friends could not do—he comforts Job and rescues him from his mourning in dust and ashes. The cynic has been debunked, for Job's faith has survived, and fear of God for his own sake, not for the blessings he bestows, is proven possible. There really is such a thing as goodness, truth, and beauty, found in God himself. Job's persevering faith testifies to it.

And in the process, the notion that people always get what they deserve, at least in an immediate and quantifiable sense, is refuted. There can be such a thing as innocent suffering, for Job did not deserve the suffering he received. Trouble comes to the righteous and the unrighteous alike.

For many, where we ended the last chapter is the perfect conclusion to our story. It reflects the reality we see in our world. The good do suffer—sometimes tragically. There is no necessary connection at all between godliness and material blessing, between righteousness and rewards. Isn't that the final lesson of Job's story?

If so, then doesn't the epilogue of Job 42:7-17 ruin it all? Doesn't God's double restoration of all that Job lost produce a "happily ever after" ending that contradicts one of the central messages of the book? As one commentator put it, "God turns out to be Father Christmas after all."[1] Some even argue that this happy ending must have been tacked on by some later writer to give this unorthodox

---

[1] R. N. Whybray, *Two Jewish Theologies: Job and Ecclesiastes* (Hull, UK: University of Hull, 1980), 5-6.

book a more orthodox resolution.[2] We will address the objection that this narrative ending doesn't fit with the rest of the book, as we look at this passage in two parts—first God's vindication of Job and then his blessing of him. Finally, we consider what this closing scene adds to this drama of Job.

GOD'S VINDICATION OF JOB (JOB 42:7-9)

The first part of our passage presents an ironic twist. All along, Job's three friends Eliphaz, Bildad, and Zophar were sure that Job must have sinned to deserve the suffering he was enduring. They were offended by his words, which, in their minds, were tantamount to blasphemy, and they urged him to repent. Now the tables are turned. In his rebuke of the three friends, the Lord refers to Job four times as his "servant"—a title of honor given in the Old Testament to the likes of Abraham, Moses, and David. And the Lord affirms twice that it was Job, and not his three friends, who had spoken rightly about him.[3] Now these three friends must humble themselves and ask Job to pray for them, and they must offer a very substantial sacrifice—"seven bulls and seven rams"—so that they might be forgiven for their false words.

Just think of it—Job has just risen from the ash heap and come out of his state of mourning, but nothing has been said about any restoration at this point. He is still poor and disgraced in the community, with his skin covered in painful boils. But he is to serve as their priestly mediator before God. The tables have turned indeed! This vindication of Job is confirmed when we read that "the LORD accepted Job's prayer" (Job 42:9).

Now there is no doubt; Job did fear God "for nothing." For at this point, he still has nothing—nothing but his faith that God is great

---

[2]See Comment 10.1, "The Epilogue as an Addition?"
[3]See Comment 10.2, "God's Verdict (Job 42:7-8)."

and God is good, and that God is worthy of our worship, our love, and our trust. The cynical satanic accuser has been proven wrong. And not only Job, but the Lord God himself has been vindicated and, we might say, glorified. God has been glorified through the faithfulness of his servant Job.

God's glory through our faithfulness. Let's step back for a moment. Has it ever occurred to you that sometimes hard things can come into your life that you may never understand, but that in some mysterious way can bring glory to God? Remember, that's how Jesus described one situation of suffering (Jn 9:2-3).

Have you ever thought that this universe is like a grand theater, and this world is a stage on which we perform as actors? Could it be that human history, and our own lives, are like a dramatic production viewed by the angels? Each day, in each little decision we make—whether to love God or ourselves, whether to choose what is good or what is bad, whether to treat other people with dignity or not—it is all on display in the heavenly realms. There is a cosmic significance of which we have no conception. We are all like Job—engaged in a mysterious cosmic battle, as every day our faith is put to the test, and God himself is honored when we trust, obey, and worship him as the great and glorious God that he is.

It is an awesome thought. But be assured, we are not alone in this struggle. We have one who is on our side—Jesus our Savior. Consider that little window into this other world that we get in Luke's Gospel. At his Last Supper with his disciples, Jesus knows that they will desert him. He says this: "Simon, Simon, Satan has asked to sift all of you as wheat. But I have prayed for you, Simon, that your faith may not fail. And when you have turned back, strengthen your brothers" (Lk 22:31-32). Be encouraged, we have one who has ascended into heaven and who ever lives to intercede for us. "I have prayed for you, Simon, that your faith may not fail." The divine director of this cosmic drama is also its author, and he is able to save us completely (Heb 7:25; Rom 8:34).

GOD'S BLESSING OF JOB

Well, you might think—*this* is where the book should end, here in Job 42:9. Job is vindicated before his friends, and God himself has been proven right before Satan. But it's not the end, though it *could* be. But, because of the character of God, it *shouldn't* be the end. For beginning in Job 42:10 we see that God not only vindicates Job, he also blesses him, richly. "After Job had prayed for his friends, the LORD restored his fortunes and gave him twice as much as he had before."

And it is entirely fitting and appropriate that this should happen. First, the Lord's consolation of Job, bringing him out of his state of mourning, finds its tangible expression, as Job's relationships are restored: "All his brothers and sisters and everyone who had known him before came and ate with him in his house. They comforted and consoled him over all the trouble the LORD had brought upon him."[4] Then Job's wealth begins to be rebuilt. "And each one gave him a piece of silver and a gold ring" (Job 42:11). Finally, "the LORD blessed the latter part of Job's life more than the former part. He had fourteen thousand sheep, six thousand camels, a thousand yoke of oxen and a thousand donkeys. And he also had seven sons and three daughters" (Job 42:12-13). His life was twice as good as before.

After his life is restored, there's no mention of him offering preemptive sacrifices for his children. Anxiety has been replaced with joyful generosity, as Job transcends cultural expectations to offer his three daughters an inheritance with their brothers. The particular attention given to the daughters in Job 42:14-15 is unexpected. First, their beauty is emphasized—"Nowhere in all the land were there

---

[4]See Comment 10.3, "God and Evil (Job 42:11)."

found women as beautiful as Job's daughters." And their names re-inforce this theme: Jemimah ("turtle dove"), Keziah ("cinnamon"), Keren-happuch ("eye-makeup"). These daughters are the epitome of loveliness.

Then we are told that "their father granted them an inheritance along with their brothers" (Job 42:15). This was highly unusual in that culture, and it may be both a sign of the abundance that Job enjoyed and of the generosity of his heart.

"After this, Job lived a hundred and forty years"—twice the usual allotment of three score and ten (cf. Ps 90:10). "He saw his children and their children to the fourth generation. And so Job died, an old man and full of years" (Job 42:16-17). The book of Job, all along a book of extremes, ends with Job as a man of extreme blessing from God.

God's blessing and God's character. God's blessing of Job at the end is not necessary, but it is certainly fitting, for it rightly displays the character of God. The God of the Bible is not a tyrant; he is not capricious, or temperamental, or whimsical. And he is certainly not wicked. God takes no pleasure in his servants' suffering. That's not who he is. And Job, despite his undeserved suffering, never cursed God, because that's not who he believed God to be. Job knew that God was just, that he was worthy of his trust, and that his purposes were good. He just didn't understand how God's goodness could be squared with how he was being treated. But when God graciously appeared to him and pointed him to the wondrous ways that he rules over and cares for his creation, that was enough for Job. He realized that God in his greatness had reasons for his actions that were far beyond Job's pay grade—"Surely I spoke of things I did not understand, things too wonderful for me to know" (Job 42:3).

That declaration of Job, in a sense, brought to fulfillment the reason for Job's suffering—he had proven that authentic faith was possible. That confession demonstrated that in Job's mind God was worthy of worship even if he didn't pour out his blessing on him. Job's fear of God had deepened such that he could trust him for what was beyond his understanding.

Job and the friends were both right in believing that God was just, but they were both wrong in thinking that he had to demonstrate that justice in immediate ways that we could always understand. That's what Job had come to see.

God didn't have to bless Job as he does in the end, but it is entirely appropriate that he did, because that blessing displays the kind of God he is. Some suggest that the double blessing that Job receives reflects the Mosaic law of restitution found in the book of Exodus that requires double compensation for theft (Ex 22:4). God somehow has to make it up to poor Job. Maybe. But that seems to put God right back in a little box similar to what Job's friends tried to put him in in the first place. God is not obligated to do anything. "Who has ever given to God that he should repay them?" (Rom 11:35). I think it better to see the double blessing as simply an expression of the abundant grace of God that flows out of his goodness—a goodness that he longs to pour out on those who come to him in faith.

Job's reward? You can call it a reward if you like—the letter to the Hebrews assures us that God does "reward . . . those who earnestly seek him" (Heb 11:6). But it is not a mercenary reward, like the money earned by a soldier for hire. No, it is a reward that is intrinsically tied up with the act itself—more like the satisfaction of victory that a valiant soldier might receive in defending his homeland from attack. I married my wife because I loved her, because I found joy in her, not for any external reward I might get. But in loving her, I have received great reward in terms of the companionship we have enjoyed over the forty years of our marriage.[5]

---

[5]On this notion of "reward," see C. S. Lewis, *The Weight of Glory and Other Addresses*, rev. ed. (New York: HarperOne, 1980 [1949]), 26-27.

In the same way, there is great reward in loving God. That is true simply because of the kind of God he is and the fact that he has made us to enjoy him. As a good and gracious God, he delights in pouring out his blessing on his children. That's what the ending sets before our eyes—in the very visible, material terms of sheep, camels, goats, lots of children and grandchildren, and long life.

God is good to Job, because he is a good and gracious God. That's the lesson that James in the New Testament takes from it— "You have heard of Job's perseverance and have seen what the Lord finally brought about. The Lord is full of compassion and mercy" (Jas 5:10-11).

Yes, this story of Job has a happy ending. And it is true that this is not the way things always end for God's people—at least not in this life. That's why James says we "have seen what the Lord *finally* brought about"—that is, "in the end."[6] The book of Job didn't have to end with Job receiving such a rich blessing, but it is right that it does. It is suitable simply because there is great reward in being faithful to God, and in the end, God will be *seen* to be just in all his ways, and he will show himself to be full of compassion and mercy. You can be sure of it.

This ending of this book points us to an even greater ending. It's the ending of the whole Bible when, at the end of this age, the risen Christ will come in glory to gather his people to himself, raise his sons and daughters from the grave, and usher in a new heaven and a new earth. He will wipe every tear from our eyes. And there will be no more death or mourning or crying or pain (Rev 21:4).

Enjoying the blessing of God forever in heavenly glory is the intrinsic reward that comes with persevering in faith to the end. That's why Paul can say, "I consider that our present sufferings are

---

[6]Greek: *to telos*, though ESV, NRSV have "the purpose" of the Lord.

not worth comparing with the glory that will be revealed in us"
(Rom 8:18). That reward of resurrected glory is fitting for all those
whose first desire is to bring glory to God.

So we've come to the end of our long journey. We've traveled
with Job on his long road of suffering and pain; we've shared in his
struggle; and now we come to his blessed end. What have
we learned?

TWO FINAL LESSONS

I close with two final lessons. First, we have learned that there can
be great mystery in the ways of God in the world. We dare not think
that we can always know what God is up to in the circumstances of
our lives. Job never did. God has his purposes in the running of his
universe that are simply beyond our limited comprehension. Our
suffering need not be the result of our sin—Job's wasn't. On the
contrary, like Job, we may suffer because of our righteousness. Jesus
called such people blessed (Mt 5:10).

God's ways are not our ways, and it is enough for us to acknowledge that fact and trust him anyway. After all, he chose to save
the world by allowing his own Son to die an unjust and painful
death. He knows our pain; he's been there. Our view of God must
be big enough that we can be satisfied in saying he is God, and I am
not. As someone has said, "If God were small enough to be understood, he wouldn't be big enough to be worshipped."[7]

But again, let me emphasize, we are not fatalists, who grudgingly
submit to some irresistible and impersonal force. The fatalist looks
at their circumstances and says, "Oh well, what will be, will be.
Tough luck." No, we are children of our heavenly Father. We know
that the God who created us and all things also loves us. We are

---

[7]Evelyn Underhill, cited in Timothy Keller, *Walking with God Through Pain and Suffering* (New
York: Dutton, 2013), 255.

encouraged to come to him with our honest thoughts and real desires. We can ask him what he is doing. And sometimes we can tell him that we don't *like* what he's doing.

Because we are not fatalists in our relationship with God, Job encourages us to be realists—we can be real in our emotional response to the real hardships we face in this fallen world.

Job may be most famous for his pious phrases in the opening chapters:

Naked I came from my mother's womb,
    and naked I will depart.
The LORD gave and the LORD has taken away;
    Blessed be the name of the Lord! (Job 1:21)

That may be what we ought to say, and what we want to say. But in the long central section of the book Job shows us in very realistic terms what we will all feel like saying and, on occasion, will say: "Why, Lord? Why are you allowing this to happen in my life? How long, Lord? How long must I wait until you make this right?" This book gives us permission to be honest with God. Job gives us a model of mournful lament and even of faithful protest.

Some people don't like that aspect of the book. They are offended by it, and in so doing, they line up more with Job's friends than with Job. In an essay by Søren Kierkegaard, a young man wonders why people want to cover up that aspect of the book. He addresses Job directly:

No, . . . you became the voice of the suffering, the cry of the grief-stricken, the shriek of the terrified, and a relief to all who bore their torment in silence, a faithful witness to all the affliction and laceration there can be in a heart, an unfailing spokesman who dared to lament "in bitterness of soul" and to strive with God. Why is this kept secret? Woe to him who . . .

would cunningly cheat the sorrowing of sorrow's temporary comfort in airing its sorrow and quarreling with God.[8]

There is a place for sorrow, for lament, and even for protest in the life of a faithful believer.

I can assure you, your faith will be tested, for in this world you will suffer. Job shows us that even in our sorrow, we have grounds for hope. So don't give up; don't give in; "as you know, we count as blessed those who have persevered. You have heard of Job's perseverance and have seen what the Lord finally brought about. The Lord is full of compassion and mercy" (Jas 5:11).

DIGGING DEEPER

10.1. The epilogue as an addition? Some readers are not happy with the happy ending that the epilogue provides to the book. For those who consider the book a denunciation of the doctrine of retribution, the reward Job appears to receive for his righteousness seems to acknowledge that the friends (and the Satan) were, in fact, right all along. And for those who envision the book to be a celebration of Job's defiance against divine injustice, Job's spiritual and social reconciliation in the epilogue is considered an anticlimax. Some, therefore, translate their preference for Job to tell another type of story than it does into the view that the epilogue is a secondary addition that mars the book's original form.[9]

No textual evidence exists that the book ever existed without the epilogue, leaving the claim of secondary addition as pure conjecture. Further, Job 42:7-9 certainly presupposes the dialogue and contributes to the interweaving of the two sections, leaving them not easily separable.[10] Even so, "incongruities" undeniably exist

---

[8]Søren Kierkegaard, *Fear and Trembling: Repetition*, trans. Howard V. Hong and Edna H. Hong, Kierkegaard's Writings 6 (Princeton, NJ: Princeton University Press, 1983), 207.
[9]See David Clines, *Job*, 3 vols. (Nashville: Thomas Nelson, 1989–2011), 3:1230.
[10]Clines, *Job*, 3:1234.

between these transitional verses and the dialogue preceding them, which, if they do not "frustrate attempts to read the book as a single coherent narrative,"[11] at least make doing so difficult. Though Newsom sees these interpretive difficulties as contributing to the book's intentional design to create a dialogue of voices that cannot be harmonized, most readers who struggle to accept the epilogue do so because it harmonizes the cacophony of voices competing throughout the previous chapters too well. But perhaps this is the point. If God is indeed good, just, and sovereign, and if Job is indeed righteous, then the prosperity Job enjoys at the end of the book is precisely what we should expect, as Job's final condition vindicates both God's faith in Job and Job's faith in God.

10.2. God's verdict (Job 42:7-8). The interpretation of the entire book hinges on the proper translation of Job's response to the divine speeches and the divine verdict declared in the following verses (Job 42:6, 7-8). The rejection of the friends' speech in Job 42:7-8 is surprising, since their consistent defense of divine justice certainly seems to ring true, but God's approval of Job's speech—shot through with protest, complaint, and even accusation—is completely shocking. Unsurprisingly, interpreters have struggled with how to interpret these verses. Many, unable to reconcile God's verdict with the dialogue, simply argue that God is not referring to what Job and the friends have said there. Frequently, scholars claim that this verdict belongs to an earlier version of the book without the dialogue. God is approving only Job's pious proclamations of faith in the prologue. Though the friends never speak in the prologue, those who take this view imagine that the friends originally made erroneous arguments, which were later replaced by those in the dialogue. Others argue that God is only referring to Job's submissive response to the divine speeches (Job 42:2-6). However, this view also runs into the

---

[11]Carol A. Newsom, "The Book of Job," in *1 & 2 Maccabees, Introduction to Hebrew Poetry, Job, Psalms* (Nashville: Abingdon, 1996), 323.

problem of the contrast God creates between Job's speech and that of the friends. Further, as David Frankel observes, "how can God blame Job's friends for failing to repent as Job does, when Job's repentance comes in the wake of a frontal assault directed squarely at him by God? Surely the friends would have similarly repented had they been so addressed by God beforehand."[12]

Even if one decides to read the text in the more natural sense of God's judgment on the dialogue between Job and the friends, the merits on which they are judged are not clear. First, the Hebrew word *nekhonah*, translated "truth" in the NIV, could be understood in a number of different ways, including as an adverb, such that God approves not of the content of Job's speeches, but his way of speaking "truthfully," "honestly," or "sincerely." This would indicate "that God values the integrity of the impatient protester and abhors the hypocrites who would heap accusations on a tormented soul to uphold their theological position."[13]

Second, the preposition *'el*, translated "about" in the NIV, more commonly has the meaning "to" in biblical Hebrew, so some argue that God is not judging the content of the speeches of Job and the friends but to whom they were directed. In the dialogue, only Job directly addresses his speech *to* God, while the friends are content to speak to Job about God.[14] Both speaking honestly and speaking to God are valued elsewhere in the Old Testament, but not universally so. In fact, at issue in the wager is whether Job will curse God "to his face"; doing so sincerely would only make this failure of faith worse. On the standard set in the book, the content of what one says sincerely to God is vitally important. There is also little to suggest that the friends are not sincere in their views or that they would be expected to speak to God, when their role is

[12]David Daniel Frankel, "The Speech About God in Job 42: 7-8: A Contribution to the Coherence of the Book of Job," *Hebrew Union College Annual* 82 (2012): 8n24.
[13]Marvin H. Pope, *Job* (Garden City, NY: Doubleday, 1965), 290.
[14]See Elaine A. Phillips, "Speaking Truthfully: Job's Friends and Job," *Bulletin for Biblical Research* (2008): 31-43.

to comfort Job. Thus, even though it violates our expectations (which, by now, should not surprise us as readers of this challenging book), these verses are best understood as an affirmation of Job's protests over the friends' pious platitudes.

However, this does not resolve the translational difficulties in these verses completely. Perhaps the most surprising feature of this passage lurks below the surface of most English translations.[15] According to the NIV, for example, in Job 42:8, God tells Eliphaz that he will accept Job's prayer on his behalf "and not deal with you according to your folly." However, that Hebrew phrase is more literally translated "not do with you a folly." Elsewhere in the Old Testament, this phrase describes outrageous acts, such as rape (Gen 34:7) and theft of consecrated goods (Josh 7:15). The act God seems to allude to here is the destruction of the friends, as the Greek translation of the phrase seems to reflect ("I would have destroyed you" [NETS]). Though attributing "folly" to God may cause some readers discomfort, other Old Testament texts describe God as deceptive (1 Kings 22:19-23; Jer 20:7-13; Ezek 14:1-14), the giver of laws that are not good (Ezek 20:25), and the creator of evil (Is 45:7). Only a few verses later in Job, the narrator will attribute "evil" to God (Job 42:11), and in the prologue God admits to allowing the Satan to afflict Job "without cause" (Job 2:3).[16] Therefore, attempting to cover up expressions of divine emotion, or "theopathism," is "exegetically foolish."[17]

However, the rhetorical purpose of this theopathism must be recognized. God is expressing the intensity of his anger with Job's friends. Significantly, this "folly" is only mentioned as a hypothetical, which God invites Eliphaz to negate via Job's intercession. There is biblical precedent for this, as well.[18] In Exodus 32:10, while

---

[15]See Philippe Guillaume and Michael Schunck, "Job's Intercession: Antidote to Divine Folly," *Biblica* 88 (2007): 457-72.

[16]See Comments 2.3, "Calvin on Satan" and 10.3, "God and Evil (Job 42:11)."

[17]Guillaume and Schunck, "Job's Intercession," 460.

[18]See Comment 7.5, "The Biblical Tradition of Defiant Faith."

the Israelites are frolicking before the golden calf, God commands Moses, "Now leave me alone so that my anger may burn against them and that I may destroy them." In so doing, God acknowledges the power of Moses's intervention to dissuade divine wrath. Though God commands Moses not to intercede on behalf of the people, by telling Moses his plan to punish the people, God invites Moses to do just that. And Moses's intercession does indeed lead God to relent (Ex 32:11-14). Similarly, God debates telling Abraham his plan to destroy Sodom and Gomorrah, but then decides that Abraham's calling to guide future generations in "doing what is right and just" legitimates including him in the divine deliberation (Gen 18:17-19). Hearing of God's plan, Abraham intervenes on behalf of any righteous people in the cities and God acquiesces. Three times, God, determined to destroy Judah for her sin, orders Jeremiah not to pray for them (Jer 7:16; 11:14; 14:11). Though God claims he will not listen, his command not even to attempt to change his mind through prayer suggests that due to the power of intercessory prayer he might, but does not want to.

On this reading of Job 42:7-8, however, God explicitly requests such intercession to turn away his outrageous anger. As Calvin, no lackluster advocate for God's sovereignty, observes, God uses means, even human means, in his providential direction of events, which could include prayer.[19] Though this interpretation is not without its theological difficulties, its alignment with this biblical tradition of defiant faith so prominent in the book invites its careful consideration.

10.3. God and evil (Job 42:11). Glinting ominously amid the gauzy account of Job's restoration is a mention of "all the evil [*ra'ah*] that the LORD had brought" on Job (Job 42:11 NRSV). The fact that the friends are not consoling Job for the "evil" that the Satan brought on him suggests either that the narrator is representing the view

---

[19]See John Calvin, *Institutes of the Christian Religion*, ed. John T. McNeil (Louisville, KY: Westminster John Knox Press, 1960), 1.17.4, 1:187.

of Job's acquaintances, who were not privy to the working of the divine council,[20] or that the narrator considers the Lord ultimately responsible for Job's afflictions despite the Satan or the Sabeans and Chaldeans being their immediate cause.[21] This attribution of evil to God is theologically problematic in light of the consistent belief in both Jewish and Christian tradition that God is perfectly good and "cannot be tempted by evil" (Jas 1:13).

Some English translations, such as the NIV, attempt to sweep this untidy detail under the rug by translating *ra'ah* as "trouble," which is a meaning the word will certainly bear (e.g., Ps 34:19; 88:4). Lindsay Wilson evades the challenging theological implications of this verse by arguing that *ra'ah* is "used widely in the OT to describe nonmoral evils like natural disasters."[22] This won't quite do, however, since the theft of Job's livestock and murder of his servants by Sabean and Chaldean raiding parties are not nonmoral natural disasters (Job 1:15, 17). Calling such deeds anything less than evil is an injustice to their victims and a failure of moral clarity. If the author wanted to avoid the suggestion that God brought "evil," there are other words he could have chosen, such as *'amal*, *rogez*, or *tsar*, translated "trouble" in, for example, Job 3:10; 14:1; and 38:23, respectively, in the NIV. Job himself attributes *ra'ah* to God in Job 2:10 with the author's approval. Other biblical texts share this view, with Isaiah presenting God forthrightly declaring,

> I form the light and create darkness,
> > I bring prosperity and create disaster [*ra'ah*];
> > I, the LORD, do all these things. (Is 45:7; also Jer 21:10)

This passage bears a striking similarity to Job's complaint in Job 30:26, in which the NIV does translate *ra'ah* as "evil": "Yet when

---

[20]Harold Henry Rowley, *Job*, rev. ed. (Grand Rapids, MI: Eerdmans, 1976), 268.

[21]Norman Habel, *The Book of Job* (London: SCM, 1985), 299; Lindsay Wilson, *Job* (Grand Rapids, MI: Eerdmans, 2015), 585; Clines, *Job*, 3:1236.

[22]Wilson, *Job*, 209.

I hoped for good, evil [ra'ah] came; when I looked for light, then came darkness."

The Lord takes credit for bringing ra'ah, using the exact Hebrew phrase used in Job, in Jeremiah 44:2 and Ezekiel 14:22 when speaking of the exile. The Ezekiel passage is particularly significant, since it speaks of "consolation" regarding this "disaster" and immediately follows the only other mention of Job in the Old Testament, as it describes him as unable (with Noah and Daniel or Dan'el) to avert it for any but themselves (Ezek 14:14-20). Further, Ezekiel claims this consolation will result from the conduct of the remnant who survived the exile, which will make clear, the Lord claims, "that I have done nothing in it without cause [khinnam]" (Ezek 14:23). This creates a fascinating parallel with the Lord's admission to the Satan in the prologue of Job, "you incited me against him to ruin him without any reason [khinnam]" (Job 2:3). Whereas, in Job, God claims that Job's piety proves that he had done nothing in the past to deserve his suffering, in Ezekiel, God claims the future behavior of the remnant will prove that the exile was not without justification. The question looming in Job is this: Will some future good ensure that Job's suffering, though undeserved, is not in vain?[23]

Human language and even human thought fails to comprehend the nuances of the perplexing relationship between God's goodness, sovereignty, and the existence of evil in the world.[24] The furthest the Bible pushes into this mystery is Joseph's response to his brothers, in which he claims that God intended good in the "harm [ra'ah]" they intended for him (Gen 50:20). This event, then, is both evil and good, and God's sovereignty is not sacrificed to maintain his goodness.[25]

Rarely, however, is the Bible this nuanced. At times, in fact, in the service of particular rhetorical purposes, Old Testament writers

---

[23]See Comment 8.4, "Suffering as Educational."
[24]See Comment 9.3, "Discounting a Dichotomous Theology (Job 40:8)."
[25]See also Acts 2:24, "The Divine Gambit" in chap. 2, and Comment 2.3, "Calvin on Satan."

emphasize divine sovereignty, even to the possible detriment of the reader's perception of God's goodness. God's claim to bring both good and evil in Isaiah 45:7 is made in the midst of the contest between the Lord and the gods of Babylon, in which Isaiah aims to make clear, as the Lord says in the previous verse, "I am the Lord, and there is no other" (Is 45:6). The repeated affirmation that God has brought the "disaster" (*ra'ah*) of the exile in 2 Kings (2 Kings 21:12; 22:16) and Jeremiah (e.g., Jer 11:11; 16:10; 19:3, 15; 35:17; 39:16; 40:2; 44:2, 11) intends to make clear that Jerusalem's fall is ultimately the result of divine punishment and not merely of Babylonian aggression. It was not for nothing (*khinnam*; though see Is 52:2, 5). As the book of Lamentations makes abundantly clear, that does not mean that the exile was not also evil; calling the Babylonians' depredations of daughter Jerusalem merely "trouble" is an injustice to her suffering. Jeremiah and 2 Kings, however, have good reason for the theological emphasis they give them.

What rhetorical purpose, then, does the attribution of all the evils Job experienced to the Lord serve in the epilogue? Throughout the dialogue, the friends have emphasized that the evil Job experienced came from Job himself, as a result of his sin, but Job claims that God is responsible. When God appears, he doesn't deny his responsibility but emphasizes his sovereignty over all that happens in his creation, including the terrors of Behemoth and Leviathan. In the epilogue, then, the narrator reinforces Job's perspective in such a way that the reader is forced to wrestle with precisely the question with which Job had to grapple: Can a God who is sovereign over the evil we face be trusted as good? Will we believe that one day, like Job or Joseph, we will see the good divine purposes behind the evils we encounter? Can we trust that our suffering will not be for nothing?

THE ULTIMATE EPILOGUE

JOB, JESUS, AND OUR GREAT HOPE

I know that my redeemer lives.

JOB 19:25

WE HAVE WRESTLED WITH JOB in his long struggle of faith, and I trust, like Jacob, we have been blessed. Job's painful affliction, which came to him "without cause," was a test of his trust in the trustworthiness of God. Even in his lament and protest, Job stands as a challenging example of faithful endurance. But as we close, we must see how our hero points beyond himself to the One who was to come. For it is Jesus, not Job, who is the supreme ground of our faith and the certain basis of our great hope, even as we live in a fallen world full of pain and suffering. The gospel of Jesus Christ provides the ultimate epilogue to Job's story, and ours.

GOD HAS PURPOSES THAT WE CANNOT COMPREHEND

In the end, God appears to Job, but in his divine speeches, he never answers Job's questions or explains the reason behind Job's suffering. Instead, God interrogates Job, and in so doing, he reveals himself in all his power and glory as the Creator and ruler of all creation who cares for even the most obscure of his wild creatures. With this humbling encounter with Almighty God, Job is satisfied that God has purposes that we simply cannot comprehend.

And aren't the mysterious ways of God on display all the more in the suffering of Jesus? To his disciples, his vicious death seemed pointless and unjustified. Jesus' suffering was evil in the deepest sense. But on that first Easter morning, the curtain was pulled back. The mysterious purpose of God was revealed. Jesus' innocent suffering was a part of a divine plan that none of us could have ever imagined. His resurrection from the grave declared that Jesus didn't die for his own sin, but for ours. The Son of God and Savior of the world had to suffer the most evil and unjust treatment humanly possible to accomplish what only God could do. The cross of Christ, which to the world is foolishness and a scandal, is a mysterious work of God displaying a wisdom grasped only in faith.

GOD CAN USE SUFFERING TO BRING
ABOUT GREAT GOOD

Let's be clear—there's nothing good about suffering itself. As C. S. Lewis reminds us, "Pain hurts. That is what the word means."[1] But the truth remains: God can use suffering to bring about great good. That happened in Job's life. He had an encounter with God that few have ever known, and his story not only brought glory to God, it has also encouraged countless millions for millennia.

How much more is that true in the suffering of our Lord Jesus, for as the Scripture affirms, "by his wounds we are healed" (Is 53:5). The world's greatest evil—the cruel crucifixion of the Son of God— brought about the world's greatest good: the redemption of God's people and the ultimate restoration of creation itself. If God can do that, then he can do anything.

He's been called the Great Alchemist, with the power to transform ugly affliction into the beauty of the refined gold of deep faith. Hymn writer Margaret Clarkson, who endured a childhood of painful

---

[1]C. S. Lewis, *The Problem of Pain* (London: Collins, 1940), 93.

headaches and crippling arthritis, expresses that well in her hymn "O Father, You Are Sovereign." In the third stanza she describes her God as "The Lord of human pain, Transmuting earthly sorrow To gold of heavenly gain." The hymn concludes:

All evil overruling,
As none but Conqueror could,
Your love pursues its purpose—
Our souls' eternal good.[2]

Back in the second chapter, I referred to the story Jerry Sittser tells in his book *A Grace Disguised* of his life after a car accident took the lives of his wife, mother, and daughter and left his son critically injured. He struggled mightily, and he writes honestly about his questions and doubts, but over time, Sittser came to recognize that God's grace can still triumph over great evil. He refers to Joseph's words to his brothers who had sold him into slavery: "You intended to harm me, but God intended it for good to accomplish what is now being done, the saving of many lives" (Gen 50:20). Sittser writes,

The Joseph story helps us to see that our own tragedies can be a very bad chapter in a very good book. The terror of randomness is enveloped by the mysterious purposes of God. In the end, life turns out to be good, although the journey to get there may be circuitous and difficult.

I have often imagined my own story fitting into some greater scheme, the half of which I may never fathom. I simply do not see the bigger picture, but I choose to believe that there is a bigger picture and that my loss is part of some wonderful story authored by God himself.[3]

[2]Margaret Clarkson, *Destined for Glory: The Meaning of Suffering* (Grand Rapids: Eerdmans and Marshalls, 1983), xii.
[3]Jerry L. Sittser, *A Grace Disguised: How the Soul Grows Through Loss* (Grand Rapids, MI: Zondervan, 2004), 118.

We can pray that when suffering comes into our lives, we can choose to believe the same things. We can be encouraged that God's bigger picture can include his mysterious work of transforming the evil of a cross into heavenly glory.

IN THE MIDST OF SUFFERING,
ONLY GOD HIMSELF CAN MEET OUR DEEPEST NEED

More than anything, in our suffering we long for meaning. I can endure the pain of the dentist's drill when I believe it will relieve my toothache. The statement attributed to Friedrich Nietzsche rings true—"It is not so much the suffering as the senselessness of it that is unendurable."[4]

A relationship with God can provide the meaning that makes any suffering endurable. But this makes the feeling of being abandoned by God, which often accompanies suffering, all the more painful. If God is indeed sovereign over his creation, and nothing happens apart from his will, then certainly he could come to our aid and relieve us of our pain. So why doesn't he?

In the midst of such personal struggle we don't need a theology seminar, we need a word from God himself. Job felt personally betrayed by the treatment he was receiving, and more than anything, he longed to meet with God. Job was convinced that since ultimately God was the source of his problem, only God could provide the solution. In the midst of suffering, God must be more than a concept, an idea, a proposition; he must become a person to you—a person you are willing to trust with your very life. Only God himself can meet our deepest need.

The gospel declares that in Jesus Christ, God has drawn near to us. The eternal Word of God has come as a human person (Jn 1:14).

---

[4]Paraphrased by Nicolas Berdyaev, *The Destiny of Man*, trans. Natalie Duddington (United Kingdom: G. Bles, 1959), 119.

God might have sent a mere messenger, an angel, to us; instead, he came personally in the form of his Son. And in a mysterious way, this Jesus Christ—who is Immanuel, God with us—makes himself known personally today by his Spirit whom he sends into the world to unite us to himself. He can shine the warmth of his light into the cold darkness of your suffering.

IN CHRIST, GOD SHARES IN OUR SUFFERING

As we consider the gospel, we see that in Christ, God not only draws near to us; in Christ, God also shares in our suffering. In Jesus Christ, God himself has entered into our world of pain. Jesus suffered physically, dying the horrible death of crucifixion—with the nails driven through his hands and feet. But even more importantly, he endured unbearable *spiritual* suffering. And here we can only speculate— based on his own Job-like cry of dereliction from the cross—"My God, my God, why have you forsaken me?" (Mt 27:46).

Undoubtedly, as John Stott comments, "The real sting of [our] suffering is not misfortune itself, nor even the pain of it or the injustice of it, but the apparent God-forsakenness of it. Pain is endurable, but the seeming indifference of God is not."[5] But that is precisely where the cross comes in. God is not distant; he is not aloof, sitting in some heavenly deck chair watching us squirm in agony in this wicked earthly life. He himself has entered into our experience; in Christ, he shares our suffering and our pain. In Christ, he has taken that pain, once and for all, on himself. And that fact changes our perception of God forever.

Helmut Thielicke, the German theologian, observes that if you look at a piece of cloth through a magnifying glass, the threads of fabric are clear in the middle and blurred at the edges. But the clarity in the middle leads us to believe that the edges must also be clear, if

---

[5]John R. W. Stott, *The Cross of Christ* (Downers Grove, IL: InterVarsity Press, 1986), 329.

only we saw them rightly. So it is with the many mysterious and confusing events in our lives—events that are a blur in our minds, events that we may never understand.[6]

How and why evil ever entered into this good world God created, and why he even chose to create a world in which evil could exist are questions that may never be answered. But the blurred edges of our experience have to be interpreted by the clarity we see in the center of our faith—the cross of Christ, which proves God's loving character for all to see. "We have to learn to climb the hill called Calvary, and from that [high] ground survey all life's tragedies."[7]

In the midst of suffering, only God himself can meet our deepest need, and in Christ, God has drawn near to us, and in Christ, God shares in our suffering.

ONLY GOD IN CHRIST CAN BRING US VICTORY

But there is still one more thing that must be said. For ultimately, we want more than a God who just feels our pain; we want a God who can do something about it. Job discovered that kind of God, for in God's grace, in the end, Job's prosperity was restored twice over. God rewards those who earnestly seek him.

But let's also remember that in the end, Job died. It may have been at a ripe old age, but still, his life ended. He was still cut off from those he loved. And those he loved surely grieved his loss. But at Easter, we see the power of God to conquer the pain and suffering of this world in a far more powerful way. For the same Jesus who hung on a cross and who was laid in a tomb, also rose from the grave on the third day and was exalted to the highest place as Lord of all. He has conquered death, and he will never die again. And by uniting ourselves to him by faith we can share in his eternal destiny.

[6]Helmut Thielicke, *Christ and the Meaning of Life: A Book of Sermons and Meditations* (New York: Harper & Row, 1965), 14.
[7]Stott, *Cross of Christ*, 329.

Job gives us an example of a persevering faith that results in God's blessing. We can look to Job and be encouraged to hold on in faith in the midst of our trials. But Jesus gives us far more than a mere example. Jesus is our Advocate, our Champion, our Redeemer, and our Savior.

And isn't this just what Job longed for—some legal advocate who could state his case, some witness who could testify on his behalf, even a redeemer who would make his claim before God? Job, in his deep pain, sees the problem, and Job, in his deep longing, points us to the only solution—the solution found in the gospel of the triune God. We now have someone who "removes God's rod from [us], so that his terror would frighten [us] no more" (Job 9:34; cf. Rom 5:8-10).

As Christians we celebrate the fact that Jesus has conquered sin and death—he has gained victory over this troubled and tragic world. In Jesus Christ, God has shown his hand; and in Jesus Christ, God has revealed his face. It is a loving face, and it is a powerful hand, for in the resurrection of Jesus Christ, our God has begun to renew this fallen world. Jesus is the first fruits of the full harvest to come; he is our champion who will lead his people to victory.

Jesus' death and resurrection transforms the Christian's view of suffering. As George MacDonald puts it, the Son of God "suffered unto the death, not that men might not suffer; but that their suffering might be like his."[8] In the light of the death and resurrection of Jesus, our present suffering is like that of Jesus himself. It is but the prelude to an eternal glory. It's in the light of the resurrection of Jesus that Paul can say, "I consider that our present sufferings are not worth comparing with the glory that will be revealed in us" (Rom 8:18), and "For our light and momentary troubles are achieving for us an eternal glory that far outweighs them all" (2 Cor 4:17).

---

[8]George MacDonald, from his sermon "The Consuming Fire," www.online-literature.com /george-macdonald/unspoken-sermons/2/.

"Where, O death, is your victory?
   Where, O death, is your sting?"

The sting of death is sin, and the power of sin is the law. But thanks be to God! He gives us the victory through our Lord Jesus Christ. (1 Cor 15:55-57)

QUESTIONS FOR REFLECTION OR DISCUSSION

1. THE BOOK OF JOB

1. Read the parable of the soils in Luke 8:4-15. What kind of testing of your faith do you find most challenging? How have you responded to those tests? How can you prepare yourself to overcome them?

2. What has been your impression of the book of Job in the past? What sorts of questions does the book raise in your mind? What do you hope to learn from it?

3. What are different reasons for suffering that we find in the Bible? How do these compare with what we find in Job's case (see Job 2:3)?

4. How have you responded to suffering in your life? Have you found that it hardens your heart toward God or softens it? What makes the difference?

5. Spend time praying for those who may be suffering now— that their faith may endure and be strengthened in the process. You might want to use Paul's prayer in Colossians 1:9-14 as a guide.

2. THE CYNIC'S TAUNT

1. What evidences of cynicism have you noticed in our culture—that "distrusting, disbelieving, contemptuous,

attitude, which holds a low opinion of mankind" and which
questions the reality of true goodness, truth, and beauty?

2. In verses 1-5 Job is displayed as a godly man. How would
   you portray a godly person if you were to write your own
   "book of Job"? Why is this portrayal of Job essential to the
   story of the book?

3. Who is responsible for Job's suffering? How do you understand the Bible's depiction of "dual intentionality"—that is,
   that in the same act, the devil can intend evil, while God can
   intend good? How does this maintain the reality of evil?
   Why is it important that we not deny that God is ultimately
   sovereign over all that happens in our lives, even when it is
   sometimes hard?

4. What is the "therapeutic gospel"? How is it like the
   "prosperity gospel"?

5. Should piety lead to prosperity? Why or why not?

6. How does God's willingness to go along with Satan's taunt
   strike you? How does it provoke you? How does it draw you
   into the message of the book?

3. THE INNOCENT SUFFERER

1. When you hear some story of horrific suffering, how are you
   most likely to respond?
   a. I'm glad that didn't happen to me!
   b. What did they do to deserve that?
   c. Where was God in all that?
   d. How can they possibly cope?

2. Would the book of Job be better if it ended with chapter
   two? Why must it go on?

3. Have you ever experienced a time when your faith was
   tested? What was most difficult about it?

4. Do you find fault in the way Job responds to his suffering in Job 3? Should you?

5. Is there a place for lament in the life of the Christian? Why or Why not? How do you deal with the many psalms in which lament is so prominent?

6. Do you sing songs in worship that are beyond or higher than your experience? Is that hypocritical? How can that be helpful?

4. COLD COMFORT

1. Have you ever experienced real suffering? What did you find most helpful? What didn't help?

2. What has been your experience trying to help people who were suffering? What have you learned from it? What have you learned not to do?

3. What was wrong with the viewpoint of Job's friends regarding his suffering?

4. What do we mean by God's retributive justice? Does God always act according to his retributive justice? Why do we want to think that God always deals with people according to what they deserve?

5. What is some way that you might be able to help someone who is suffering now?

6. Who can you pray for now that God may be their comforter?

5. A SUFFERER'S PROTEST

1. In times of suffering and trial, which of these options would you be most tempted to follow?

   a. a superficial religious piety

   b. an anger toward God and a denial of God's goodness

   c. a suicidal despair in your condition

   d. an abandonment of God

2. Why do you think laments are so common in the Bible? How can lament be a helpful response to suffering?

3. Has Job gone too far in the way he addresses God? Why or why not?

4. What do you make of the idea that ultimately the problem of suffering and evil in the world goes back to God and that therefore only God can solve it?

5. Read Job 9:32-35 (also Job 16:19-21; 19:25-27). How does that point us to the gospel?

6. Read the parable of the importunate widow (Lk 18:1-8). How does this relate to the story of Job? To situations you've faced in your life?

7. Pray for persevering faith.

6. A DRAMATIC ASIDE

1. What is the difference between knowledge and wisdom? Why can't science give us wisdom? Why must wisdom ultimately come from God?

2. Why is wisdom so valuable? How much do you value wisdom?

3. What does it mean to say that wisdom is a relationship? Why is wisdom necessarily "personal"?

4. How is God's wisdom related to creation? How does that affect your view of the natural world?

5. How is Jesus the embodiment of wisdom? How does that encourage you to seek to know him and to follow him?

7. JOB'S CLOSING ARGUMENT

1. Is there a time in your life for which you are sometimes nostalgic? What was joyful about it? What happened to it?

2. Do you believe that every human being has an intrinsic dignity that comes from God? Why do we treat our dogs like people and people like dogs? How should our common creation by God affect the way we deal with people, whatever their social status?

3. How is dignity related to the #MeToo movement? How about problems related to racial conflict?

4. How has the story of Job encouraged your faith?

5. Does the model of a godly life found in these chapters fit your conception of what holiness means? As you look at Job's example, what is most challenging to you?

8. THE MYSTERIOUS ELIHU

1. What are your impressions of this fellow Elihu? How would you describe him? Does he remind you of anyone?

2. What do you find in what he says that is true? What does he get wrong?

3. Have you seen Christians claim to know things that they don't really know? How do you respond to that?

4. Why are arguments never enough when it comes to our wrestling with pain and suffering?

5. What does it mean to say that God draws near to us personally? Has that happened to you? How?

9. GOD SPEAKS

1. Have you ever had someone you trusted let you down? How did it feel? Have you ever felt that God has let you down?

2. When are you most tempted to doubt that God is on your side? How do you deal with that temptation?

3. How does the first divine speech depicting the physical and animal worlds speak to you of God's majesty and his wise

governing of this world? How should it affect the way you view the world around you? How should you respond to that revelation?

4. What forces do the Leviathan and Behemoth represent to you? Do you believe that they are merely God's creatures he can subdue and control? How does that relate to the hostile forces of this world that seem so threatening?

5. How do you understand Job's reaction to God's speeches in Job 41:1-6? How do you respond to them?

6. Do you expect to know why God allows hard things to come into your life? Can you trust him even when it is hard to see what good could possibly come of them?

7. Why did you put your trust in God in the first place? What are the grounds of your faith?

10. JUSTICE AFTER ALL?

1. What do you think of the ending to the book of Job?

2. Why are we not to be fatalists in our view of God's rule in our lives?

3. In what sense is God's blessing of Job a reward? What is the difference between a mercenary reward and an intrinsic reward? What is your reward in being faithful to God?

4. What do you think of this idea: "There is a cosmic significance to what we do that we have no conception of. We are all like Job—engaged in a mysterious cosmic battle, as every day our faith is put to the test, and God himself is honored when we trust him and obey him and worship him as the great and glorious God that he is"?

5. How does the book of Job help us to be realists in our understanding of living in faith in a fallen world?

6. What are your key takeaways from our study of the book of Job?

7. What would it mean for you to "fear God for nothing"?

THE ULTIMATE EPILOGUE

1. Why do you think people can so easily get caught up in a "health and wealth" gospel?

2. How do you find the message of the Bible to be "true to life"? As reflecting "the real world"?

3. Paul says "the foolishness of God is wiser than man's wisdom" (1 Cor 1:25). What does he mean by that? How does it relate to the story of Job? And how does it apply to you?

4. Read John 16:33. How does the resurrection of Jesus give you courage, strength, and comfort as you face the trouble of this world?

Take time to pray through Paul's prayer in Ephesians 1:18-23.

SCRIPTURE INDEX